SH

Swami Sai Sharan Anand (1889-1982)

Published by
Sterling Publishers Private Limited

SHRI SAI BABA

SWAMI SAI SHARAN ANAND

Translated from Gujarati by
V.B. KHER

A Sterling Paperback

STERLING PAPERBACKS
An imprint of
Sterling Publishers (P) Ltd.
A-59, Okhla Industrial Area, Phase-II,
New Delhi-110020.
Tel: 26387070, 26386209; Fax: 91-11-26383788
E-mail: sterlingpublishers@airtelmail.in
ghai@nde.vsnl.net.in
www.sterlingpublishers.com

Shri Sai Baba
© 1997, Swami Sai Sharan Anand
ISBN 978-81-207-9453-5
Reprint 1998, 2008

Printed and Published by Sterling Publishers Pvt. Ltd.,
New Delhi-110 020.

CONTENTS

PREFACE

It is eighteen years since India attained independence. The warped slavish mentality of Indians now shows the proper improvement. Ignorance about Truth, lack of faith in God or saints, and scepticism about incredible (supernatural) powers of the *Poorna Jnanis*, all resulting from wrong or incomplete Western education, are reduced to some extent. Dr Connan, Monsieur Coho and the researchers of the National Laboratory of Psychical Research show that a divine Master or adept can exercise control over matter and living beings. This was recognised by our ancestors from time immemorial, but the belief was lost in the sands of time, and is now regaining ground. I wish to tell the readers that the living personification of this belief was Sai Baba who had attained union with the Brahman. Going one step beyond even the dicta propounded by scientists and by researchers, I have attempted to establish that the individual who attains this state never perishes. On the other hand, he manifests himself even now for those with firm faith and also for the world-weary, the seeker of knowledge, the seeker of something he treasures and the man of vision or spiritual discrimination, and helps them. Out of crores of people who inhabit the globe, even if a few seekers of knowledge persevere on the path and attain self-realisation, they will be blessed and the writer will have the satisfaction of knowing that his objective in writing this book has been fulfilled.

This book is based on the writer's own experiences (which are true to his knowledge) and the published experiences and references to the sources, have been given wherever necessary.

Finally, I dedicate this sixth edition of the book to Lord Sai for inspiring and directing me to author this book.

Sai Sharan Anand

INTRODUCTION

In June 1974, when I visited Shirdi for the second time, I was in search of a Mahatma who was closely associated with Sai Baba. There, I heard from K.S. Pathak, the then Court Receiver of Shirdi Sansthan, the name of Swami Sai Sharan Anand of Ahmedabad, a living link with Sai Baba. So, my wife and I went to Ahmedabad in November 1974, in pursuit of our objective. We called on Swamiji, then eighty-four plus, who received us warmly and with loving kindness. In our morning and afternoon sessions with him lasting for three days, he answered all our queries candidly and with utter frankness, and removed all our doubts and misconceptions. He also enlightened us about the true nature, mission and powers of Shri Sai Baba.

At the end of our marathon discussions he placed in my hands as Sai-prasad, a copy of the book in Gujarati on Sai Baba, authored by him, which had run into six editions by 1966 since its first publication in 1946. My translation of the book into Marathi was published in 1982.

Since Swamiji had been moulded, shaped and guided in the prime of life between 1911 and 1918 by Sai Baba, his testimony is of great significance to Sai devotees all the world over. Even after Sai Baba's *mahasamadhi* in 1918, the Master continued to guide him and reveal himself in many ways, which has been documented by Swamiji in his other works in Gujarati, published posthumously. Moreover, as I discovered, Swamiji was an adept in spiritual matters and was utterly truthful in his speech and deeds. He had been a witness to many extraordinary phenomena of Sai Baba as averred by him in his preface to the book. As such, his testimony about Sai Baba is first hand and authentic.

Being desirous of sharing this precious treasure with a wider audience, I have translated this book into English for the benefit of readers all over the world. How far I have succeeded in my efforts I leave to the readers to judge. Before I close, a word of thanks is surely due to Dr. Marianne Warren but for whose invaluable help this translation would not have seen the light of day. I, therefore, acknowledge my immense debt of gratitude to her.

Vishwas B. Kher

SWAMI SAI SHARAN ANAND
A Biographical Sketch

by V.B. Kher

Shri Sai Baba had no disciples though he had, and has, innumerable devotees. One such devotee, a holy person who shunned the limelight, was Swami Sai Sharan Anand. Prior to his being ordained as a *sannyasi* he was Vaman Prangovind Patel. He was born on April 5, 1889 in a well-to-do and educated Brahmin family at Mota, a village in Bardoli Taluka (famous for the *satyagraha* of peasants in 1928) of Surat District which was then a part of the composite Bombay Province. His father, Prangovind Lalbhai Patel, was employed in the Excise Department (Salt Branch) of the Government of India. His mother, Manigauri, was the daughter of the well-known educationalist, Tuljaram Somnath. Vaman's grandfather had served as a Talathi in Navasari and was known as an honest, upright government servant who practised and enforced discipline. His grandmother, Nandkuvar, was a very religious lady and so was his mother, Manigauri.

Vaman studied up to the sixth form in his village, Mota, and for the seventh form he came to stay at Kheda with his uncle-Ramgovind, who was a head clerk in the Collector's office. From 1899, he commenced his secondary education at Ahmedabad where his father had been transferred. In 1903, his father had been transferred to Bombay. So Vaman joined the New High

School (which was later renamed after its Principal, Bharda, as the Bharda New High School) in Bombay, and passed the matriculation examination in 1905.

At that time there were three colleges in Bombay: Wilson College, St. Xavier's College and Elphinstone College. Their fees for one term were Rs 36/-, Rs 48/- and Rs 64/-, respectively. As Vaman's father was a government servant, he preferred to put his son in Elphinstone College from which he graduated in 1909 in Arts with Philosophy. Manu Subhedar, who later entered the field of commerce and industry and represented that Constituency in the Central Legislative Assembly in 1934, was a co-student and friend of Vaman. Vaman passed LL.B. examination in 1911 and signed articles with a solicitor's firm in Bombay known as Messrs. Jehangir Gulabbhai and Billimoria.

According to the custom at that time, Vaman was married at the age of thirteen to Kalavati, the daughter of Ambaram Krishnashankar Shukla. From his childhood, Vaman had a religious bent of mind which was nourished by the religious atmosphere in his household. In his childhood, he learnt to recite *Ramraksha, Vishnu Sahasranam* and *Aditya-Hriday Stotra*. When he was about five years old, his father was posted for some time at Dharasana Salt Depot where they stayed in a tent. Since many months, Vaman was suffering from diarrhoea and everyone had given up hope of his survival. Once Vaman's mother was sitting outside the tent with him in her lap, sighing for her infant, when suddenly a fakir appeared and the following conversation ensued between her and the fakir.

Fakir: Your child is very fortunate.

Vaman's mother: What fortunate! He gets so many loose motions that we feel he is a companion of only four days.

Fakir: No, No, don't say that. He is very fortunate. In his right armpit is a wart and a mole on his right side.

(Here, Vaman's mother raised his frock and found that Vaman did have those identification marks. So the conversation further proceeded.)

Vaman's mother: What you say is correct. But what about his sick condition?

Fakir: Take this *udi* and put it in his mouth and all will be well.

Swami Sai Sharan Anand records in his Gujarati autobiography *Sainathne Sharane*, published posthumously in 1983 (pp. 19-20), that thereafter his health improved rapidly and his parents were relieved. His mother had told him so.

When Vaman was seven years old and was schooling at Kheda, early morning he would visit the temple of Somnath Mahadev with his mother and sisters, where he would meet a fakir who would playfully tease him. Vaman would also pass him on his way to the school, when the fakir would again indulge in some such pranks. In 1911, when Vaman first visited Shirdi, he recognised at once that the fakir he used to meet at Kheda in his childhood was none other than Sai Baba. Similarly, once in 1913, holding his two palms opposite each other a few inches apart, Sai Baba remarked to Hari Sitaram Dikshit that he had known Vaman since he was as small as a mouse. When Vaman told his mother about this remark of Sai Baba, it was then that she told him about the sudden appearance of a fakir at Dharasana, when she was sitting outside the tent in the incident which has been narrated above.

When Vaman was in Inter Arts class, he lost interest in his daily religious rites, like *sandhya-puja*, and stopped performing them. However, since he was habituated to some regular ritual, his mind was not at rest and he continued to recite the *stotras* after the morning bath, and started reading the *Bhagavad-Gita* before retiring to bed, as he found that it infused mental strength into him. He was also convinced by studying

Neetishatak and *Vairagyashatak* by Bhartruhari, that
the ideal of Aryavarta was the realisation of God through
renunciation. As he got first class marks in logic in Inter
Arts examination, Vaman chose Logic and Moral
Philosophy as his subjects of study for B.A. R.S. Mars
was then the Professor of Logic and Moral Philosophy in
the Elphinstone College. He was a scholar of German and
Greek and had read works of Kant in the original. As
such he was very popular with students. The study of
Kant's philosophy unsettled Vaman's mind and he
wondered whether God really existed or was merely the
creation of man's mind; whether the universe was
sustained by a conscious creative power or was created
accidentally. The more he thought, the more he became
eager and anxious to unravel the mystery of life and to
see God face to face, like Swami Vivekananda had done.
When he was in this state of mind, his father took him to
Balakrishna Maharaj. Vaman told Balakrishna Maharaj
that he would only accept him as his *guru* if he would
enable him to get a direct perception of God. Now Vaman
longed to meet a Mahatma who would finally resolve his
doubts. His prayer was answered. His father, who had
just returned from a visit to Sai Baba, told him that the
latter was capable of meeting all his demands. So on 10
December, 1911, after his second LL.B. examination was
over, Vaman left for Shirdi. The account of his first
meeting with Sai Baba is narrated in detail in his
Gujarati autobiography *Sainathne Sharane*. After the
first meeting with Sai Baba, Vaman visited Shirdi
frequently, right up to Sai Baba's *mahasamadhi* on
October 15, 1918. However, his two visits in 1913 and
1916 were particularly significant and productive from a
spiritual point of view.

Vaman went to Shirdi in May 1913 and Sai Baba
detained him for nearly eleven months. Initially Sai
Baba made him do *Gayatri Purascharan* to wipe off his
past *karma*. He would also send him on his behalf to the

four or five houses for alms. He also put him through the necessary spiritual discipline, made him read *Jnaneshwari* and other spiritual works, and gave him spiritual experiences. He treated him with affection, like his own son, and would call him by the pet name of Babu. One day, Sai Baba told him to go home. So he returned to Bombay in March 1914.

Due to his long stay in Shirdi, Vaman's period of articled clerkship was interrupted. On his return to Bombay, he met Jehangir, the senior partner of the firm, who told him that the period of 13 months earlier put in by him, was now wasted as his period of training was interrupted, it would not be counted and he would have to put in two years afresh. About this time he received two offers of employment, one of Police Prosecutor and another as an Assistant Teacher in C.J.N.L. High School, Navasari. On the advice of Sai Baba, he accepted the latter and served over a year in that post. In the following vacation, Vaman consulted Gulabbhai, another partner of the firm, who advised him to apply to the Chief Justice of the Bombay High Court for condonation of the break in his articles. On making the necessary application, an order was passed by the Chief Justice condoning the break and Vaman was permitted to serve for the remaining period of eleven months to complete his period of articled clerkship. This is said to be the only instance of its kind in the history of the Bombay High Court. Accordingly, Vaman completed his period of articled clerkship and started preparing for the solicitor's examination.

In October-November 1916, Vaman spent three weeks in Shirdi which were very important from his point of view, for he had many invaluable spiritual experiences of a high order, and he became fearless. He would go anywhere at midnight and sit for meditation for long hours, near the stream or in the jungle. Once in the afternoon, he started with Kakasaheb Dikshir for the

masjid. At that time construction work was going on in
the Butiwada. Dikshit skirted the Butiwada and went to
the masjid. Vaman took the short-cut through the
Butiwada, and while doing so, a heavy stone fell on his
head which made him unconscious. It was a serious
accident, but Sai Baba sent an ointment for application
on Vaman's head and shoulder. With one application, the
pain ceased at once and the wounds healed naturally
after some days without any further treatment. During
this period, Sai Baba opened his seventh chakra
Brahmarandhra and united his *prana* with the universal
prana.

Between 1917 and 1935, the career of Vaman was full
of vicissitudes as will be seen from what follows. From
March 1917 to January 1921, he worked as the Principal
of Model High School at Ahmedabad. Then he returned to
Bombay and was for some time an Assistant in Kanga
and Sayani, a firm of solicitors. For a year thereafter he
joined the Pioneer Rubber Works of his friend, Manu
Subhedar. In 1923 he passed his Solicitor's examination
and from January 1924 conducted a firm of solicitors,
Nanavati & Co, for a year and a quarter. Next he worked
as an Assistant Solicitor in Choksi & Co., Solicitors.
Between 25 July 1925 and 15 September 1926 he was a
partner of Paralkar in a firm of solicitors called Paralkar
& Patel. Once again the pull of Ahmedabad proved
stronger and he joined Model High School as Principal.
He left Ahmedabad in 1929 to take up his appointment
as a Professor in Law College, Bombay. During this time
he published a commentary on the Companies Act and a
commentary on the Insolvency Act.

Within a year thereafter, he took up his appointment
as an Assistant in Crawford Bayley & Co., Solicitors, to
which he stuck on for two years. That was the end of his
legal career and his residence in Bombay as well. He
went back to Ahmedabad, and from January 1935 served
for fifteen years as Principal of Umreth High School,

Umreth, in Nadiad District from which he retired in 1950.

Even after Sai Baba's *samadhi*, Vaman's *upasana* and *tapas* continued with vigour and he lived in the world but was not of it. Mentally he had renounced all attachment to the world. In 1951, his wife Kalavati passed away after forty-nine years of married life. She had given birth to a son, Meghashyam, who died prematurely, and a daughter, Triveni, who was married happily. She too expired on 1 August, 1978.

After his retirement from the educational field, Vaman turned his hand to literary activity, authoring religious books. He joined the Sastu-Sahitya Mandal and published the following fourteen books in Gujarati between 11 December, 1950 and 31 March, 1953.

1. *Shri Sai Baba* (2nd edition)
2. *Shankaracharya*
3. *Manushyadharma*
4. *Nitoyapath*
5. *Sati Savitri*
6. *Shri Prahlad*
7. *Jadabharat*
8. *Ambarish*
9. *Shukadevji*
10. *Gajendramoksha*
11. *Mastaram*
12. *Jnandev ane Changdev 'Pasashti'*
13. *Dharmakatha*
14. *Japa ane Namasmaran*

Besides these he has authored a poetical work, *Sai Leelkhyan*, in 24 chapters, describing the various *leelas* of Sai Baba which he published independently in April 1962. His book, *Sai Baba*, was very popular in Gujarat and ran into six editions until 1966.

His commitment to worldly affairs was now at an end and on 12 July 1953, he took *sannyasa* at Dakor as per Sai Baba's directions. Thereafter, he lived an austere and virtuous life for twenty-nine years and experienced complete unity and oneness with Sai Baba. He attained *nirvana* at Ahmedabad at twenty minutes past midnight on Wednesday 25 August, 1982. His body was interred and a *samadhi* has been erected over it.

Swami Sai Sharan Anand had supernatural powers which he used sparingly and judiciously in hard cases, without ever speaking about them. After his *nirvana* the following books of his were published posthumously:

1. *Sainathne Sharane*, 1983, being his spiritual experiences.
2. *Brahma Parimal*, November, 1986.
3. *Siddhamrit*, February, 1987.

1. BIRTH, CASTE AND FAMILY

Although I am unborn, everlasting, and I am the Lord of all, I come to my realm of nature and through my wondrous power I am born.

Bhagavad-Gita IV:6 trans, Juan Mascaro

For the fulfillment of desire of those worshipping the One without a second assumed many forms, of which the principal are the Sun, the Moon, Ganesh, Brahma, Vishnu, Shiva and Shakti. Of these forms I bow to the most excellent Light.

Shri Rang Avadhoot
Datta Sayam Smaranam, 4

God is beyond the three states (waking, dreaming and sound sleep) and is independent of maya (the creative power); He is free from anger and hatred. To such God I bow. Neither deities, nor men, nor sages are able to know the uttermost extent or reach of maya; You humbled the pride of the mighty demons. When the subjects are put to the greatest hardships in the world, Oh Vaikunthrai, You come at that time and manifest Yourself.

Bhagwat (Gujarati) composed by Vallabh,
Sections: 4 & 8, Chapts 8 & 17

Moved by compassion and, of course, due to the moral or religious merit of the devotees, the formless Supreme Spirit, Sadguru, well-known as Shri Sainath or Shri Sai Baba, manifested himself by his self-existing power. If asked, he would only say, "Brahma is my father, Maya my mother, and this universe my home." There is no reliable information so far available about the parents of this incarnation.[1] From the articles, books and experiences of devotees published so far, it becomes clear beyond doubt that he was a great incarnation — about this there are no two opinions.

Some opinions of those who regarded Sai Baba as the perfect Absolute Brahman or an incarnation of God are reproduced herein below:

1) The late Hon. Hari Sitaram Dikshit, B.A., LL.B., Solicitor, Bombay High Court, former member of the Bombay Legislative Council, whom Sai Baba referred to as Kaka, wrote in *Shri Sai Leela*, Vol. II, issue No. 5, p. 1:

There is no reliable information about the native place of Sai Maharaj or his parents. However, it is certain that he was much connected with Moglai (the Nizam's territory). In his talk there were frequent references to Sailu, Jalna, Manvat, Pathri, Parbhani, Naurangabad (Aurangabad), Beed, and Bedar - all located in Moglai. Once a man from Pathri had come for the *darshan* of Sai Maharaj. Sai Maharaj asked him for the news of Pathri, and taking the names of prominent people in Pathri, enquired about them individually. From this it can be deduced that he had particular knowledge of Pathri, but it cannot be stated authoritatively that he was born there.

It cannot also be stated with certainty that he was originally a Brahmin or was born a Muslim. Nay, it cannot also be stated whether the belief of some of his devotees that he was not born as others are born — no woman bore him—is correct or not. To those who are not his devotees, the theory of his not being born as others are, may seem impossible, but the present writer does not feel so. Sai Maharaj has exclaimed to the present writer, "Now when I go I will come back as eight years old". It is narrated in the *Puranas* that when Shri Krishna incarnated near mother Devaki, he was eight years old. The eight-year-old figure cast such dazzling splendour that it lighted up the ten directions and the moon and the sun hid themselves (*Hari Vijay*: Chap. 3 verse 126).

Many devotees of Sai Maharaj do not believe that he rose to be a *siddha* (seer) from the stage of a *sadhaka* (seeker). They regard him in indisputable reality as an incarnation (of the deity) and observing his *leelas* and supernatural powers, consider that he is Shri Krishna incarnate. Of course, Sai Maharaj did not arrogate to himself this authority. In his conversation he would refer to himself as the servant or slave of God (*Shri Sai Satcharita*, pp. 1-2).

2) In the book, *Sri Saileelamrit* by Prabhakar S Agasakar, published by Shri Sai Baba Sansthan in 1953, the following opinion is expressed on page 43:

Shri Sai Baba was not born out of the womb (of a mother). He was not born in any family or in any religion. Such an event is not an impossibility in world history. Like Saint Kabir and Namdev, Shri Sai incarnated himself in Shirdi as a perfect Sadguru. He was ever in the state of Brahman - consciousness (God-consciousness). So he did not make any distinction between Hindus and Muslims. So, without probing further into his birthplace and religion, let us regard him as an incarnation of Brahman and place our heads at his holy feet.

3) After practising severe austerities Shri Upasani, who came into contact with Shri Sai Baba, composed a *stotra* (hymn) which is known as *Shri Sai Mahimna Stotra*. It is sung at the noon *arati* at Shirdi.

I bow to Sadguru Sainath, birthless, foremost unique self-evident Supreme Spirit, Ram-Incarnate, who has originated on his own (on this earth). Oh Lord, I am indeed purified by your *darshan* (sacred sight). (verse 8).

4) In verses 110 to 115 of Chapter IV of *Shri Sai Satcharita*, the late Govind Raghunath alias Annasaheb Dabholkar, former Magistrate of Bandra, Bombay, has said:

Just as by good fortune, Saint Namdev was found by Gonai as a child floating in the River Bhimrathi, and Kabir by Tamala in a shell in the River Bhagirathi, so did Sainath appear for his devotees in the village of Shirdi under a neem tree (*Melia azadirachta*) at the young age of sixteen years. He was a born *Siddha* (self-realized soul) and sensual desires did not arise even in his dreams. The veil of *maya* was swept aside by him and salvation lay in the hollow of his palm. No one knew where, or in which pious family or of which parents, Sai Baba was born. No one knew of his antecedents, and people were at their wit's end trying to find out who his parents were. Leaving behind his parents, family, kith and kin, caste, in fact, all worldly ties, he appeared in Shirdi for the good of the people.

Further, in verses 14-18 of Chapter VII of *Shri Sai Satcharita*, it is stated in support of the foregoing:

If it be said of him that he is a Hindu his abode is always the *masjid*; if it be said that he is a Muslim, fire is alight day and night in the *masjid*. In the *masjid* is the grinding wheel for corn; in the *masjid* there is also sounding of bell and blowing of conch, an oblation to the fire. How can he be a Muslim? At all times in the *masjid* there is *bhajan, annadan* (distribution of food), an oblation to and worship of the feet (of Venerable Sai Baba). How can he be a Muslim? If it be said of him that he is a Muslim, the best of the Brahmins worship him. *Agnihotris* (Brahmins maintaining a perpetual fire), abandoning the pride of their silk cloth of purity, prostrate themselves before him. People thus astonished who came to discover through personal observation follow the same course and are silenced in his presence.[2]

After exhaustive discussion, Dabholkar comes to the conclusion in Chapter XXIV:5, of *Shri Sai Satcharita*:

Sai is indestructible and ancient. He is neither a Hindu nor a Muslim. He is without caste, family, and *gotra* and is ever absorbed in his Self.

5) The present writer has already expressed his agreement with the above view, in his words 'by self-existing power'. What Sai Baba had said in this matter is this: "I left my parents when I was eight years old and came to the banks of the Ganga (Sai Baba invariably referred to the River Godavari as 'Ganga')". Many a time Sai Baba would say "I will return as a child of eight." This narration accords with the account of the birth of Krishna given in *Hari-Vijay*. Moreover, in the reports published about the parents and birthplace of Sai there is much disparity. We shall discuss this in detail at the appropriate place. But the present writer feels that Sai Baba was an incarnation of the same class as Shri Krishna.

6) Shri Amidas Bhawanidas Mehta writes in his book entitled *Purna Parabrahma Srisadgurusainath Maharajni - Janavajog Vigato Temaj Chamatkaro* (Gujarati), p. 8:

There is no reliable information available regarding the year in which, and the place from which Shri Samarth Sadguru Sainath Maharaj came to Shirdi, where he was born, who his parents were, etc. When his devoteees questioned him in the beginning he only replied: "This *pinda* (gross lump) is called the body, the universe is my *gaon* (place), Brahma my father and Maya my mother". This is a matter of wonder. It is really strange that even though many scholars, judges, barristers, solicitors and doctors are his devotees, they should not be able to obtain any

clarification about the above questions in spite of·
their attempts. The moral is that men of the highest
education in the twentieth century are not capable of
carrying out such research about real incarnations.

7) In pages 1-2 of *Shri Sainath Prabha* or *Dharam
Rahasya* (Editor: Lakshman Balwant Petkar, B.A.,
LL.B., High Court Pleader, Vol.I. Issue No. 11 (1918)), it
stated as under:

There are many people in the village [Shirdi] of the
same age group as Sai Maharaj. But the account of
each individual being different, there is no
harmonious consistency between their accounts. But
they are agreed on one point, viz., that Maharaj was
an incarnation and just as Samarth Ramdas came to
the banks of Krishna from the Godavari, similarly,
Shri Sainath Maharaj must have come to the banks
of Godavari on the direction of Shri Rama.

Further on pages 13-14 it is said:

As described in verses 2-3 of Canto X of the
Bhagavad-Gita, Sai Maharaj was a divine
incarnation. It is the belief of the devotees that just as
Ramdas was an incarnation of Hanuman, similarly,
Sainath Maharaj was an incarnation of Shiva, Rama
or Dattatreya. There is a continuous regular
succession of Navanaths beginning with Adinath or
Shankar. Many believe that Sainath Maharaj is the
tenth Nath in this succession.

8) The Late Rao Bahadur Moreshwar W. Pradhan,
J.P., former Member of the Bombay Legislative
Assembly, wrote in his book entitled *Shri Sai Baba of
Shirdi* (Shri Sai Baba Sansthan, 7th Edn., 1973, p.25 pp.
25-26):

Shri Sainath Maharaj (alias Sai Baba), the saint of
world fame, first appeared in Shirdi as a very
handsome lad of sixteen about the year A.D. 1872 .
Shirdi is a small village abutting on Agra Trunk Road

in the Kopargaon Taluka in the Ahmednagar District. Up to now there is no reliable information about the place, birth or parentage of Shri Sai Baba. This much is certain that Sai Baba was familiar with several places in the Nizam's territory. In his talks several times he used to mention Shelu, Jalna, Manvad, Pathri, Parbhani, Nowrangabad (Aurangabad), Beed, Bedar — all Moglai places. Once a man from Pathri had come to take Baba's darshan. Baba's enquiries made from this man about Pathri village and several of its well-known residents showed that he knew the place very intimately; but this alone does not warrant that Pathri was Baba's birthplace.

9) Shri G.S. Khaparde, former Member of the Central Legislative Assembly, in his Introduction to the first edition of *Shri Sai Baba of Shirdi* by M.W. Pradhan says:

Our Sadguru Sai Maharaj of Shirdi... to my mind represented perfection so far as it can possibly be conceived by an imperfect being like myself. No praise that I can bestow is too high for him... I count it as the greatest piece of good fortune that circumstances led me to his feet, and the moment I approached them as humbly as I could, all the load of my worldly cares disappeared though only a few minutes before it was felt to be exceedingly oppressive and such as to excite disgust of life.

This is not only my experience but that of tens of thousands of others whom I met there during a rather prolonged stay. Among them were many highly educated gentlemen and ladies, a large number of hard-headed businessmen, many who had renounced the world and led a life of devotion and piety. The whole of the countryside worshipped him and gathered round with the instinct with which ants surround a big lump of sugar. While many came long distances at great expense and trouble, each went away satisfied and anxious to repeat his or her visit as often as it could be managed. It was a sight to see and enjoy.

The wonder of wonders is that, of the personage so universally admired and worshipped, not even a single human being knew the real name. He dropped into the village, so to say, from the blue, helped a person to find his lost horse and took up his residence there for a whole lifetime, helping everybody that came along without any distinction, securing the love and reverence of all without exception. He appeared to know the innermost thoughts of everybody, relieved their wants and carried comfort to all. He fulfilled my idea of God on earth.

10) Rao Saheb Yeshwant J. Galvankar states in his Preface to the second edition of *Shri Sai Baba of Shirdi* by M.W.Pradhan:

If biography of saints is difficult, that of Shri Sai Baba is attended with difficulties almost insuperable. A cloud of mystery hangs over all the affairs of his life and completely veils off his birth, parentage and early life. None knows definitely anything about that period.

Many well-known devotees of Sai Baba regard him as a holy person who had realised the perfect unconditioned Soul but believe that his body was Muslim! Let us now investigate the truth of this view.

11) Shri Ganesh Dattatreya Sahasrabuddhe was at one time employed in the Police Department and spent his spare time in singing *lavanis* in *tamashas* (farce full of songs and dance) to the accompaniment of a tambourine. By the grace of Sai Baba he gained recognition as a poet and came to be known as Das Ganu. He was a staunch devotee of Sai Baba. He has composed several poetic tales with a moral which are useful for *kirtana, pavadas*

(ballads), *subhashita* (fine discourses), long poems, *stotras* (hymns) and written tales from the *Puranas* and lives of saints in verse form. Out of these, in *Bhaktaleelamrit* (1906), *Santakathamrit* (1908) and *Bhaktasaramrit* (1925), there are accounts of Sai Baba. *Shri Sainath Stavan Manjari* (a poem of praise) devoted only to Sai Baba is tasteful, full of divine love and touches the deepest chords of the devotee's heart. In verses 69-70 and 72 thereof, Das Ganu says about Sai Baba's parentage and birth as under:

But superficial are these differences
Of interest only to pedagogues;
For those devotees desirous of knowledge
They are of no consequence. 69

Your state is that of unity with Brahman
Caste and creed ye have none;
You are the Guru Supreme
And the primal cause of the creation. 70

You are beyond caste and creed,
You are Brahman, the essence of Truth;
You are That, verily,
You are beyond human conception. 72

Whenever any one asked Sai Baba about his parentage he had one constant answer: "This universe is my abode, Brahman is my father and Maya my mother." There is hardly any reference to Sai Baba's external appearance and birth in Das Ganu's works. His attention is riveted on Sai Baba's state of unity with the Supreme Spirit. Time and again Sai Baba brought this state of his to the notice of Das Ganu who considered himself blessed in describing it, or singing his praises, or in offering prayers to him. When trickles of waters of the Ganges and the Jamuna flowed from the toes of Sai Baba, which were sufficient to fill a *lota*, Das Ganu purified his body with that *tirtha* (holy water) and overpowered with

emotion broke into a poem to which we will have occasion
to refer later in Chapter Six on Supernatural Powers.

12) After Sai Baba took *mahasamadhi*, one devotee,
Shri Upasani, accompanied by other devotees went to
Benares and carried out all obsequies, food-distribution,
etc., involving considerable expense.

13) Shri Sathya Sai Baba, residing at Puttaparthi in
Anantapur district of Andhra Pradesh astonished his
companions by his *leelas*. From the age of fourteen he has
declared a number of times that he is an incarnation of
Sai Baba of Shirdi. He has related the history of his past
incarnation which is briefly stated below: His father
Gangabhav and mother Devagiramma lived in Pathri on
the banks of the Godavari. They were pious, generous,
religious-minded and were staunch devotees of Shiva-
Parvati. They were unhappy as they had no issue.
Bhagwan Shankar subjected them to a trial a number of
times but they stood the test. So Shiva-Parvati
manifested themselves and gave them a boon whereby
Shiva took birth in their family as the third son. That son
was Sai Baba. In the meantime Gangabhav developed so
much aversion or indifference towards worldly matters
that he decided to leave his household. Devagiramma
insisted on accompanying him. Ultimately both of them,
leaving the child Sai under a tree, retired into a forest for
penance. After some time a fakir and his wife who were
childless were passing by. The abandoned child attracted
their attention. They accepted him as a gift from God and
brought him up until he was twelve years old.

It is indisputable that Sai Baba regarded himself as a
Brahmin. In 1912 the present writer's father developed
abdominal dropsy and doctors gave up all hope of his life.
In December, when I went to Shirdi, I could not help
thinking of my father's condition which caused anxiety.
The moment the thought arose in my mind Sai Baba
said, "Get that person with bloated stomach here." I said

to myself, 'What Baba says is correct, but my father is orthodox in his views! So, how will he agree to come to Sai Baba who looks like a Muslim?' Immediately Sai Baba exclaimed, "What, am I not a Brahmin?"

Sai Baba's oldest and most devout devotee was Mhalsapaty. For approximately thirty to forty years he would sleep in the *masjid* along with Sai Baba. Sai Baba once told him that he (Sai Baba) was born in a Yajurvedi Deshastha Brahmin family of Pathri and his father gave him away to a fakir.[3] Madhavnath and the foremost devotee of Baba Sri B.V. Narasimhaswami have accepted the truth of this statement of Mhalsapaty.

A Marwadi Brahmin named Megha, employed by Hari Vinayak Sathe, went to Shirdi much against his will at the bidding of his master. When he went for Sai Baba's *darshan*, Sai Baba flew into a temper, took a stone in his hand and thundered, "How dare you step in? You are born in the highest Brahmin caste and I am only a *Yavana* (Muslim)!" Megha was stunned! He thought, "How far Kheda (in Gujarat) is from Shirdi! Yet Sai Baba has knowledge of my conversation in privacy with my master by his second sight!" We will see later how Megha came to regard Sai Baba as Shankar and served him with love and devotion.

From the above it is clear that if Sai Baba was born, he was born in a Brahmin family. Whether he was born or not, it is a fact that he regarded himself as a Brahmin and showed his displeasure to those who considered him a Muslim.

There is still another account given by Suman Sundar in his article in *Shri Sai Leela* of July-September 1942, on pp. 359-372. It is based on what he heard from his guru, Madhavnath. Briefly stated, there is a town called Pathri in Moglai (Nizam's Dominions). A Yajurvedi Brahmin lived there. He had three sons. The eldest son was Sai Baba. When the boy was five, a *fakir* came to the

Brahmin and said, "Give mine to me." The Brahmin
replied. "Whatever I have is yours." Then asking for the
eldest boy he took him away. He brought the boy back to
his father when he was nine years old, and partaking of
milk at his place, again took him away for another three
years. The period between the years twelve and eighteen,
the boy spent in seclusion, and at the age of nineteen he
appeared in Shirdi beneath the neem tree.

From the above accounts we can say along with Sri
B.V. Narasimhaswamiji: "Baba's birth and his parentage
are shrouded in mystery and we haven't yet met any
individual who has a direct perception thereof." Citing an
enigmatic aphorism supposed to be from the *sastras*, to
decide the question whether Sai Baba was a Hindu or a
Muslim, some assert that Shudras and Muslims were
born from the lower half of the *Virat-Purusha* (The
Universal Deity, with a glorious and variously
magnificent body - the Demiurge and Pervading Spirit of
the Universal system). And on the basis of the saying:
'There is none meaner than *Yavana*', they despise
Shudras and Muslims and regard only Brahmins as
worthy of respect. This kind of reasoning is reproachable.
The *Vedas* are revealed scriptures. How will God-inspired
Vedas ever say: 'Only my head is useful and the lower-
half is useless?' On the other hand, it is the divine will
that even Shudras are a part of his body. If the head non-
cooperates with the lower half of the body, it can perform
no action. So if Brahmins, Shudras, Musalmans do not
work in cooperation, there cannot be harmony in the
world. Cooperation is to be expected from all. So no one
should regard anyone as low or inferior. If at all, there is
the saying, 'There is none lower than a *Yavana*', the word
Yavana is to be construed not as a Muslim but one, who,
straying from the narrow, straight path succumbs, to his
evil tendencies. This is also the intention of the *Vedas*
and it is strange that learned men cannot appreciate this

truth. It is certain that *shrutis* which proclaim the doctrine of *Advaita* (non-duality) and *Abheda* (non-differentiation) cannot make any distinction such as Hindu-Muslim.

On the Vijayadashmi day in the year 1916, i.e., two years before he lay down his mortal coil, after the evening round, Sai Baba, the knower of the heart within, became angry, his eyes turned red, and he threw his *kafni* in the *dhuni*. In this naked state he called out loudly, "Open your eyes wide and see clearly whether I am a Hindu or a Muslim" (*Shri Saileelamrit*, p. 157: *Shri Sai Satvharita*, Chap. XXXXII, verses 20-28). Those who were present then testify that Sai Baba had not been circumcised.

In his last days, Sai Baba got a devotee by the name of Vaze to do two to three *parayanas* (complete reading) of *Ram Vijay*. The edifice which had been constructed after interring Sai Baba's body in Butee-Wada is also constructed according to Hindu style (of architecture). Thereafter, a spire was constructed on the Samadhi Mandir and in 1954 a marble idol of Sai Baba was installed with ceremonial rites on Vijayadashami Day in 1954, which was unveiled at the hands of the present writer. It is natural that a person who considers all these details dispassionately should be convinced that Sai Baba was a Hindu and a Brahmin at that. Yet the present writer does not insist on the acceptance of any particular view, for he believes that the welfare of a reader lies not in indulging in an acrimonious controversy on this point but in the remembrance of the Supreme Being, Sai Baba, and the practice of his message.

The account of Sai Baba's parents as related by Madhavnath has already been given earlier. That Madhavnath had fellow-feeling for Sai Baba is clear from verses 109-110 of Chapter 22 of *Madhavnath Deepprakash* excerpted below:

Shri Paramhamsa Sheelanath, Shri Sadguru Sainath
Dhundiraj in Palus, Gajanan in Segaon
    and Gopaldas (Narsing Maharaj) in Nasik;
Bonds of intimacy united this group of five Naths
And they communicated with each other by their
    internal (yogic) powers.

In support of the above statement the writer of
Deepprakash has cited evidence that at the very time
Gajanan Maharaj passed away in Segaon, Sai Baba, who
was standing in Shirdi, suddenly fell to the ground,
unconscious for a long while. This fact was also narrated
to the present writer by many devotees in Shirdi.

Some devotees of Sai Baba regard him as an
incarnation of Dattatreya and try to place him in the
traditional framework of Dattatreya sect. They believe
that their well-being lies in this. Sai Baba established his
identity with that great Deity by reminding a Brahmin of
his *navas* (prayer and vow) to Dattatreya and asking him
for Rs 15 on its fulfilment. Baba also established this fact
by giving *darshan* to some in the form of Dattatreya. As if
not satisfied with this, some devotees speak of continuity
of regular succession of Dattatreya incarnation with
Akkalkot Swami and assert that Sai Baba and Akkalkot
Swami are one.

Datta devotees also believe that Akkalkot Swami is
an incarnation of Narasimha Saraswati. The following
examples are quoted in support of the identity of Sai
Baba and Akkalkot Swami:

1) Giving Rs. 2 to Pitale, Sai Baba reminded him of
his father having been given Rs. 3 earlier by Akkalkot
Swami.

2) When the father of R.K. Naik asked Akkalkot
Swami to whom they should look for guidance after him,
Swami gave them his leather padukas and told them
clearly that hereafter his residence would be in Shirdi,
and their welfare lay in serving Sai Baba as devotedly as

they had served him till then. From these instances they show the continuity of succession from Narasimha Saraswati to Sai Baba and regard Sai Baba as an incarnation of Dattatreya. In his book, *Sai Baba Avatar Karya* (Marathi), A.Y. Dhond, in order to establish that Sai Baba was an incarnation of Dattatreya, cites the contemporaneity of Manekprabhhu of Humanabad and Akkalkot Swami, and then strains every nerve to show the tradition of unity between Sai Baba and Akkalkot Swami. Though all these attempts may be laudable from the point of view of *sadhana* (spiritual practices) of devotees, such attempts to link them ascribes secondariness to Sai Baba which is undesirable.

Even after decades of Sai Baba's passing away, his devotees continue to get experiences similar to those which his devotees got when Sai Baba was in the embodied form. In the past, mahatmas, saints and yogis with miraculous powers lived in India. But very few out of them have taken the trouble after their physical existence ceased, to remove so readily the sorrows and misfortunes of their devotees. No one except utmost compassionate God Himself can be ever so anxious. He alone, on passionately calling upon him for succour, responds instantaneously and removes difficulties and calamities. That is why all over India in towns and villages, and in Africa, Sai Baba is remembered and his praises are sung. Temples have been raised to him in Madras and Mysore. So all devotees believe with good reason that God Himself incarnated in the form of Sai Baba. The *Vedanta* which describes Him as beyond words and all scriptures and the *Bhagavad Gita* which regard Him as the Controller of the Universe, Birthless, Indestructible, resorting to His material nature, comes into being by His mysterious power. Some by rare chance get experience of this Eternal Principle which assumes form, as described in the *Bhagavad Gita, Canto* 2, 29:

There are some who have actually looked upon the Atman, and understood It, in all Its wonder. Others can only speak of It as wonderful beyond their understanding. Others know of Its wonder by hearsay. And there are others who are told about It and do not understand a word.

(Translation by Swami Prabhavananda and Christopher Isherwood)

or

One sees him in a vision of wonder and another gives us words of his wonder. There is one who hears of his wonders; but he hears and knows him not.

(Translation by J. Mascaro)

In *slokas* 1-3 of *Shri Sai Mahima Stotra*, it is stated:

I bow to God incarnate Sadguru Sainath who is ever the Absolute Reality, fountain of knowledge and joy, the cause of existence, preservation and destruction of the universe, who has assumed the form of a human being by the wish of his devotees. (1)

I bow to God incarnate Sadguru Sainath, destroyer of *samsar*, the cycle of birth and death, the darkness of ignorance; powerful as the sun, beyond thought and speech, comprehended by sages in meditation; pure without attributes, who pervades the universe. (2)

I bow to God incarnate Sadguru Sainath, refuge of the suffering mankind drowned in the ocean of *samsar*, fond of devotion of his (the Supreme Principle), who has come to this world in the Kali Yuga[4] for the salvation of his devotees. (3)

Those who regard such Being as a collection or seat of elements are sinners and their company should be avoided as stated in the *Mahabharata* similarly as in the case of those who regarded Lord Shri Krishna merely as an embodiment of elements. So what is the point in superimposing a family, *gotra*, caste, religion, etc., on such Being? In the case of incarnations like Shri Krishna, Sai Baba, instead of coming to the conclusion 'not this, not this' after a fruitless search for their family, caste and *gotra*, let us regard them all as manifestations of God. Caste, religion, etc., are all spoken only of the body. The soul that remains is ever free. Hence, there is no question of Sai Baba being a Hindu or a Muslim.

In the case of those regarded as incarnations by the Hindus, there are some who were born of human parents and others who manifested mysteriously with a specific purpose. All incarnations are forms of Godhead. Because of the diversity of the cause and task and according to the times, there is variation in the divine incarnation and there is no place in these manifestations for gradations or classes.

In the mysterious manifestations were Narasimha incarnation for the killing of Hiranyakashopu, Vaman incarnation for the salvation of Bali, Shikhandi, etc. Of this class was Sai Baba. It is no wonder that many devotees of his believe this to be so. The practical ways for resolving Hindu-Muslim hostility, conflicts, riots provoked by trifles prescribed in Hinduism or Islam are similar. To show this by example and also to guide the simple, straight-forward loving devotees on the right path, Sai Baba manifested himself in Shirdi. So it is humbly urged that the highest goal can be reached by thinking of Sai Baba in the same way as one's feeling about the chosen deity of worship and walking on that path.

Followers of diverse religions such as Hindu, Muslim, Parsi, Christian, etc., came for Sai Baba's *darshan* and became his devotees. All of them had the same experience and have it even now. It is that Sai Baba pervades everything, is the ruler of the heart and knows what is good and bad. He is well aware of our inner unexpressed thoughts as well as the most secret acts. But he is the storehouse of mercy. He does not forget anyone who remembers him. Irrespective of caste, *gotra*, family, religion, *karma* of the devotee, he hastens to his succour on the devotee calling out to him passionately. He saves him imperceptibly from dangerous disease, calamity, practical difficulty, occasions or circumstances of disgrace or dishonour. And if the need arises he manifests himself and protects his devotee.

The kind God who cleared the *hundi* of Narsi Mehta of Junagadh, became a Mahar for the sake of Damajipant and remitted to the King's treasury the full value of the grain distributed among the poor from the Government stores, helped Janabai to beat into shape cowdung cakes and complete the whole job, told and solved riddles for the amusement of a great devotee while he was grinding-pounding corn, saved Kabir Kamal from a thorny death, the same Lord Sai assumed form and gave Balakram Mankar a railway ticket, at his own expense, and at the time of the delivery of the daughter of Nanasaheb Chandorkar sent Ramgirbua from Shirdi to Jamner with *udi* and the text of his *arati*, drove the tonga from Jalgaon to Jamner in the garb of a sepoy of Nanasaheb and reached Ramgirbua to Jamner in the nick of time. After he had abandoned his mortal coil, he affixed a thousand signatures of Pleader Dhumal on local board papers as the President of the District Local Board, assumed the form of a peon and the name Ganapati Shankar and accompanied Nachne to Nasik by train to help him to complete the obsequies pursuant to his wife's death. To satisfy the cravings of his devotees and for their protection, Lord Shri Krishna incarnated on this earth as Shri Sai Baba, and helped the devotees to accomplish the end of their existence.

The devotees feel the need of this incarnation, the necessity to love him and the desire to attain his favour. How are those who have knowledge of Sai Baba's actions and have experienced his grace concerned with the question of his parentage and caste? Their goal is one.

Even though the Lord is formless, if he assumes form out of compassion, to benefit from him, to experience bliss in his company and to attain their weal, let the logicians, so-called intellectuals and pragmatists and rationalists indulge in speculation. The devotees have only one conviction. It is this. God of all castes, sub-castes, religions is only One. According to their faith and taste, He appears in different forms. The perceptible evidence of this is the incarnation of Sai Baba.

Notes

1. In June 1975, V.B. Kher paid a visit to Marathwada (formerly Moglai, Nizam's Dominion), visited the towns of Pathri, Sailu, Parabhni and researched into the origins—parentage, family, etc., of Sai Baba. From all the information available, he came to the conclusion that Sai Baba may have been born at Pathri in the Yajurvedi Deshastha Brahmin's family of the surname of Bhusari. On the basis of his findings he wrote an article entitled "A Search for the Birthplace of Shri Sai Baba" which was published in the January 1976 issue of *Shri Sai Leela*, the official organ of Shri Sai Baba Sansthan of Shirdi.

2. At page 82 of the Urdu Manuscript (unpublished) of the devotee Shri Abdul (personal attendant of Shri Sai Baba from 1889 to 1918), there is an entry of which the following is an English translation:
    Friends, how is it possible to fathom the inner mind of Sai Baba if one cannot understand even the outward appearance (form) of Sai Baba? If it be said that he is a Muslim, his ears are pricked; if it be said that he is a Hindu, he dwells in the *masjid*, repeats the name 'Allah Malik' and distributes cooked meat as *prasad* (consecrated food). In his inner being does he contemplate the *Vedas*, the *Puranas*, the *Gita* or the *Koran*, Fakah? Only God knows. So Sai Baba's *leela* (sport) is wonderful. Amir, a Muslim devotee, wishes to sing the prasises of Sai Baba but does he have the capacity to do so? Sai Baba's *durbar* is that of a *Kalandar* (Muslim fakir). It is not a *Math* (monastery) of a Hindu Swami. His slave Abdul regards him as his *Murshid* (Guru).
    R.B. Purandare has also stated (*Devotees' Experiences of Sri Sai Baba, Part I*, pp. 104-114) that Sai Baba's ears were pierced and observed Sai Baba while bathing naked, that he was not circumcised.

3. The allegorical meaning of this saying can be as follows:
   Pathri = Turya (the transcendental stage). *Brahmin* = One
   who has a direct perception of the Brahman and is absorbed in
   it. *Fakir* = One who follows the path of renunciation and
   disengagement from worldly affairs, i.e., disengaging himself
   from worldly affairs and transcending the lower three states, I
   did not take to the path of *pravritti* (activity) like King Janak
   of Vaidehi.

4. *Kali Yuga* - the fourth age of the world, the iron age or that of
   vice. It commenced, according to some, 300 years ago,
   according to others 3,101 years ago, and according to yet
   others 1,370 years before the Christian era. Its duration is
   through 432,000 years; at the expiration of which period the
   world is to be destroyed.

2. ADVENT IN SHIRDI

In every age I come back
To deliver the holy.
To destroy the sin of the sinner,
To establish righteousness.

Bhagavad Gita, IV:8
(Swami Prabhavananda & Christopher Isherwood)

He who subjugated Kaliya and lifted on his little
finger the Govardhan mountain to protect (the
people) from the wrath of Lord Indra, was small in
years but excelled in bravery.

(Bhalan)

As a corollary to the account of Sathya Sai Baba about
Shirdi Sai Baba's birth given in Chapter One, he says:

In my last birth I appeared as Sai Baba of Shirdi. I
stayed with the aforesaid fakir until I was twelve. I
would play in the company of my friends, many kinds
of games. Once while playing a game of marbles with
the son of a *sowcar* (banker), he lost all his marbles.
So I called upon him to stake any other thing round in
shape. He ran to his house, brought a round *linga*
worshipped in his household and staked it. He lost the
bet. So he gave it to me and I swallowed it. The
sowcar's son raised a hue and cry and the news spread
everywhere. When the *sowcar's* wife heard it she
came running to the spot with a stick and threatened
me. I immediately opened my mouth and showed her
all the divine forms of Vishnu's various incarnations.

with the result that she prostrated before me. This became a topic of discussion in the whole town. Sitting in the mosque I would worship the *linga*. The local Muslims were agitated and boycotted the *fakir* who was my guardian. The Hindus drove me away from the temple thinking that I was a Muslim. The *fakir* was pained by all these events and asked me to leave. So I left his house and took to the road but did not give up the worship of the *linga*. While worshipping it I would keep a lamp before it which I would fill with water instead of oil. Yet it would burn like a lamp of oil.

Once while wandering along the bank of Godavari I encountered a *nabab* who had lost his horse. I told him that his horse would arrive there shortly. While we were thus conversing, the horse appeared there. The *nabab* was pleased. He became my follower and addressed me as 'Sai'. Thus wandering I arrived in Shirdi and camped in the courtyard in front of Khandoba's temple.

The present writer has already stated in Chapter One that while wandering along the banks of Godavari, Sai Baba appeared as a youth in Shirdi in District Ahmednagar.[1] He came into contact with a Mahatma and looking upon him as his *guru*, served him for twelve years with his heart and soul. Sai Baba would say, "My *guru* would sit at one place. He would never leave his seat and perform all his bodily acts there. Feeding him and cleaning the faeces and urine were my responsibilities. Whatever you see in me is the result of that service (to the *guru*)."[2] There are many paths for the direct perception of the Divine. Among them Sai Baba regarded devotion to *guru* as the principal means. In his discourse on *Bhagvat*, Section 11, Chapter 12, Stanza 12, this well-known and well-accepted doctrine has been taught by Lord Shri Krishna to Uddhav.[3]

As his *guru*'s time for *samadhi* came near or after the *guru*'s *samadhi*, Sai Baba constructed an edifice under the neem tree to the left of *Guru-padukasthan* and spent many many years in the underground cell (*hypogeum*) opposite, in loving memory of his *guru*.[4] This *samadhi* was first noticed when Rao Bahadur Sathe, the owner of the place, was all ready to erect a staircase to the verandah of the upper storey. When asked what should be done about it, Sai Baba said: "It is the *samadhi* of my ancestors. Do not disturb it. Make a bay-window and construct a staircase over it. God will bless those who burn incense before it on Thursdays and Fridays." It is learnt on enquiry that the underground cell (*hypogeum*) when first noticed, extended from Sathewada to the *masjid* and the *chavadi*. There was a small door behind the *chavadi* for exit. Sai Baba once told the present writer, "At that time I grew matted hair and beard which touched the ground!" Pointing to the column near the *dhuni* (fire) in the *masjid*, Sai Baba once said, "There was an underground cell where I would spend the day. Though people would move about nearby, I would not come out. Only when a virtuous man came I would emerge and hold discourse with him."

Since his advent in Shirdi, Sai Baba spent his whole life there right up to the time of his *samadhi* in 1918. During all these years he never went out of Shirdi except for occasional visits to Chandrabhan Sheth at Rahata, three miles away, and to Babasaheb Dengle at Nimgaon, a mile away. So it appeared that physically he was in Shirdi. But for the love of his devotees he would materialise and become manifest in any place by his yogic powers.

Twelve years before Sai Baba arrived in Shirdi, a *sadhu* called Devdas made his abode there. He had bright eyes and a good physique. Appa Bhil, Mhalsapati, etc., from Shirdi would often visit him. Kashiram would

provide him with undressed rice, or corn. His fame spread
like the waxing moon. He would write *Venkatesh Stotra*
(Hymn to Venkatesh) on a slate for Appa Bhil and others
and get it recited by them. He was a seer. Kashinath
Shimpi and Tatya Kote accepted him as their *guru*.
Moreover, *sadhus* of different sects came to him and Sai
Baba also liked their company.

As Shirdi was on the route to Rameshwar,
Pandharpur and other places of pilgrimage in the south,
many *sadhus* would come to Shirdi. A holy person by the
name of Janakidas of the Mahanubhava sect was also
residing in Shirdi then. Sai Baba would also spend some
time in his company. Gangagir, head of the *math*
(monastery) of Puntambe who had a large following,
would often come to Shirdi. Gangagir and Anandanath, a
disciple of Akkalkot Maharaj, had observed about Sai
Baba, "Whence comes it that this individual is here? He is
a gem of a man and of a very high order. Verily, it is the
good fortune of Shirdi that the Kohinoor diamond is
amidst them."

When Gangagir first came to Shirdi, Sai Baba would
keep two unbaked earthen pitchers filled with water
opposite the neem tree near his *guru's samadhi*. As soon
as he kept the pitchers on the ground the water in them
would drain away. A devotee was willing to supply baked
pitchers to Sai Baba but he would require only unbaked
pitchers. Sai Baba's devotee, Vamantatya, would give
him two unbaked earthen pitchers daily. Sai Baba would
keep them filled with water near the *Guru-samadhi*.
During this period Sai Baba also raised a garden opposite
the *Guru-samadhi*. The *Guru-samadhi* and the garden
are the symbols of Baba's love for his *guru* and his *tapas*.

During the day Sai Baba would wander in the fields
outside the village as he wished. While thus wandering
he met Mhalsapati who addressed him as Sai Baba and,
as the latter did not object, he came to be known by that

name. Because of Mhalsapati and others, Sai Baba began
staying in the dilapidated mosque. If anyone invited him
for a meal he would go. He would prescribe and give
medicines without charging any fees. In fact, he nursed
any patient himself if he found that the patient was
neglected. Once a patient died because he did not follow
the prescribed regimen. It is said that from that day Sai
Baba stopped administering medicine and instead
distributed *udi* (sacred ash). About this particular
change, Sai Baba once remarked to a devotee, "First, I
would give medicine to people but later I stopped this and
began repeating the name of Hari. In this process I saw
Him face to face."

After he had ceased to administer medicine, there
was a natural change in his lifestyle. Now he began
wearing tattered garments and begged for alms as many
times as he liked. He would carry a *dhoti* on his shoulder
and gathering one end of it, he would convert it into a
jholi (bag) and put dry *bhiksha* like rice, *bhakri*
(unleavened millet bread) in it. In another hand he would
carry a tumbler in which he would accept all liquid or
semi-liquid substances like *amti*, cooked vegetable,
chatni, milk, curds, etc. He would then keep all the
bhiksha in a *kundi* (open-mouthed jar). Crows, dogs and
cats would take away morsels of food from it and no one
would shoo them away. The person sweeping the masjid
would also take away 10-12 *bhakris* from the *kundi*
without any objection being raised. If any poor, hungry or
an unexpected visitor arrived, he also would be fed from
it. To keep visitors away Sai Baba would sometimes feign
anger; so the villagers called him a mad *fakir* and did not
go his way or trouble him. But there was a pious Maratha
lady who knew his worth. She was aware of his spiritual
eminence. So she had vowed not to take her meal unless
Sai Baba was first fed. By day, Sai Baba would be either
near *Guru-samadhi*, or in the fields, or in the jungle

nearby, or in Nimgaon. But Bayajabai would carry Sai
Baba's meal in a wicker basket over her head and after
seeking him out she would feed him and only then have
her meal. How would such a person send away Sai Baba
empty-handed if he came for alms? We will see later how
Sai Baba favoured her son Tatya Ganpat Kote, and
helped him in his difficulties, raised his prestige and
ultimately laid down his life in exchange for Tatya's.[5]

Mhalsapati, who first named him as Sai Baba, took
him to the village and introduced him to his two friends,
Kashiram Shimpi and Appa Jagale. This trio received all
sadhus, gosains, bairagis, fakirs, etc., who visited the
village and served them. The three became Sai Baba's
devotees and served him with their bodies, mind and
wealth. It is they who arranged for his stay in the *masjid.*

At that time Sai Baba did not accept *dakshina* from
anyone. So he would not accept even from Kashiram.
Kashiram would then be sad and would be in tears. In his
psychological state there was a subtle feeling of his being
the donor and Sai Baba being the recipient. Of course he
would be unhappy. Seeing this Sai Baba began asking
him *dakshina* repeatedly. In the beginning he would take
a pice or two. Slowly and gradually he raised his demand.
Since Sai Baba began accepting *dakshina*, Kashiram's
financial position deteriorated. In a few days he was
beggared. No one would even lend him any money for
giving *dakshina* to Sai Baba. When he was reduced to
such a sorry plight, he realised that both the donor and
the recipient were fractions of His radiance and in order
to remove his egotism Sai Baba had reduced him to
penury. The day he realised this and abandoned the ego
of differentation of himself as the donor and Sai Baba as
the recipient, his monetary condition started improving
and he attained a happier state of mind than before.
Thereafter, whether Sai Baba asked him for *dakshina* or
not, he did not lose the equanimity of his mind.

Kashiram was a vendor of cloth and on the bazaar day in the surrounding areas, he would set up his shop. Once, while returning from Naur Bazaar he had an encounter with an armed party of Bhil freebooters. Kashiram gave away all that he had except a small bundle which he would not part with. The plunderers thought that the bundle contained the most valuable things and that's why he was refusing to part with it. Actually, the bundle contained only powdered sugar which Kashiram always carried on Janakidas's advice to feed the ants. So when the looters tried to snatch away the bundle, he resisted them. He picked up a sword of one of the looters which was lying on the ground and put two robbers to death. In the meantime, a third robber hit him on the head with an axe. Kashiram lost consciousness and fell to the ground. Considering him as dead, the rest of the robbers fled from there.

But Kashiram was not dead. He regained consciousness after some time. He was asked to go to a doctor by others but as he had boundless confidence in Sai Baba, he did not heed this advice and returned to Shirdi. After taking the treatment prescribed, he was restored to health within a few days. Kashiram received the sword as a reward from the Bombay Government for his act of bravery.

At the very time the struggle between Kashiram and the robbers was going on, Sai Baba was abusing and uttering a cry of distress or trouble, bellowing, and at the same time beating his mouth with his hand. From this conduct of Sai Baba the villagers of Shirdi surmised that some dear devotee of Sai Baba was in trouble and Sai Baba was raising a hue and cry to save him. And so it happened. The armed party of Bhil robbers was a large one and escaping from their clutches was impossible without divine help.

Many years after this incident this bhakta passed away on *Ekadashi* day. Appa Jagale also died one

Ekadashi, many years after serving Sai Baba devotedly. Of the three devotees, the contact with the *pujari* of Khandoba, Mhalsapati, lasted right up to the *samadhi* of Sai Baba. Until the last he was engaged in the service of Sai Baba.

Every alternate night Sai Baba would sleep in the *masjid.* That day Mhalsapati would also pass the night in the *masjid* with Sai Baba. On that night, he would go to the *masjid* at nine o'clock, sit the whole night reclining against a pillar and conversing with Sai Baba. If Mhalsapati drowsed off Sai Baba would immediately wake him up. For fourteen years Tatya Patil also slept in the *masjid.* Sai Baba would engage them in conversation and keep them awake the whole night.[6]

On the full-moon day in the month of *Margashirsha* (November-December), in *Sake* year 1807 (A.D. 1885) as he had a severe bout of Asthma, Sai Baba said to Mhalsapati, "I entrust my body to your custody. I am going into *samadhi.* Please take care of my body for three days." So saying, Sai Baba went into *nirvikalpa samadhi.* At that time Mhalsapati sat by Sai Baba continuously for three days and nights. Seeing the motionless body (resembling a corpse) ignorant people began talking of preparing for his funeral. But remembering Sai Baba's words, Mhalsapati scotched all that talk. As said by Sai Baba, he came down to normal consciousness from his *samadhi* on the appointed day and time. If Mhalsapati had not taken care at that time the devotees would have been deprived of Sai Baba's company for the next thirty-three years.[7]

When we think of the monetary condition of Mhalsapati we are reminded of Krishna's devotee Sudama, how poor he was at the time of his going to Dwaraka. But it appears from one incident that Sai Baba wanted him to be content with his lot. Once a rich man offered a platter filled with gold coins to Sai Baba as *dakshina*. But Sai Baba declined the gift without even touching the coins. At that time Mhalsapati had come to worship Sai Baba. Seeing him, the man asked leave of Sai Baba to offer the coins to Mhalsapati. Sai Baba flatly refused permission and said, "In *fakiri* (freedom from worldly encumbrances and care) lies true sovereignty. *Fakiri* is of long-standing, ancient, while dukedom is transitory."[8]

The authority of this devotee of Sai Baba who ever performed the *japa* of *Om Namah Shivaya* was not ordinary. Because of his having had the benefit of Sai Baba's companionship even in Sai Baba's lifetime, many devotees got their doubts cleared by Mhalsapati if they did not understand the meaning of Sai Baba's words. After Sai Baba had passed away he was the source of obtaining satisfaction and assurance. Since he had a premonition of his end he had intimated to all his fellow devotees in advance about it. The edifice of his *samadhi* is in his own house. The *puja* of Khandoba is now performed by his son, Martandrao.[9]

Notes

1. How and when the advent of Sai Baba in Shirdi took place is narrated in the article entitled 'Shri Sai Babanche Shirdit Agaman' (Marathi), by V.B. Kher, which was published in the issue of Navashakti dated April, 1979. It is translated into English under the title *The Advent of Shri Sai Baba in Shirdi*.

2. *Shri Sai Satcharita*, Chap. XIX, pp. 61-68 and Chap. XXXII, pp. 66-68, 75-79, 88-89. V.B. Kher visited Sailu Pathri, parbhani in Marathwada in June 1975 and investigated who Sai Baba's *guru* was. From all the information available to him, he came to the conclusion that Venkusa or Roshanmia was not his *guru*. In fact, it is doubtful whether Sai Baba had any *guru* and it is likely that, like the saints of Maharashtra, Tukaram and Ramdas, he too must have had a direct perception of the Divine. On the basis of his research, B.V. Kher wrote an article entitled "The Guru of Shri Sai Baba", which was featured in the April and May 1976 issues of *Shri Sai Leela*.

3. Thus endeavour to establish a living relationship with your Sadguru. This is the highest form of *bhakti*. By the sword of knowledge produced by such *bhakti*, sever the ignorance of *jiva* and realise your Self. Then give up all your activities involving (new) *karma*.

4. About these *padukas* all the information is detailed in V.B. Kher's article entitled "Shri Akkalkot Swami Maharaj and Shri Sai Baba", published in the July 1976 issue of *Shri Sai Leela*.

5. *Shri Sai Satcharita,* Chap. VIII, pp. 105-109.

6. Ibid., chap. VIII, pp. 116-122.

7. Ibid., chap. XLIV, pp. 62-64.

8. Ibid., chap. VIII, p. 112.

9. Martandrao passed away a few years ago. At the time Swami Sai Sharan Anand published the sixth edition of this biography of Sai Baba in 1966, Martandrao was still alive.

3. DEVOTION TO SADGURU

He (true *Guru*) removes the veil from the eyes,
And gives the true vision of Brahma:
He reveals the worlds in Him, and
Makes me to hear the Unstruck Music:
One Hundred Poems of Kabir
Translated by Rabindranath Tagore, No XXII

It is the mercy of my true *Guru* that
has made me to know the unknown;
Kabir says: 'The *Guru* is great beyond words,
and great is the good fortune of the disciple.'
One Hundred Poems of Kabir
Translated by Rabindranath Tagore, No XXVII

For Sai Baba, a born *Siddha,* who manifested himself in order to perform his mission of incarnation, there was no need or expectation of a *Sadguru.*[1] Where was such a need or expectation for Shri Rama or Shri Krishna? Yet, according to the spirit of the times, they followed the practice of sitting at the feet of the *guru* (for the sake of gaining knowledge) and did *leela*. Sai Baba must have done likewise. As said earlier, from his childhood to youth, he served his *guru* in the *chavadi* with his heart and soul. After his *guru* took *samadhi*, Sai Baba spent years in the loving contemplation of his *guru* in the underground cell (*hypogeum*) opposite the *samadhi*.

In this connection the aged mother of Nana Chopdar, a resident of Shirdi, narrated a wonderful tale. She said, "Initially, this fair and handsome lad was seen sitting

under the neem tree. People were astonished at the sight
of this beautiful youth. He practised severe austerities.
Cold or heat did not affect him. When first sighted he was
a knower of Brahman. Even in his dreams he was
desireless. His renunciation was firm as if he had
abandoned *maya* completely. People from near and far
came for his *darshan*. By day he kept no company; he was
not afraid of the darkness at night. Where could this
youth have come from, was the thought that filled the
minds of all. His form was so comely that it would be a
case of love at first sight for anyone. He did not visit any
household. He was mostly seen sitting under the neem
tree. Everyone would wonder on seeing this
personification of renunciation."

An astonishing thing happened one day. It was the
day of Khandoba's fair. Two to four persons began to
shiver, heave and chatter as if possessed by the Spirit (of
the god Khandoba). People began asking questions to
him: "Who are the fortunate parents of this lad? Where
does he hail from? Oh God Khandoba, please tell us." The
Spirit replied, "Get a hoe, dig at the place I point out, and
you will know." One man brought a hoe and began to dig
at the spot opposite the neem tree as pointed out. After
digging for some time at the place, a layer of bricks was
noticed. Below the layer of bricks was found one stone
disk of a grinding wheel. On removing the stone disk an
underground cell (*hypogeum*) was seen which was
plastered with lime and in its four corners were four
lighted *samais* (upright lampstand usually made of brass
or silver with a hollow disk at the top which is filled with
oil and a wick); a *pat* (a low wooden stool); a *gomukhi* (a
glove, shaped like a cow's mouth by which the hand is
covered in telling beads); and a rosary were also found
there. The Spirit also said, "This boy practised penance
here for twelve years."

Then people plied Sai Baba with question after
question. He replied, "This is the shrine of my *guru*. Take

care of it."[2] As commanded by Sai Baba the underground cell was closed securely. Many years thereafter Sai Baba told Hari Sitaram Dikshit, "This is the place of our forefathers. Burn incense here every Thursday and Friday and it will conduce to your welfare." Mhalsapati and other old residents of Shirdi regarded this place as the shrine of Sai Baba's *guru* and would bow to it. That Sai Baba performed penance for twelve years near this shrine, is the general belief in Shirdi. On behalf of the Shirdi Sansthan, incense is burnt here every Thursday and Friday evening.

Who was this powerful and mighty *guru* of Sai Baba? No reliable information is available regarding what family he was born in, when his forefathers came to Shirdi, and when and how he and Sai Baba came to know each other. In Chapter XXVI of *Bhakti Saramrit* (Marathi)[3], Das Ganu infers that the name of the *guru* of Sai Baba may have been Venkusa. Based on this information, Sri Narasimhaswami imagines from the obscure and uncertain replies which Sai Baba gave in his examination on commission by a first class magistrate in a theft case, that he had stated the name of his *guru* as Venkusa. This great devotee of Sai Baba forgets that in this very deposition when asked what his caste was, Sai Baba replied, "My caste is *Parvar Digar*", i.e., God. This clearly means 'I am God — Rama, Krishna, Eshwar of the Hindus, Allah of the Muslims, Zoroaster of the Parsis and Jesus of the Christians. There is no necessity to ask about me, about my caste, *guru,* etc.' Rao Bahadur Hari Vinayak Sathe says in his statement, "Sai Baba gave me his *guru*'s name. It ended with '*Shah*' or '*Sa*'. I have forgotten the rest of the name." In the presence of the present writer Sai Baba had said, more than twice, that his *guru*'s name was Roshan Shah Miya. The object of this was to remind the present Brahmin writer that he should remember the sun which lights up this world, and

so faithfully carry out his ordained duties. As urged by
Sai Baba, the writer carried them out but thinking a
little more it occured to him that *Roshan* was a word
frequently occurring in Sai Baba's conversation. In
Tamaso ma jyotir gamaya (Lead me from darkness to
light), the word *jyoti* (light) has been used and in this very
sense Sai Baba would use the word *Roshan*. The term
'Roshanshahmiya' suggests that Self-effulgent Spirit is
real (*Shah*) in this world and this world appears (real)
due to ignorance. Similarly, there is no exaggeration in
the statement that Sai Baba said by way of advice that
'there is life in death', when he offered his own life in
exchange for Tatya Kote's and demonstrated the truth
thereof.

Whenever Sai Baba talked about himself to anyone
whom he was advising, he did so not in order to tell about
his past life, but to remind the latter about his chosen
deity (*Ishta* or *Upasya Daivat*). So if Sai Baba told anyone
that his *guru* was Venkusa, it referred to the chosen deity
of the latter.

The Responsibility of a Sadguru
Sai Baba would tell Nanasaheb Chandorkar that these
days many are fond of becoming *gurus*. But the
responsibility of the *guru* is onerous. Until his disciple
attains salvation the *guru* has to follow him from birth to
birth and ultimately set him free. By merely giving
advice one does not become a *guru*. There are many
erudite scholars who can give plenty of learned
discourses, but thereby they cannot become *adhyatmic*
(spiritual) *gurus*. Only he is a *guru* who does not rest
content merely with giving a lesson to his disciple, but
watches over him carefully to see how the lesson is being
practised. Not only that, he also encourages him, corrects
him whenever necessary, sets him on the virtuous path
and monitors his progress from birth to birth until the
latter is liberated. For this very reason omniscient (lit.

Trikalajna, knower of the past, present and future) *guru* Sai Baba attracted by visible means all those persons who were bound to him by ties of past births (*rinanubandha*) and carried them further from the last stage of their past birth or in the present birth from where their progress was held up. He kept a vigilant eye on how far his advice was being acted upon. He once said to Nanasaheb Chandorkar, "If anyone calls on you for help in a public cause you should do whatever you can. If you are not in a position to help or do not wish to help you should decline courteously but should not make fun of the person seeking help or get cross with him. Will you remember this?" Nanasaheb promised to do so. Sai Baba commented thereon, "This lesson is not as easy to follow in practice as it seems." However, Nanasaheb assured him that he would certainly abide by his advice. Thereafter, the following incident happened.

Whenever Nanasaheb went to Shirdi from Kopargaon, on his way he would visit the Dattatreya *mandir* for the Lord's *darshan* and spend some time there. He would also meet the caretaker of the *mandir*. Once, due to a pressing request of the caretaker, Nanasaheb agreed to give monetary assistance of Rs 300 for the construction of a *ghat* (landing platform with steps). The caretaker was happy. After some days Nanasaheb started for Shirdi with his *sadu* (husband of wife's sister). However, as he could not arrange to take Rs 300 with him, he decided to avoid the caretaker of the *mandir* on the way, and instead of taking the regular road for reaching Shirdi, went by a by-road. The by-road was in a bad condition and a thorn entered Nanasaheb's foot which gave him a lot of trouble. When he reached Shirdi, Sai Baba appeared to be angry and did not talk to Nanasaheb.

When asked why Sai Baba was silent, he said to Nanasaheb, "You feared that the caretaker would ask

you for the promised monetary help and in the process
you missed *darshan* of Dattatreya. You also took
recourse to a by-road instead of the regular one. Is this
how you follow my lesson? If you did not carry Rs 300
with you or could not arrange for it, what was the harm
in telling the truth to the caretaker? What was the
necessity of coming by the by-road and suffering the
pricks of a thorn in the foot instead of following the
straightforward course? Why should I talk with such a
person?" Nanasaheb was astonished at Sai Baba's
omniscience. He admitted his fault and assured Sai Baba
that he would not be guilty of its repetition.

Sai Baba astonished Nanasaheb by testing him once
again to see how far he had learnt his lesson! He had once
cautioned Nanasaheb thus: "If anyone approaches you
for help, give according to your capacity. If the recipient is
not satisfied you should politely decline to give anything
more. But do not get angry with him or show off your
wealth or power to him." Nanasaheb agreed to conduct
himself accordingly. A few months after this
conversation, a beggar woman came for alms at
Nanasaheb's residence at Kalyan. She was offered alms
as usual but she asked for the pitcherful of *bhajani* (flour
made of four or five kinds of grain, parched and ground
together) prepared by Nanasaheb's wife. Nanasaheb's
wife gave also a little *bhajani* to her but she was not
satisfied and asked for more. Nanasaheb's wife then gave
half the quantity to her. Yet the beggar woman was
dissatisfied. Then Nanasaheb's wife was agitated and
said to her angrily, "Take what is given or get out." But
the beggar-woman not only refused to accept anything
less than the pitcherful but would not budge from her
place. So Nanasaheb's wife called her husband and
apprised him of the facts. Nanasaheb called his *chaprasi*
and said, "She is a beggar-woman and yet she has the
audacity to ask for all the *bhajani*! Isn't she ashamed? It

is well if she accepts what is given or else throw her out forcibly." Hearing this the beggar-woman said, "If you don't want to give the whole *bhajani*, don't, but why ask your *chaprasi* to throw me out forcibly? I will myself go." So saying she left. After some months Nanasaheb went to Shirdi for Sai Baba's *darshan*. This time too, Sai Baba appeared to be cross and would not talk to Nanasaheb. When asked the reason for this, Sai Baba said, "What's the use of talking to somebody who does not conduct himself according to the advice given to him? Did you not want to throw out by force, the beggar-woman asking for the *bhajani*? She would have sat on your doorstep for some time and left. Instead of persuading her by sweet talk, where was the necessity of threatening the use of force?" Nanasaheb did not immediately recall the incident which had happened some five or six months ago. But when he remembered it he was filled with remorse. He did not ever imagine that Sai Baba would test him in the garb of a beggar-woman! Nanasaheb's respect and esteem for Sai Baba grew multifold by this incident and the conviction grew upon him, that he could never tell in what garb and when Sai Baba would put him to test. This brought about the necessary change in his attitude and behaviour.

Two Guru-mantras or Bhakti-sutras

Sai Baba often said, "For a human being, a *guru's* place is pre-eminent. By keeping utmost faith in him, by being devoted to him alone, everything is obtained. A devotee's whole strength is due to his *guru*. Devotion to a *guru* is superior to devotion to gods or goddesses. *Guru* is the Supreme Being." And he would praise and commend devotion to a *guru*. From his aforegoing utterances and the boundless love with which Sai Baba practised penance in the underground cell under the neem tree for several years, raised a garden, his sentiment that it was a place of his forefathers, his statement that burning incense would conduce to the well-being of the devotee, we get some idea of his love for, service of, and surrender to his *guru*. For the born-*siddha*, Sai Baba, there was no need of any *guru* or a long course of spiritual practices. But in accordance with time-honoured practices of incarnations to set a standard and example for seekers, he undertook the course of devotion to the *guru*.

Out of those who came for his *darshan*, he would gladly tell the ones whom he considered as seekers about his *guru's* powers, kindness, single-minded contemplation or unexcelled changeless state of meditation and his own singular service to his peerless *guru*. Similarly, he would clearly explain the two great precepts of *bhakti yoga*, pointed out by his *guru*, and would command to the seekers to faithfully adhere to them.

Food, pleasure and merriment, happiness and sorrow in life are dependent on one's *prarabdha* (*karma* constituting the occasion of the present birth). When Nanasaheb established that he was a true seeker of spiritual emancipation and not mere worldly pleasures, Sai Baba spoke to him of these two precepts or steps. Through Nanasaheb, many devotees came to know of them, and knowledge thereof was communicated to Annasaheb Dabholkar, author of *Shri Sai Satcharita*. We will trace that incident and Sai Baba's easy and superb way of instruction.

Once Dabholkar was sitting near Sai Baba. In his presence Sai Baba told one Sathe, who had finished one *parayana* of *Guru Charitra*[4], that he should complete one more *parayana* thereof so that God would favour him and he would be liberated. Hearing this Dabholkar was filled with *sattvic* spirit of competition - that Sathe would be freed from the cycle of birth and death in one *parayana* and he who had been reading *Gurucharitra* for forty years, should be without any such reward! Sai Baba read

the thought passing in Dabholkar's mind and said to him,
"Go to Madhavrao Deshpande and get fifteen rupees."
Dabholkar went to Madhavrao and conveyed Sai Baba's
message to him. Madhavrao immediately replied, "How
can a poor man like me have money to give to Sai Baba?
Moreover, how am I qualified to instruct a learned person
like you?" So saying, Madhavrao began narrating various
experiences of Sai Baba to him. One such experience
related to Radhabai. Hearing that tale Dabholkar's mind
was quietened and he was overwhelmed by the lovable
art of Sai Baba to confer favour. In this tale, too, there
was instruction regarding two spiritual precepts.
Thereafter, Madhavrao and Dabholkar went to Sai Baba,
and Sai Baba asked Dabholkar, "Have you brought the
Rs 15 from Madhavrao?" In reply Dabholkar began
narrating what he heard from Madhavrao and added
that Radhabai's tale is the one through which you have
certainly showered grace on me. Sai Baba then urged
Dabholkar to remember this one lesson which would be
conducive to his welfare. Then he gave the whole
quantity of sugar received by him as *prasad* to Dabholkar
and said, "If you keep this one thing in mind, your mind
will become saturated with sweetness like sugar." From
this Dabholkar was convinced that Sai Baba desired to
instruct him through the medium of Madhavrao. The
thought of *sattvic* competition in his mind vanished and
he was happy that Sai Baba's concern and solicitude for
him was no less than for Sathe.

The tale of Radhabai is as follows: Once Khashaba
Deshmukh's mother, Radhabai, came to Shirdi for Sai
Baba's *darshan* along with some folks from Sangamner.
At the sight of Sai Baba's she was instinctively drawn
towards him and felt that if he were to become her *guru*,
through his instruction, she could advance spiritually.
Cogitating over this, she came to the firm conclusion that
at any cost, she must get a *mantra* directly from Sai

Baba, and began fasting. After three days' fast she became weak. One devotee of Sai Baba felt concerned at her condition and told Sai Baba that unless the old woman was pacified, she would suffer and may even die. So Sai Baba called her, bade her sit opposite him and said:

Mother, I will tell you the truth. My *guru* was a great Master, full of kindness. I served him with all my being, but he would not favour me with a *mantra*. I had an intense urge to receive a *mantra* from him and felt that I must never leave him. He had accepted me as his disciple from the start. He had taken two pice from me. My desireless *guru* never wanted material wealth. He demanded two things: *shraddha* or *nistha* (faith, trust) and *saburi* (courage combined with patient waiting). I gave these two pice to him at once. It is rare to find a *guru* like mine. I would look at the living embodiment of devotion and love, ever lost in medititation, with admiration, day and night. In the process, I lost all sense of hunger or thirst. He became the centre of my observation, attention and meditation. If he were out of my sight I would become restless. My *guru* had no other expectation from me except *shraddha* and *saburi*. I had already committed them to him. So he never neglected me and ever protected me from danger. Sometimes I would stay in his company and at other times away from him. Yet he looked after me with a kind eye just as a tortoise nourishes her young one by her mere sight. I speak the truth. My *guru* never initiated me with a *mantra*. So how will I initiate you or give you a *mantra*? But follow this fundamental precept of singular trust and courage. And do not torture yourself by fasting.

This advice sank deep into Radhabai. She gave up her fast and began practising this form of devotion faithfully.[5]

The Debt to Guru

The ties of Nanasaheb Chandorkar with Sai Baba were very old. When Nanasaheb was the Collector's Personal Assistant in 1887, the Kulkarni of Shirdi had to go to the Collector's office in Ahmednagar in connection with work of land revenue. Sai Baba sent a message with him to Nanasaheb to meet him at Shirdi. Sai Baba would say many times, "I will willy-nilly drag anyone who is my man, here, even if he is hiding in the seventh nether world." Moreover, an incarnation is eager as well as in a hurry to complete his mission. In accordance with this Sai Baba sent an invitation to Nanasaheb. But, Nanasaheb would not believe Appa Kulkarni. On the other hand he also remarked that, even if what he said was true, he would not go, and so did not. A second time Sai Baba invited Nanasaheb, but still he did not go. However, when Sai Baba sent an invitation the third time, Nanasaheb agreed to go. He was perplexed and wondered whether Sai Baba was a *fakir* or a *sadhu*. He could not come to any conclusion. He put on a jacket of alpaca and went for Sai Baba's *darshan*. On the way he remembered that one should not go empty-handed while visiting the place of a saint or God. He had not taken anything with him and there was no possibility of getting anything in a village like Shirdi. He did not know what to do but discovered in the pocket of his jacket a *pudi* (a small packet consisting of a folded sheet) containing a few almonds and sugar crystals which he always kept in his pocket. He felt better by the thought that he had something to give by way of offering.

On reaching Shirdi with his companions he bowed to Sai Baba and placed before him the offering. A few people were already sitting with Sai Baba. Thus in all there were twenty-five men. Yet the *prasad* in that *pudi* of offering which was distributed, sufficed for all! Nanasaheb took a seat facing Sai Baba and put a

question to him, "Why did you send for me?" Sai Baba
replied, "Well there are any number of men in this world,
but instead of calling them, when I call you there must be
a reason for it." "What is it?" asked Nanasaheb. Sai Baba
said, "There is a relationship between us going as far
back as four births. You are not aware of it but I am. So I
called you.[6] Come again at your convenience."
Nanasaheb said that he would, but did not believe in Sai
Baba's word. Many days thereafter, an epidemic of
plague broke out at Ahmednagar. The Collector
requested Nanasaheb to get himself inoculated against
plague, so that, by his example, others would also get
themselves so inoculated. Inoculation against any
disease for immunisation was a new experiment at that
time. It was the popular belief that inoculation is
harmful. Nanasaheb asked for a week's time to think
over the matter and in the meantime met Sai Baba and
sought his counsel. Sai Baba said, "What is the objection?
Get yourself inoculated. There is nothing to fear."
Nanasaheb informed the Collector of his decision to get
himself inoculated. The Collector was pleased.
Nanasaheb got himself inoculated and his example was
followed by all other employees in the Collector's office.
No harm came to them. From that time, Nanasaheb
came to believe in Sai Baba, and every fortnight when he
camped near about Shirdi, he would spend the weekend
in Sai Baba's company. On such occasions, late into the
Saturday nights, Sai Baba would talk to him about
philosophy, *Bhagavad Gita* and matters religious. The
tale of the two pice - *shraddha* and *saburi* -was one such
tale narrated to him by Sai Baba.

Sai Baba manifested himself for the sake of
advancing on the righteous path, those who were
connected in their past lives with him. He contacted them
and influenced their lives by his company, love and words
of advice. Similarly, he won over by love a learned *fakir* of

Ahmednagar, named Javar Ali, and then humbled his pride of being a *murshid*. This *fakir* from Ahmednagar had settled down in Rahata, five kilometres away from Shirdi. He was well-versed in the *Quran*. He began constructing an *idgah* (place of prayer) in Rahata, but in the process attracted the charge of having polluted the temple of Veerabhadra. So he left Rahata and came to stay in Shirdi with Sai Baba. Javar Ali was a sweet talker and soon impressed the villagers of Shirdi with his learning. It appeared as if Sai Baba's friendship with him had increased. When Javar Ali shifted his residence to Rahata again, Sai Baba accompanied him. He served Javar Ali in every way and even carried water for him. Sai Baba would visit Shirdi occasionally but his devotees were dissatisfied at his having left Shirdi. So they went in a deputation to Rahata. When they reached Rahata, Javar Ali was out and Sai Baba was alone. He said to them, "It is good that the *fakir* is not here. He is a hot-tempered man and if he knows that you have come to take me away, he will curse you." While they were thus engaged in conversation, Javar Ali arrived. He asked all of them in a friendly way, "What, you have come to take this lad away? If you wish to do that, take me also with him." He said so because he had come to depend on Sai Baba for his so many services that he would otherwise miss him. They consented and so both Sai Baba and Javar Ali returned to Shirdi. Once Javar Ali and Devadas engaged in a debate in which Javar Ali was defeated. Crestfallen, Javar Ali slipped away to Vaijapur. Many years later, he visited Shirdi in a chastened mood and filled with repentance for having considered himself a *murshid* and Sai Baba his *chela*, and saluted Sai Baba. It is comparatively easy to put away the pride of wealth, but difficult to give up pride of learning, knowledge, wisdom and righteousness. To relieve Javar Ali of such pride, Sai Baba won him over by love, and then humbling

him in a debate through the agency of Devadas, he
brought him to his senses. Similarly, he assumed the
form of an old man and advised Upasani Baba, who was
emaciated through mortification of flesh, to partake of
food, and brought him to Shirdi. Upasani did not wish to
remain in Shirdi and left for Dhulia. But Omnipresent
Sai Baba, exercising control over all the faculties of
Upasani, brought him forcibly to Shirdi and assured him
that if he stayed in Shirdi for four years he was sure to
attain liberation.

Testing the Righteous

As faith, trust, devotion and love strike firm roots, m'
calamities descend, as if God were testing the righteou..
Every devotee has to face the test, either to gauge the
depth of his trouble, or to enable him to pass the test
successfully and furnish him an opportunity to
strengthen his virtues. Mirabai had to face many
troubles one after the other; Kabir-Kamal had to stand
the ordeal of being led to the hangman's noose; Narsi
Mehta had to be ready to face the indignity of being
called a thief; Madalasa, a devotee who was a courtesan's
daughter, had in the garb of a merchant to be prepared to
die as a *sati* for concealed Shiva, etc. Guru is God,
Parabrahma. So it is no wonder if Sai Baba, in order to
test the faith of his devotees, had to put them through an
ordeal. The late Hari Sitaram, alias Kakasaheb Dikshit,
had turned his back on a flourishing legal practice and a
promising political career to serve Sai Baba, with his
body, mind and wealth.

Once Sai Baba tested his faith in a strange way. One
day a goat on the border of death was tied to a post near
the masjid by someone. At that time Bade Baba, a *fakir,*
was sitting near Baba. Sai Baba asked Bade Baba to kill
the goat with one stroke, but he demurred. So Sai Baba
asked Madhavrao Deshpande to get a knife and finish
the   job.   Madhavrao   brought   a   knife   from

Radhakrishnaai, but when she came to know the purpose for which it was required she demanded it back. In the meantime Dikshit came there. Sai Baba then asked him to get a knife to strike down the goat. Dikshit had immovable faith in Sai Baba. He had firm faith that Sai Baba would never ask him to do any wrong sinful act. Dikshit, to whom the word of Sai Baba was the law and guiding principle in his life, brought a knife from Sathe Wada and waited for a signal from Sai Baba to strike. At that moment Sai Baba exclaimed, "Let it be, Kaka, turn back. How cruel you are! You call yourself a Brahmin and commit violence! Don't you have any compunction?" Dikshit threw away the knife in his hand and said to Sai Baba, "Your nectar-like speech is my *dharma*. I do not know any other religion. Your word is law as far as I am concerned." Then Sai Baba said, "Take this jug of water. I will myself kill him by *halal*." After some time he only stated, "Instead of killing him here, take him away to the *fakir's takia*." There the goat died a natural death. Everyone knew that the goat would die on its own, but Baba used this as an occasion to test the faith of his devotees and separate the goat from the sheep. He also showed thereby that he had to protect Dikshit and his family from accidents, diseases and calamities as Dikshit had single-minded devotion toward him and had surrendered and sought refuge in him.

He who has faith and confidence that his *guru* is omniscient, omnipresent and omnipotent; he is his *guru*'s child; that it is not necessary to ask and beg of anyone else for knowledge; the mighty *guru* will, at the appropriate time, give him the appropriate thing and advice; and so the devotee lives peacefully and courageously and gets the required temporal and spiritual knowledge when the need arises. This knowledge may be obtained through a book, natural utterance of any individual or from within on attention being concentrated on some aspect of material object or action of living creature. But for that it is not necessary for a devotee to approach any person other than his *guru*; in fact, such approach indicates lack of faith in his *guru*; it is not a sign of total surrender to him. In time of difficulty or calamity, worldly persons consult as many persons as possible and chart out their course of action. If a suit is filed in a court, besides the advocate on record, a senior lawyer may be consulted and his advice sought. If a patient is sick, other specialists may be consulted, besides his family doctor. But this rule of conduct in worldly affairs is not applicable to secure release from the cycle of birth and death. Think a hundred times before accepting and enthroning in your heart any person as *sadguru*. However, if you wish to benefit spiritually from him, then like a chaste and virtuous wife, you cannot install anyone else in that place; if you do, know that your faith is shaky and wanting.

And if your unresolved difficulty is solved through a book, natural utterance of an individual, concentration on some aspect of material object or action of living being, do not be under the mistaken belief that the said book, individual, material object or living being is your *guru*! On the other hand, you must always entertain the feeling that through the grace of your *sadguru*, the said book, individual, etc., were instrumental in resolving your doubt. When this lesson sinks in, you may be said to have taken the first step on the path. Then, and then only, you may be said to have given the *guru-dakshina* of faith and trust. This statement is supported and underlined by Sai Baba's strong disapproval of any devotee fishing for knowledge from other devotees instead of directly approaching him.

Once Sai Baba's devotee, Deo Mamledar of Dahanu, came to Shirdi. During the day, due to preoccupation with official duties, he had no time. He had intense desire to do some reading of religious books at night. Many a time he commenced reading *Jnaneshwari*, but some obstacle or the other would crop up and he would be unable to do regular reading of *Jnaneshwari*. So Deo was unhappy. At last he decided that he would start the reading of *Jnaneshwari* only when Sai Baba directed him so that no obstacle could thwart the regularity. In this frame of mind he arrived in Shirdi. There he met Balakram Mankar. Mankar had dedicated his body, mind and wealth to Sai Baba, and made Shirdi his abode. Sai Baba had permitted him to dress like him, i.e., don a *kafni* and tie a scarf round his head. This privilege had been extended only to three devotees, one of whom was Mankar. Naturally, there was a belief among the devotees, that they were the ones specially favoured by Sai Baba. In accordance with this belief, Deo asked Mankar, "How did you earn the grace of Sai Baba?" Mankar agreed to tell the whole story to Deo the next day and, in fact, did so. Then Deo asked him, "How did Sai Baba inspire you to do *upasana* (objective meditation)? Did he not tell you how to meditate on Brahman? Please tell me all about it."[7] Before Mankar could even reply, a messenger suffering from black leprosy, came there from Sai Baba with a message that Deo was wanted by Sai Baba. Deo immediately went to the masjid. It was as if Sai Baba was waiting for him near the compound wall. On seeing Deo he asked, "With whom and about what were you conversing?" Deo stated that he was conversing in the Dikshit Wada with Mankar about him. Then Sai Baba asked him for Rs 25 as *dakshina* which Deo readily gave. Thereafter, Sai Baba led Deo up the steps of the masjid and both sat facing each other. There was no one in the masjid besides the two of them. After a short while Sai Baba said, " The strip of cloth in which I keep the *dakshina* received by me has been stolen." Deo replied, "I do not know anything about your strip of cloth." Still Sai

Baba asked him to look for it in the masjid. Deo searched carefully but did not find it. Then Sai Baba became angry and flying into a temper denounced Deo and accused him of stealing the strip of cloth and demanded to know whether he came all the way to Shirdi to commit theft. Seeing all this Deo was astounded and stood up. He was ordered by Sai Baba to retire to the Wada. After two to three hours Sai Baba called his devotees and said to them, "What I said sometime back must have hurt old man Deo, but I could not help speaking as the theft was committed." Then he again asked for *dakshina* from Deo. Deo paid it and sat by Sai Baba. Sai Baba then turned to him and said, "What do you do in the Wada?" "Nothing," said Deo. Then Sai Baba said, "Make a rule to sit regularly in the Wada for reading *pothi*. When I am sitting here to give you the whole *jari shela* (a cloth composed of four breadths depending from the shoulders loosely over the body), what is this bad habit of stealing a shred of cloth?" Like the *chataka* bird which is delighted at the sight of clouds, Deo was also pleased but did not understand the cryptic reference to *shela*. Suddenly it dawned on him that Sai Baba may be referring to his direct enquiry with Mankar about meditation on Brahman as the theft of a shred of cloth. What Sai Baba wished to emphasize was that when the ground is ready for sowing, the *guru* on his own leads the devotee to the higher step. For that it is not necessary to run hither and thither without the *guru*'s approval, for nothing is achieved thereby; it only inhibits progress.

After this event no obstacle arose from the day of commencement in the regular reading and exposition of *Jnaneshwari* by Deo in accordance with Sai Baba's direction. Before the completion of one year, on Thursday, April 2, 1914, Deo had a pleasant experience in his dream of Sai Baba's grace. He saw Sai Baba sitting on the upper storey of his home. Sai Baba asked him, "Do

you understand the *pothi?*" Deo replied in the negative.
"When will you understand?" asked Sai Baba. Overcome
with emotion, Deo said, "It is no use reading the *pothi*
unless your grace descends on me." Then Sai Baba said.
"Sit by me and read in my presence." "What shall I read?"
questioned Deo. Sai Baba stated, "*Adhyatma* (discourse
on the Deity as the pervading and ruling Spirit)." Then
Deo commenced reading the *pothi* in his dream. Soon
thereafter the dream ended and Deo woke up. Deo's story
is a telling example of how Sai Baba cares for his
devotees and leads them on the righteous path when they
devotedly carry out his orders.

Notes

1. *Shri Sai Satcharita*, Chap. IV.
2. Ibid., Chap. IV, pp. 124-131.
3. Publiched in English by the All India Sai Samaj, Madras, in 1945 under the title *Sai Hari Kathas.*
4. *Gurucharitra*, a Marathi Pothi, is the religious biography of Shri Narasimha Saraswati, regarded as an incarnation of Lord Dattatreya, authored by Gangadhar Saraswati.
5. *Sri Sai Satcharita*, Chap. XVIII, 129-163 and Chap. XIX, pp. 35-104, 111-118.
6. *Bhagavad Gita*, IV, 52.
   You and I, Arjuna, have lived many lives
   I remember them all: You do not remember.
   *Translation into English by Swami Prabhavananda &
   Christopher Isherwood.*
7. Attention of the reader is drawn in this connection to *Brahma Sutra*, III, (iii), pp. 59-60; IV, (iv), pp. 15-16 and the commentary of Shankaracharya, *Bharat Teertha*, which is summarised below:
   Upasana is of two types: (1) *Ahamgraha Upasana* and (2) *Pratika Upasana. Ahamgraha Upasana* or meditation may be on *Saguna Brahma* (Brahman with form) or *Nirguna Brahma* (Brahman without form). In both, Brahman is regarded as not different or separate from Self, i.e., as its own Self. But when the presence of Deity is invoked by religious rites in an object without soul, meditation on such an object is called *Pratika Upasana*. By *Ahamgraha Upasana*, Brahmaloka can be attained, but it cannot be attained by *Pratika Upasana. Upasanas* enumerated in the *Upanishads* such as *Shandilya*

Vidya, Bhooma Vidya, Sat Vidya, Dahar Vidya, Upakoshal Vidya, Vaishwanar Vidya, Udgeetha Vidya, Anandmaya Vidya, Akshar Vidya, are all forms of *Ahamgraha Vidya.* The object of all these *Vidyas* or *Upasanas* is realisation of Self or Brahman. A seeker may select any one of these *Upasanas* of his choice and should then stick to it until the Self is realised. This is the rule of *Ahamgraha Upasana.* If a seeker goes after many *vidyas,* his attention will be divided and thereby his spiritual progress will be retarded or interrupted. Once the object of *Upasana* is realised, study of other *Upasanas* will be unnecessary.

Pratika Upasana is meant for the fulfilment of worldly desires. Hence, the above rule of *Ahamgraha Upasana* is not applicable to it and for satisfaction of various desires Upasana of more than one object or gods is permissible. Single-minded devotion of *Sadguru* is meant for Self-realisation. Worldly desires can be fulfilled by devotion to *Sadguru,* gods or goddesses, who have the power to grant such desires. But Swami Sai Sharan Anand is of humble opinion that it is advisable to stick to one object of *Upasana* even in this matter.

4. MEANS FOR THE UPLIFT OF DEVOTEES

Worship the feet of Hari, O my mind,
Beautiful to look upon, soft and cool as a lotus,
Able to remove the three kinds of pain.
When Prahlad grasped those holy feet
He was elevated to the rank of Indra.
When Dhruv took refuge in them
He was transported to the motionless realm.
In the fair body of the holy Dwarf
They measured the universe.
Their touch saved the wife of Gautam
They tamed the serpent Kaliya
When Krishna sported as a cowherd.
They supported the Govardhan Mountain
When Indra was put to shame.
Mira is the servant of Lal Giridhara,
The raft on which to cross the unnavigable sea.

The Devotional Poems of Mirabai, No 1.
(translated by A.J. Alston)

Even a material object which comes into contact with an individual whose heart beats continuously day and night in tune with *Logos*, bursts into speech. His speech discourses to the devotees and directs them. Let us now examine the means which are available to the *Sadguru* who is omnipresent (literally, envelops the atom, dust, individual and universe) and protects his devotees, ever and anon, by manifesting in gross, subtle, great or atomic form.

On account of the *keertanas* (celebrating the praises
of God with music and singing) of Das Ganu and
propagation of Nanasaheb Chandorkar and Kakasaheb
Dikshit, devotees, educated and uneducated, began to
flock to Shirdi. Sai Baba would instruct them according
to their capacity. In the instruction of Sai Baba, sayings
or quotes from *Jnaneswari, Eknathi Bhagwat*, or from
Samarth Ramdas, would be used with advantage. His
mastery of Sanskrit would put to shame even *shastris*
and *pundits*. This was proved by the way Sai Baba took a
sloka (stanza) from the *Bhagavad Gita* and expounded it
to Nanasaheb Chandorkar, and explained the meaning of
a Vedic hymn to a devotee. One Kharkar was unable to
understand the meaning of a Vedic hymn. Sai Baba
asked him to recite the hymn immediately before and
after the one in question, showed him the correlation of
the three hymns and clarified lucidly the meaning of the
middle hymn.[1] His Muslim devotees would extol his
profound knowledge of Arabic, Persian and Urdu. How he
was able to acquire all this knowledge is a great mystery.
For ever since he came to Shirdi in his youth, right up to
his end, he never had any books or means of writing.
Hence, many a devotee says, 'What can be unattainable
or unknown to him from whom the deity of learning
originates?' Others opine that it is the fruit of his long
penance and supreme devotion to his *guru*. Still others
believe that it is beyond the ken of the limited human
intellect to master all the scriptures in Sanskrit, Persian,
Arabic, Hindi, Marathi, etc. And as Sai Baba had such
knowledge, they assert that it is a proof of his
incarnation.

After he ceased administering medicine, Sai Baba's
reputation in Shirdi village was that of a mad *fakir* and
villagers kept away from him. In this period of his God-
intoxicated life, for many years, he would sleep at night
on a narrow plank of 10" breadth suspended from the

rafter of the roof and secured by rags. At the head and foot of the plank *panatis* (earthen saucer-form receptacles for the oil and wick of a lamp) would be lighted. No one ever saw Sai Baba getting up on the plank at night or getting off the plank in the morning. He would be seen on the plank only in the lying posture. He would pass the whole night in such posture. Even if a weak man were to step on the suspended plank it would come crashing down. People wondered how he could lie on it through his yogic powers! Slowly the news spread and crowds began to gather to see this marvel. So, one day, Sai Baba removed the plank for good.

Many years thereafter Sai Baba once narrated lovingly to Kakasaheb Dikshit, the story of his penance, and Dikshit was so moved that he asked him, "If you are so fond of sleeping on a plank, I will suspend one plank here for the night." Sai Baba said, "Never mind. How would it do for me to sleep up while Mhalsapati by my side sleeps on the ground?" To which Dikshit replied, "We will put up another plank for him." Exclaimed Sai Baba, "Kaka, it is not for any ordinary person to sleep on a suspended plank. It is possible only for him who is wide awake and who can do without sleep.[2] I say this to Mhalsapati, 'Keep your hand on my heart and watch the continuous *nama-smaran* which goes on there. Wake me up the moment it stops.' But he falls asleep while doing this and his hand becomes heavy like a stone. How can he sleep on the plank? He alone who is ever awake, watchful and absorbed in devotion can sleep on the plank at a height!" This utterance reminds us of the following lines from Mirabai's devotional poem:

Friend, I have lost all sleep.
I spend the whole night
Watching and waiting for the Beloved.

Sai Baba thus hinted at the sounding of the drum of the beginningless eternity within the soul which is referred to by the yogis as *Anahat* and by Suns as *Saut-e-sarmadi* - in order to draw attention to the fact that the loving devotee is ever watchful and every single breath of his is accompanied by *nama-smaran*. It is no exaggeration to say that not only in his heart but from every limb, every bone and every pore of his body *anahat* sound emerges. In an ordinary individual his limbs and bones are in a state of torpor. But in Sai Baba's body these were not only active but permeated with the divine essence and so he exclaimed, "Though I may no more be in flesh and blood, my bones will assure you from the grave, my tomb will communicate with you and will sway with him who surrenders to the Spirit [in it]. Do not ever think that I will be lost to you. Remember me with intense devotion and you will be blessed."[3] This assurance is not illusory, but a thing of everyday experience for those who come to Shirdi for *darshan* of Sai Baba's *samadhi*. There are thousands of cases of devotees whose difficulties, calamities, doubts and questions have been resolved and their number grows as every day passes.

Sai Baba would also use other *hatha yoga* practices besides sleeping on the narrow plank. It is said that he would go to the stream north of the *masjid* in privacy, take out his intestines, clean them and hang them up for drying. It is also said that he would practise the more difficult act of *khand yoga* (severance of various limbs of the body) at night in the *masjid*. The act was like this. If anyone visited Sai Baba at night in the masjid, he would not find him there, but various parts of his body would be found lying separately in the masjid at different places. If his head were at one place, his hands would be at another place, the trunk at the third and legs at the fourth. A person looking at the sight would be frightened and would not report lest he were involved. In the morning there would be a complete change of scene, and Sai Baba would be seen sitting in his usual place, and the person would wonder! After many days the word spread that it was a play of Sai Baba's yogic powers.[4]

In order to lose consciousness of the body, to experience that oneself is not the body, but separate from it, yogis resort to many practices. For example, enduring the heat of the sun or fire, sleeping on a bed of nails, living only on air without intake of food, remaining naked, consuming five kinds of fire, are all means to experience vividly that one is not the body but the soul. But Sai Baba's means to experience this truth was unique. He believed that his body was that of a single-minded devotee or servant of God. So if his devotee were suffering from an ailment Sai Baba would take the *karma* of the *bhakta* upon himself, and remove the devotee's ailment. Thereby, even if his *bhakta* had to go through his *prarabdha karma*, the intensity of it would be considerably reduced to make it bearable. A thing which is considered as impossible by science is possible for a yogi, and the effect of such power has been experienced by Sai Baba's many devotees.

At the time of delivery of his devotees' wives, Sai Baba would say that he experienced the pains himself. And by the time he told of his pains and moaned and groaned in the masjid, the delivery pains of the women would begin to subside and they would deliver. In 1911, when the epidemic of plague broke out in Shirdi, seven or eight buboes were seen on Sai Baba's body, and he began to get fever. Seeing this, devotees were concerned and asked him what the remedy was for cure. Sai Baba suggested that burnt cottonwool should be dipped in *ghee* (clarified butter) and applied to the buboes. He followed this remedy himself and assured his devotees that nothing would happen to him and also to anyone in Shirdi village, as he had taken the calamity upon himself. And so it happened. There was no case of death reported in Shirdi. More wonderful was the fact that in spite of so many buboes on his body there was no change in his daily routine - his morning and evening rounds, visit to Lendi, begging for alms and sitting in *dhyana* in the masjid near the railing.

At that very time, Sai Baba's devotee, Dadasheb Khaparde, had suspended his legal practice and was staying in Shirdi. As long as Sai Baba did not permit him to leave Shirdi, he was determined to camp there. Khaparde's young son who was with him got high fever and was in great pain. The boy's mother was frightened as there was an epidemic of plague in Shirdi. One day when Sai Baba was on his evening round, Mrs Khaparde asked Sai Baba to bless her son. Sai Baba said, "Mother, do not fear. The sky is overcast with clouds, it will rain and the sky will be clear." So saying, he raised his *kafni* up to his hip and showed four egg-sized buboes and added, "Look, I have taken the ailment of your son upon me. You have nothing to fear. I am suffering all this for your son and he will be all right soon." Mrs Khaparde was relieved and the boy was cured as assured.[5]

On *Dhanatrayodashi* day, the same year, Sai Baba was sitting in the *masjid* opposite the *dhuni*, stoking the fire. Suddenly, Sai Baba put his hand in the fire and sat quietly. When the devotees in the *sabhamandap* outside saw what was happening, a devotee went up, clasped Sai Baba round his waist and pulled him back. Seeing the burns sustained by the whole hand, the devotees asked him with grief in their heart, "What have you done?" Hearing this Sai Baba came to his normal consciousness and said, "What shall I tell you? A child, sitting on its mother's hollow above her hip, fell into the fire. I pulled her out. While doing so my hand was burnt. Let it be. But the life of the girl was saved. The thing is that the wife of a blacksmith, while blowing the bellows of the fireplace, forgot the existence of her child on the hollow above her hip. The child fell into the fireplace. I gathered it up."

As soon as Nanasaheb Chandorkar heard of this incident, he rushed to Shirdi along with Dr. Paramanand of Bombay. Sai Baba told him that God was his physician and did not get his burns examined by the doctor. He would have his burns dressed by a devotee suffering from black leprosy, who would regularly massage the burns gently with *ghee*, place a leaf over them and bandage the hand. With this treatment the hand was healed.[6]

It had become a second nature with Sai Baba to take up the *karmic* suffering of his devotees and thus lighten their burden. This service of devotees, he would regard as service to God, and considered himself fortunate on that account. This becomes clear from the following dialogue with his devotees.

Once some of his devotees said to him, "We are blessed by your *darshan*." Sai Baba replied, "Brothers, I deem myself fortunate that I came to know you and I am grateful to God for it." It is no wonder if he, who has thus vowed to serve humbly, has no consciousness of his body, and is ever absorbed in *sahaj samadhi*, wears himself out in the fulfilment of his vow of service. That is his daily spiritual practice and a rule of his life. Yogis give up the ghost at their sweet will. Death cannot touch them. And it was thus in the discharge of his vow of service that Sai Baba gave up his life for the sake of Tatya Kote Patil, a devotee of his since a long time.

Sai Baba had already foretold that on the tenth day of the month of *Ashwin* (i.e., Dusshera) in *Sake* year 1840 (A.D. 1918), Tatya Kote would die. As *Ashwin* approached, Tatya Kote Patil got high fever and was laid up in bed. He had full trust in Sai Baba. Lying in bed he would remember Sai Baba. He would not go to the *masjid* for Sai Baba's *darshan*. Sai Baba also simultaneously developed fever. The tenth day of *Ashwin* arrived. Tatya Patil's pulse slowed down. His relatives, who knew of Sai Baba's prophecy, realised that there was no hope for

Tatya Patil. Sai Baba, on the other hand, looked all right. He was laughing and joking on that day and behaved as if his health had improved. But it so happened that Sai Baba passed away suddenly ¬nd Tatya Patil's condition began improving from that ᴜay.[7] When we consider all these facts and appreciate them in the light of the service rendered by Tatya Patil's mother (Bayajabai) to Sai Baba and the latter's love for Tatya Patil, then we come to the conclusion that in exchange for the service rendered by Tatya Patil's relatives, Sai Baba, out of his sweet will, abandoned his mortal coil and thus fulfilled his vow of service to God.

Notes

1. *Shri Sai Leela*, Vol. 30, (1953) 1st issue.
2. *Shri Sai-Sat-Charita*, Chap. XLV, p. 136.
3. Ibid., Chap. XXV, pp. 104-108.
4. Ibid., Chap. VII, p. 60.
5. Ibid., Chap. VII, pp. 100-109.
6. Ibid., Chap. VII, pp. 73-90.
7. Ibid., Chap. XLII, pp. 45-67.

5. MISSION OF INCARNATION

He who knows the nature
Of my task and my holy birth
Is not reborn.
When he leaves this body
He comes to me.

Bhagavad Gita, IV, 9
Translation by Swami Prabhavananda &
Christopher Isherwood

Who sees his Lord
Within every creature,
Deathlessly dwelling
Amidst the mortal:
That man sees truly.

Bhagavad Gita, XIII, 23

Seeing all things equal,
The enlightened may look
On the Brahmin, learned and gentle,
On the cow, on the elephant,
On the dog, on the eater of dogs.

Bhagavad Gita, V, 18

In Bharatiya society there is diversity. Here exist many languages, many religions and many castes. Hence the essence of Bharatiya philosophy is in unity. On account of this philosophy, the great men who are born in Bharat wish to establish a state of equality. The roots of divisions or distinctions have gone deep down due to diverse customs and rules of conduct.

Really speaking, without attaching too much importance to externals, Bharatiya philosophy strives for the attainment of Truth. Thanks to the great men in Bharat, the stream of this philosophy has been flowing uninterruptedly.

Adapted from the Hindu translation of
Rabindranath Tagore

God does not belong to any individual, society, caste, sect, party, people or country. Men-women, poor-rich, unhappy-happy, foolish-wise, bad-good, atheist-theist - all these believe in Him in some form or other according to their own nature and temperament. If a man, unable to obtain freedom from threefold afflictions[1] or physical or mental pleasure through his own limited strength or intellect, gets it through the agency or instrumentality of a higher power, he accepts it with thanks and tries to propitiate his benefactor for such constant help. Such attempts vary according to the nature and temperament of individuals. But the aim of everyone is alike - to keep the higher power pleased so that it may render him help. Whatever caste or country to which a man belongs, in the life of every individual, there arise occasions when all his efforts fall short and he is not able to see his way ahead. In such times he struggles to get help from any quarter and if he gets such help, he acknowledges it gratefully and tries to keep his benefactor pleased for such help also in the future. This is the ordinary tendency, not of any caste, sect or individual but all human beings.

So, when any great personality arises which succours all, irrespective of their caste, country, etc., and strengthens the faith of the righteous, people of many castes, creeds and sects, forgetting their differences, come to him. They do not think of his caste, family or religion as they are worshippers of the divine radiance. These devotees respect the brotherhood as well as their object of worship and carry on their devotion peacefully, with understanding, reason and accommmodation. In such brotherhood are to be seen the seeds of growth and progress of society.

Sai Baba's personality was of the above kind. Persons of various faiths - Hindus, Muslims, Parsis and Christians - would come to him to have their desires fulfilled. Even today people of these faiths visit his *Samadhi Mandir*, which is open to all. Sai Baba would look on all visitors with an equal eye and not care for caste, family or sect of the devotee and make no distinction between them. When he was embodied, he had given various spiritual experiences to his devotees and convinced them that his personal state transcended all human distinctions and differences and was worthy of respect. We shall narrate some such experiences as proof of this statement.

During the Christmas of 1909, a medical practitioner went to Shirdi with his friend who was a *tahsildar*. This doctor was an orthodox Brahmin and was strict in his observance of religious rites like bath, *sandhya*, etc. He was a great devotee of Shri Rama. Being of the view that Sai Baba was a Muslim, he said to his friend that he did not feel like going with him. The *tahsildar* friend told him that he would not be asked by anyone in Shirdi to prostrate before Sai Baba and Sai Baba himself would expect nothing of the kind. So, reluctantly, the doctor accompanied his *tahsildar* friend. When they reached Shirdi and stood at the entrance of the *masjid*, it appeared to the doctor that Lord Ramachandra himself was sitting before him, and he immediately prostrated before him (Sai Baba). On coming out of the *masjid*, the doctor narrated his experience to his friend and resolved that unless Sai Baba blessed him (with spiritual experience) he would not touch food or go to the *masjid*. On the fourth day, the doctor met a friend of his from Khandesh unexpectedly, and forgetting his resolve entered the *masjid* along with his friend from Khandesh. When the doctor prostrated before Sai Baba, the latter asked him, "Well, doctor, why have you come? Who called you?" The doctor melted completely after being reminded of his resolve. The same midnight Sai Baba favoured him. In his sleep, the doctor experienced indescribable bliss and this state of his lasted for fifteen days even after his return home.[2]

Like the staunch Shri Rama devotee above, Mule Shastri, an equally staunch devotee of his *guru* Gholap, had once been to Shirdi to see Gopalrao Buti, a rich *Malgujar* of Nagpur, who was devoted to Sai Baba. Mule Shastri did not intend halting in Shirdi for long but was to return to Nasik after meeting Buti. He met Buti and thereafter along with others went to visit Sai Baba. At that time Sai Baba was distributing plantains as *prasad* to all assembled devotees. Mule Shastri had studied the six systems of philosophy (*darshanas*) and was proficient in astrology and palmistry. He extended his hand to take up Sai Baba's palm for reading but Sai Baba paid no attention and instead placed four plantains in Mule Shastri's hands. What did a fakir like Sai Baba have to do with palmistry? Seeing that Sai Baba was a holy person without any desire, Mule Shastri returned to the Wada where he was staying. Thereafter, he had his bath and wearing a silken *dhoti* sat down for his ritual of *agnihotra*. In the meantime, Sai Baba started for the *lendi* and remarked, "Take geru with you. I have to don an ochre-coloured robe today." No one around him understood the significance of this remark. By the time Sai Baba returned from the *lendi* and it was time for the noon *arati*. Bapusaheb Jog, who conducted the *arati*, asked Mule Shastri whether he would accompany him to the masjid for *arati*. Mule Shastri had strong scruples about pollution by touch and so he was reluctant to leave his *agnihotra* and go to the *masjid*. Sai Baba was now seated in the *masjid* and *arati* was about to commence when he said, "Go to the Brahmin who has newly come and get *dakshina* from him." Buti approached Mule Shastri for *dakshina*. Since he had sat down in his silken dhoti for *agnihotra*, Mule Shastri's mind was unsettled, but out of deference for Buti he accompanied the latter to the *masjid* with his *dakshina*. Lest the *masjid* should pollute him he remained at a distance in the *sabhamandap*, saluted Sai Baba and showered flowers on him.

Then a strange thing happened. While everyone saw Sai Baba in his seat, Mule Shastri saw. his *guru* Gholap in an ochre-coloured robe instead. He was perplexed. Gholap guruji had expired years ago. So he was wondering whether to trust his eyes or not; whether what he saw was a fantasy or the reality; whether he was awake or asleep. He pinched himself and convinced himself that he was awake and what he saw was the actuality. He ran up the steps of the *masjid* and overcome with emotion embraced the feet of his *guru*, and stood up with his hands folded. Others now began reciting the *arati* of Sai Baba while Mule Shastri with his eyes half-closed sang loudly the *arati* of Gholap guru. And when he opened his eyes after he had finished singing *arati*, he saw Sai Baba sitting in his usual place asking him for *dakshina*. By the miraculous power of Sai Baba, he had *darshan* of his *guru*. Mule Shastri was overjoyed and with tears in his eyes prostrated himself before Sai Baba. People around marvelled as Mule Shastri narrated his experience.[3]

Sai Baba would wear a *kafni* made of coarse *manjarpat*, tie a piece of cloth around his head and grow a beard. People knew him by the name of 'Sai Baba'. Most of the Hindus visiting him, before and also after coming to Shirdi, were haunted with doubts and debated in their minds whether they were on the righteous path, or were

being led astray. They would weigh and consider whether
they should derive some immediate benefit or accept him
as their guide. And everyone, according to his capacity
and ability, would determine whether he should
establish a temporary or lasting relationship with Sai
Baba. Among those who, acquired knowledge step by
step, of these matters by personal experience and became
his permanent devotees was one Brahmin by the name of
Megha from Marwar, who was domiciled in Gujarat.

Megha came into contact with a devotee of Sai Baba,
Rao Bahadur Hari Vinayak Sathe. The latter was a
Deputy Collector of Kheda district. Megha was a
Brahmin only in name for he knew next to nothing about
Gayatri, and much less about *Sandhya-puja, Brahma
yajna, Vaishvadev, Rudra,* etc. Sathe took him in his
employ and entrusted to him the daily *puja* of Shiva.
Sathe made him aware of his ignorance, explained to him
the duties of a Brahmin and taught him the *Gayatri
mantra*. The mutual affection between the two increased
and Megha accepted Sathe as his guide. After some days
Sathe described to Megha the greatness of his *sadguru*
Sai Baba, and said to Megha with emotion, "I desire that
my *guru* who is Shiva personified should be bathed with
Ganga water and worshipped with religious rites. I am
much pleased with your progress and feel that if you were
fortunate enough to come into contact with my *guru*, you
will be blessed amd it will conduce to your welfare."

Megha asked him, "What's the caste of your *guru*?"
Sathe replied, "I do not know his caste. Both Hindus and
Muslims claim him as their own. His permanent abode is
in a *masjid*, a *dhuni* (fire) is perpetually lighted before
him, and to that fire he offers oblation of the alms he
receives." Megha was frozen and said, "As he resides in a
masjid and Muslims consider him as their own, he must
be a Muslim. What, can a *yavana* ever be a *guru*? No,
never." Sathe did not know what to say. However, on

being much pressed by Sathe he agreed to visit Sai Baba
at Shirdi. On reaching Shirdi, before he could enter the
masjid, Sai Baba assumed a ferocious look, picked up a
stone and shouted, "Dare you step in! I am the lowest of
Yavana and you are a high class Brahmin! Go away, you
will be polluted if you touch me." Megha was stunned.
Ahmednagar was so far from Kheda and yet Sai Baba
knew what he had said in his private talk to Sathe! But
there was no time to think. Sai Baba had chased him out
of the *masjid*. Megha ran out. But Sai Baba's anger was
feigned. He only wanted to suggest to Megha that he was
aware of his thoughts. Shortly thereafter Sai Baba was
pacified and Megha could come freely to the *masjid*.
Megha stayed in Shirdi for many days and served Sai
Baba. He observed Sai Baba's powers, his way of life,
from close quarters but yet could not put his firm faith in
the latter. He returned to Kheda but fell ill and was
confined to bed.

One day he went for Shiva's *darshan* but instead of
the *pindi* he saw Sai Baba. Now he longed to return to
Shirdi. Soon after he recovered, he proceeded to Shirdi.
There Sai Baba got him to do the *Gayatri Purascharan*.
This time he not only relished his life in Shirdi, but came
to believe in Sai Baba and became his staunch devotee.
He began worshipping him in the belief that Sai Baba
was Shankar incarnate. Day and night Megha would do
japa of Shankar. He did not mix much with others. He
was straightforward and simple. He always had a joyous
expression on his face. In Shirdi there was no tree of *bela*
(*Aegle marmelos* or *Cratoeva religiosa*) which is sacred to
Shiva. So Megha would get *bela* leaves from one and a
half miles away, worship all gods of the village and would
then come to the *masjid* to worship Sai Baba.

Initially, Sai Baba would not allow anybody to
worship him. If anyone approached him with necessary
things for worship, he would get angry. But ultimately,..

seeing the devotion of Mhalsapati, he first accepted *puja* at his hands. Later, Nanasaheb Chandorkar's son, Mahadev, and thereafter, all other devotees began worshipping him. Once the custom of *puja* was established, sometime later the beginning of *arati* in the Chavadi at night and in the morning and in the *masjid* at noon was made by Nulkar, retired *munsif* of Pandharpur. After Nulkar expired, his place was taken by Megha. Megha performed this task with excellence. The fair-complexioned, robust Megha with matted locks and beard would first worship village gods and then worship Sai Baba and, standing on one leg, perform *arati* with total concentration.

Once Megha went to the *masjid* after worshipping all the village gods except Khandoba, as the temple door was closed. Before he could commence the worship of Sai Baba, the latter stopped Megha and said to him, "There is a breach in your daily practice. Go, complete the *puja* of all the village gods and then come here." Megha told him that as Khandoba *mandir* was closed he could not worship there. Baba said, "Go again, the door is now open. Complete the remaining *puja* and then we can have the *puja* and *arati* here as usual." The door of Khandoba was now open. Megha returned to the *masjid* after worshipping Khandoba. Thereafter the *puja* and *arati* of Sai Baba took place as usual.

Experiences like the above strengthened Megha's faith. Once on *Makar Sankranti* day (the passage of the sun from Sagittarius to Capricorn), Megha felt the desire to bathe Sai Baba with water of the Godavari river (ten miles away from Shirdi) for which he obtained Sai Baba's permission after much persuasion. On the *Sankranti* day, Megha got up very early in the morning, made his way to the bank of the Godavari and filling his copper/brass vessel with its water, returned to Shirdi and approached Sai Baba. Sai Baba did not get up. The noon *arati* over, all the devotees returned to their places. Then Megha said to Sai Baba, "Now it is afternoon, at least now get ready for your bath." Sai Baba replied, "What has a *fakir* like me to do with Ganga water bath (Sai Baba would always refer to Godavari as Ganga)?" Megha would not budge from his stand. He said, "I know one thing. Shankar is propitiated by a bath with Ganga water. Today is *Sankranti.* So I must bathe my Shankar with Ganga water, isn't it?" Giving in to his importunity Sai Baba said, "O.K. If you insist, I will remove my head cover. Head is the prime organ of the body. Pour a little water over my head so that it will be as if my whole body has been bathed." No sooner were these words out of Sai Baba's mouth, than with the shout of *Har Gange*, Megha emptied the whole vessel of water on Sai Baba's head. With the feeling that he had bathed Shankar with his clothes on Megha was overjoyed. But what wonder did he see? Only Sai Baba's head was wet while the rest of his body was dry and there was not a drop of water on his *kafni.* Megha was astonished and remembering this he rejoiced again and again saying to himself, "What a remarkable characteristic of Sai Baba that he pleased me and yet saved me from the blame of violation of *guru's* order."

Sai Baba gave Megha another incomparable experience which won him completely. It was about one year after Megha had commenced serving Sai Baba. One day, early in the morning, Megha saw clearly in his dream the figure of Sai Baba who threw consecrated rice on his bed and said to him, "Megha, trace the *trishul*," and vanished. Megha woke up and found consecrated rice all over his bed. The door of his room was bolted. So Megha went to the *masjid,* and narrating his experience to Sai Baba, asked him, "Shall I trace the *trishul,* according to the vision in the Wada where your picture is hung up?" Sai Baba replied. "What vision, did you not

recognize my voice?" Megha said, "First, I also thought so
but as the door of my room was bolted from within, I was
perplexed." Sai Baba then exclaimed, "I do not require a
door to pass through. I have neither shape nor size. I am
omnipresent." The same day, in accordance with Sai
Baba's direction, Megha drew with red lead the *trishul* to
the right of Sai Baba's picture. Next day a Ramadasi
from Poona arrived in Shirdi and presented a *Shivalinga*
to Sai Baba. Megha happened to come there at that time.
Sai Baba said to him, "Look, Lord Shankar has come.
Take care of him." Megha was overwhelmed on seeing
the *Shivalinga*. He had no doubt whatsoever now that
Sai Baba was *sadguru* Lord Shankar himself and
considered himself blessed that he got an opportunity to
serve him.[4] For a long time he resided in Shirdi and
served Sai Baba loyally and faithfully. When he died, Sai
Baba remarked, "He was my true devotee" and caressed
his corpse and arranged for his funeral and obsequies,
including the feeding of Brahmins.

Hearing reports that Sai Baba distributed much
money among the poor a party of four Ramadasis
(consisting of the husband, wife, daughter and wife's
sister) broke their journey on their way to Benares at
Shirdi. After having Sai Baba's *darshan* and staying in
Shirdi for two days, they found that Sai Baba distributed
Rs 50 to Rs 100 daily. So, except for the wife, all others
became greedy and thought if they stayed in Shirdi for
long and ingratiated themselves with Sai Baba they
would be well off. They began to perform *bhajan* every
day before Sai Baba with this motive. Only the wife was
selfless.

Once after the noon *arati*, Sai Baba gave the wife
darshan in the form of Rama wielding the bow.
Immediately she clapped and shed tears of joy. When the
party returned to its habitation the wife was asked why
she behaved as she did. She described how Sai Baba had

given her the *darshan* of Rama wielding the bow. Her
husband was selfish. He ridiculed her and told her that
what she saw was not true. The same night the husband
dreamt that he had surrendered himself to Sai Baba and
admitted to him that he considered the latter as Muslim,
and had a grudge against him in the belief that the latter
converted Hindus to Islam. Sai Baba reminded the
husband that he worshipped the *panja* (the iron hand of
the Muhammadens, representing their five holy
personages) at home and on the occasion of marriage,
worshipped Kadbibi, a Muslim divinity. He repented and
begged of Sai Baba to give him *darshan* of Ramdas
Swami and in his dream, Sai Baba did favour him with
the *darshan* of Ramdas Swami. Sai Baba thus showed
those who were greedy the path of virtue and convinced
them that he (Sai Baba) transcended all differences such
as caste and religion and was a divine incarnation. Then
the party began to do *bhajan* with unalloyed devotion.
Sai Baba also treated them with consideration. Thus,
though their desire to benefit financially by their
residence in Shirdi did not materialise, they received the
higher fruit of devotion and with contented hearts they
proceeded on their onward journey to Benares.[5]

A foreign educated medical officer in Government
service and a friend of one Kashinath Shankar Dubey
entertained a suspicion about Sai Baba being a Muslim.
Sai Baba gave him *darshan* of a mixed Hindu-Muslim
divinity in his dream and removed his doubts. The dress
of this divinity was white and a white cloth was tied
around its head. This divinity advised him as follows:
"Sainath Maharaj and Dattatreya are both one. Do not
be guided or deceived by external appearance or dress.
Identify the inner reality and perceive it." The doctor's
faith was strengthened by this divine appearance in his
dream. Also the ailment with which he was afflicted for
six months and which was not subsiding was slowly

cured by his faith, Sai Baba's worship and partaking of
prasad. Thereafter, this doctor accepted Dattatreya as
his *ishtadaivat* (chosen deity) and by his devotion to Sai
Baba and the latter's sympathy and help, he made good
progress.[6]

One out of the two visitors from Goa who came for Sai
Baba's *darshan* also had a similar experience. This
individual had vowed to offer his first month's pay to Shri
Dattatreya if he secured a job. Then he secured
employment on a monthly salary of Rs. 15. With years of
service his pay increased and at the time of his visit to Sai
Baba it was Rs. 700 per month. But he had forgotten his
vow and was not released from his debt to Dattatreya. As
soon as he prostrated before Sai Baba, the latter said to
him, "Give me my fifteen rupees." The visitor gladly paid.
Seeing this the other visitor who also prostrated before
Sai Baba offered Rs. 35 to him, but Sai Baba did not
accept the money. Madhavrao Deshpande, a favourite
devotee of Sai Baba, who was sitting near him said to Sai
Baba, "Why do you make such distinction? You ask for
Rs. 15 from one and refuse Rs. 35 from the other, who
voluntarily wishes to make an offering." Sai Baba
replied, "You do not understand. I take nothing from
anybody. This *masjid* Dwarakamai (as Sai Baba would
refer to it) asks and that too to the extent the debt is due.
The man who pays his debt becomes happy. What do I
need money for when I have neither home nor any
sansar? I am detached in every way." When the visitor
who paid Rs. 15 narrated the tale of his forgotten vow
and non-payment of his 'debt' all were delighted and got
some idea of Sai Baba's unity with the Supreme Being
and his powers.[7]

Kakaji Vaidya had an experience of the oneness of Sai
Baba with Saptashringidevi of Vani in Nasik District. He
was the priest of Saptashringidevi and regarded her as
his chosen deity. Since a calamity befell him he was

restless and full of care. So, he entered the Devi's temple and prayed to the Devi intensely. The Devi was pleased, appeared in his dream and told him that he would get peace of mind if he approached Baba. Kakaji immediately woke up and began thinking who Baba could be. Considering Triambakeshwar as Baba, he went to Trimbak. Every day, on waking up he would first have *darshan* of Triambakeshwar and after a bath would perform *rudra* with *abhishek*. He did this for ten days but there was no change in his condition and his anguish was unabated. So, he returned to Vani and again taking the Devi's *darshan*, complained piteously, "Why was I sent to Trimbak? There is no change in my condition. At least now please steady my mind." The same night the Devi came in his dream and said, "The Baba I referred to was Sai Baba of Shirdi. Go to him. Why did you unnecessarily go to Trimbak?" Kakaji got up wondering where Shirdi was and how to go there.

Iu the meantime, it so happened that a proficient astrologer who visited Shirdi told Madhavrao Deshpande's younger brother, Bapaji, that, as his elder brother, Madhavrao, had not fulfilled the vows of his mother as per her wish, he had incurred the displeasure of the Saptashringidevi. After Bapaji reported this to Madhavrao, the latter remembered that in his childhood he was once ill when his mother had vowed to take Madhavrao for the *darshan* of Saptashringidevi. Similarly, when their mother suffered due to formation of tumours in her nipples, she had vowed to present two silver nipples to the Devi if her suffering was removed. Madhavrao had promised his mother on her deathbed to fulfil her two vows. Madhavrao's *ishtadaivat* was *sadguru* Sai Baba. So he got two silver nipples made by a silversmith, prostrated before Sai Baba and said, "You are our Saptashringidevi. Please accept these in fulfilment of my mother's vows." Sai Baba advised him

that he should personally visit Saptashringidevi's temple
and place the offering at her feet. Accordingly,
Madhavrao proceeded to Vani and in his search for the
priest arrived at Kakaji's house. In Vani, Kakaji was
eager to meet Sai Baba of Shirdi, and when he got to
know who Madhavrao was, he was overjoyed. After
Madhavrao had fulfilled both the vows of his mother, he
and Kakaji started for Shirdi. As soon as Kakaji arrived
in Shirdi, he went for Sai Baba's *darshan*. He neither
asked anything of or conversed with Sai Baba, nor did Sai
Baba bless him. But by mere *darshan* of Sai Baba Kakaji
was pacified, his restlessness vanished and he obtained
peace of mind. He stayed in Shirdi for twelve days and
with Sai Baba's blessings returned to Vani.[8] From this
tale we get some idea of the unity of the Devi and Sai
Baba, and the unique art and power of the latter to get
his devotees to fulfil their obligations and make them
happy.

Similarly, Sai Baba showed his wonderful identity
with Akkalkot Swami, the famous and powerful
incarnation of Dattatreya, to the devotees of the latter
who would visit Shirdi. Once Harischandra Pitale, a
resident of Bombay, went to Shirdi with his wife and son
for the *darshan* of Sai Baba. His son was epileptic and in
spite of the best medical treatment there was no
improvement in his condition. There was only one
remedy left - *darshan* of a holy person and his blessings.
At this time Das Ganu was making known to the public
the name, the place, the greatness and fame of Sai Baba
through his *keertanas*. Hearing of his renown, Pitale
arrived in Shirdi with his wife and son. He and his family
took *darshan* of Sai Baba. He was going to place his son
at the feet of Sai Baba, but the son himself attempted to
do so. Sai Baba and Pitale's son looked at each other and
the latter collapsed to tne ground foaming at his mouth.
Pitale was perplexed and frightened. A stream of tears

began to flow from the eyes of his wife. Assuring them, Sai Baba said, "Take him to your place. He will revive after half an hour. Do not worry." The Pitales returned to their habitation. The son soon came back to consciousness and felt all right. Then Pitale along with his wife went for Sai Baba's *darshan* and began pressing his legs. They stayed happily in Shirdi for some days serving Sai Baba with devotion.

On their day of departure to Bombay, they prostrated before Sai Baba, took his permission to leave and received *udi-prasad*. At that time, taking out three rupees from his pocket, Sai Baba gave them to Pitale and said to him, "I had given you two rupees before. Keep these three rupees along with them for *puja* and you will be blessed." This was Pitale's first visit to Sai Baba. So he did not follow how he could have received two rupees earlier but said nothing. He returned home eager to find out what the reference to two rupees meant. He narrated his experience to his aged mother and asked her if she could enlighten him. Pitale's mother thought for some time and then observed, "What Sai Baba told you is true. As you took your son now to Shirdi for Sai Baba's *darshan,* your father had taken you to Akkalkot for *darshan* of Akkalkot Swami, who was pleased with the devotion of your father and as *prasad* gave your father two rupees which he asked him to keep in daily worship. As long as your father was alive the two rupees were in the shrine and your father would worship them with faith. But after his passing away the articles used in *puja* became the playthings of the children who had no faith in God and who were ashamed of doing *puja*. In the years that have elapsed the two rupees were lost. Never mind. But now know that in the guise of Sai Baba you have met Akkalkot Swami. Give up your doubts, remember the devotion of your father and humbly accepting the three rupees as *prasad* of a holy person, worship them." Pitale took his mother's advice to heart and remembering Sai Baba started worshipping them with devotion.[9]

At the time of *nirvana* of Akkalkot Swami, Keshav Naik asked him, "Maharaj, to whom should I and my son Ramachandra look for guidance after you are gone?" The Swami hurled his leather *padukas* at him and said, "Worship these and go to Shirdi in the district of Ahmednagar where there is my incarnation. Give him your love in the same way as you have loved me, and you will not be in want for anything." After Akkalkot Swami took *samadhi* (1878) Keshav Naik went to Shirdi with his son Ramachandra along with some companions. There all of them had *darshan* of Sai Baba and sat down. At the behest of Sai Baba, Ramachandra Naik plucked some leaves of the neem tree which Sai Baba gave to the Naiks and their companions for eating. They tasted so sweet to Naik that he ate a number of them and was filled. As Akkalkot Swami had rendered half of the neem tree at Akkalkot and showed his unity with Narasimha Saraswati to pilgrims from Gangapur, similarly Sai Baba also demonstrated his oneness with Akkalkot Swami. Shri Ramachandra Naik narrated to the present writer how Sai Baba had obliged him by his kindness. When Ramachandra Naik was in urgent need of money for the marriage of his daughter and was greatly worried about it, Sai Baba on his own arranged for the required sum Rs. 600 to be given to Naik in a strange way and thus the marriage was solemnised. Akkalkot Swami also used to help his father in a similar way.[10]

Sai Baba convinced every visitor, whatever his chosen deity, a god, goddess, incarnation or holy person that he was fully identified with that chosen deity. A Parsi contractor of Nanded Seth Ratanji Shapurji Wadia, had an experience of this in a comparable way. Wadia was rich but he had twelve daughters and no son. So he was unhappy and desired that he should have a male successor. He had great faith in Das Ganu who asked him to travel to Shirdi for Sai Baba's blessings. Wadia came to Shirdi and went to the *masjid* with the offerings of baskets of fruit and flowers, had *darshan* of Sai Baba and then said humbly to him, "Hearing of your fame I have come to take refuge in you, for you help people who are in distress." Sai Baba replied, "Well, you have come at last. Give me whatever *dakshina* you wish to give in addition to Rs 3-14 annas, which you have already given me and your desire will be fulfilled." Wadia gave *dakshina*, received Sai Baba's blessings and returned to Nanded. Then he narrated the whole account of his visit to Das Ganu and said that he did not understand how, where and when he had given Sai Baba Rs 3-14 annas. Das Ganu reminded him that after the latter had decided to pay a visit to Shirdi, Maulisaheb (a holy person who earned a humble living by carrying loads, i.e., by *Hamali*) had come to the household of Wadia when he was presented with garland and fruits and served a light repast, and the expense on that account may be computed. On adding the sums spent on various items, the total was found to be exactly Rs 3-14 annas. Wadia was astonsihed at the powers of Sai Baba and felt that a higher power always watched over minute acts of an individual and the good that one did was recorded in its books! His wish for a son was also fulfilled by Sai Baba's blessings.[11]

Christians visiting Shirdi also experienced that Sai Baba had divine powers and so they looked upon him with reverence. Chakra Narayan, a Christian, was Police Fouzdar at Kopargaon in 1918. He says in his statement: "I was not a believer in Baba. We were watching Baba through our men. Even though I watched him sceptically, the result was to create in me a high regard for him. First and foremost was the fact that he was not moved by women or wealth. Many women would come to him and

place their heads on his feet and sit before him. But he
was unmoved; he would not care to cast one glance of
admiration, or of lust at them. He was clearly and
unmistakeably unattached. About money also, we
watched him. People voluntarily gave him money. If any
did not give him money, Baba would not curse or hate or
be displeased with him. The same held good about his
begging for bread. He did not care for what he got.
Whatever he got, he scattered with a liberal hand. When
he died, we took possession of his cash; that was only
Rs.16. Yet daily he was paying or giving away hundreds
of rupees. Often we noticed that his receipts were smaller
than his disbursements. Wherefrom came the excess for
him to disburse or pay? We could not make out. This
made me conclude that he had divine powers."[12]

A Christian nurse working in Thakar Hospital in
Girgaum, Bombay, had an experience of the unity of Sai
Baba with the Holy Ghost, even after he had passed
away. Her boss rejected her application for leave to go to
Shirdi. By her chanting of Sai Baba's name
(*namasmaran*) her boss was influenced by Sai Baba
imperceptibly to change his mind and reverse his earlier
order. So her leave was sanctioned and her desire to go to
Shirdi was fulfilled. Similarly, Mirabai Satyavir, a
Christian teacher in a Methodist school, wrote to the
present writer that a copy of this biography of Sai Baba
came into her hands and on reading it, she came to
believe in Sai Baba and to remember him. Thus, all her
difficulties were removed. Later, in her letter dated 29
November 1950, she conveyed that she went to Shirdi a
second time and she recovered her lost wristwatch valued
at Rs. 100 through the wonderful help of Sai Baba. Sai
Baba secretly helps and guides her in her difficulties. Her
friend, Smt. Parmar, the wife of Deputy Collector, has
also received similar experience.

Muslims visiting Sai Baba regarded him as a *Pir
Avaliya* of a high order and respected him accordingly.

Kabir says: "Those devotees who are true and even-minded are immortal." There is an ancient belief among Muslims that an *avaliya* never dies. Such an experience was given by Sai Baba thirteen years after he laid down his body to Rajabally Mohammed, a Khoja contractor. Rajabally's she-buffalo became ill and, in spite of the treatment of a veterinary surgeon, showed no improvement in her condition. Rajabally remembered Sai Baba and administered Sai Baba's *udi* (holy ash) to the buffalo as a result of which the ailing buffalo recovered. Abdulla Jan, a Pathan from Tarabel in Hajra District of North-West Frontier Province, had an educative experience. After Sai Baba shed his mortal coil, he showed Abdulla that he was still looking after the latter's welfare and that Abdulla need not approach any other *Murshid*. Abdulla recognised Baba as his *Murshid* in his first meeting and accepted him as such. But after Sai Baba passed away Abdulla felt frustrated as he had no idea of the former's divine powers. Abdulla felt that as Sai Baba was no more in body he could not look after him. So with a dejected heart he proceeded to the North-West Frontier. On his way, in Swat valley, he came across the tomb of Syed Akunbaba, a descendant of the Prophet. While lying down near the tomb one night, Abdulla prayed to Akunbaba to take him under his protection. That very night he had a dream in which he saw Sai Baba seated in a chair near his head. Sai Baba did not say anything. But from this experience Abdulla realised that though Sai Baba had abandoned his mortal frame, he was still concerned about him and looking after him.

Similarly, a broker called Amir Shakkar, had an experience which convinced him that Sai Baba is an *avaliya* of a high order. So when Gopalrao Gund and Damuanna Kasar decided to hold in consultation with prominent men in Shirdi an annual fair and asked Sai Baba when it should be held, the latter suggested the day

of Ramanavami. So every year on Ramanavami, a
procession is taken up to the *masjid* (Dwarakamai) and
flags are put up. Muslim devotees, too, according to their
custom, take a *sandal* procession through the village up
to the *masjid*. *Sandal* means that levigated and
powdered sandalwood is placed in a metal vessel of a
certain form and size, and incense is burnt before it and
agarbatti lighted, and it is taken in procession up to the
holy place, and then palm impressions of levigated
sandalwood are put at that place. Amir Shakkar would
every year organise with pomp a *sandal* procession at
night. After him, his widow has continued the practice for
the last several years. The flag procession of Hindus and
sandal procession of Muslims are organised on the same
day and followers of both faiths participate in each
other's procession.

Equal regard and respect for religions was a precept
of Sai Baba's life. To whatever caste, faith or sect a visitor
belonged, to create, nurture and stabilise this feeling of
equal respect was the prime mission of his incarnation.
Normally, people in this country behave with
consideration with followers of other religions or observe
detachment. When false religious propaganda is carried
on, controversies which break out are on the verbal
plane. But two main communities inhabiting this
country, namely, Hindus and Muslims, indulge in mutual
hatred, enmity and clashes. Wise people have attempted
to end these clashes and establish friendship between
them but without the desired success.[13] To all well-
wishers of this country making such efforts, the life of Sai
Baba is a guide.

It is because of Sai Baba's influence that Bade Baba,
alias Fakir Baba, to whom Sai Baba gave between Rs. 25
to Rs. 55, daily arranged to feed the poor, needy,
deserving Hindus. It is again because of this influence
that Balaji Nevaskar, a Hindu devotee, nursed Dagdu, a

Muslim devotee, during the last month of his life. Similarly, Adam Dalal of Bandra, who was involved in a criminal case, approached Sai Baba's devotee, Raghunath Tendulkar, a resident of Bandra, and entreated his wife to pray to Sai Baba for him to be discharged. Accordingly, she prayed for him and Adam was discharged. These are all instances of how Hindu and Muslim devotees interacted with each other in a spirit of friendship and goodwill and in a spirit of loyalty to their common *Guru*, Sai Baba. The above-mentioned Abdulla Jan says in his statement:

> My stay with Baba brought about some changes in my mentality. When I came to Shirdi, I regarded Hindus as enemies of mine. After remaining about three years with Baba, this feeling of animosity passed away and I was viewing Hindus as my brethren. Now, for instance, I see with regret that, at Bombay, Hindus wish to destroy Muslims and their mosques, and Muslims wish to destroy Hindus and their temples. If both suceed in wiping out each other, they will only make room for persons of other faiths to establish themselves in the place of these two.[14]

By his inner vision Sai Baba once foiled a plot of Fakir Baba to convert Hindu devotees and taught him a lesson that by such dubious means one does not attain salvation. While Sai Baba had once gone to Lendi, taking advantage of the absence of Hindu devotees in the *masjid*, Fakir Baba mixed some water tasted by him in the water stored for Hindu devotees and waited for Sai Baba to return! Sai Baba had already perceived this through clairvoyance. So, on returning to the *masjid*, he flew into a temper and broke the pitchers in the *masjid*, and shouted abuses. When it became known why Baba had done so, all the devotees were delighted. Fakir Baba felt ashamed of his conduct and never again indulged in such behaviour.

Many fundamentalist Muslims considered that by applying levigated sandalwood to Sai Baba, playing instrumental music, sounding conch and performing *arati* of Sai Baba, his Hindu devotees were compelling him to act against religion. All this sinning against Islam which Sai Baba did for the sake of his Hindu devotees would be ended if the said devotees were anyhow removed. With this belief they would plead with Sai Baba to stop all the above practices. Seeing this had no effect on Sai Baba, they would get angry and would give vent to their anger in their relations with Hindu devotees and Sai Baba himself. In 1894, some intolerant Muslims in Shirdi summoned the Kazi of Sangamner and positioned themselves near the *masjid,* armed with *lathis,* under the leadership of the Kazi for obstructing the devotees going to the masjid for worshipping Sai Baba. In the meantime, Mhalsapati, who worshipped Sai Baba daily, arrived there with articles of *puja*, but noticing the armed Muslims, worshipped Sai Baba mentally from a distance and was about to leave when Sai Baba himself called him in the *masjid* and got himself worshipped. The armed Muslims stood transfixed and could not prevail against Sai Baba. Slowly they dispersed and never again did they indulge in such fundamentalist behaviour.

Twenty years after the above incident (1914), a fundamentalist Pathan, who also did not relish the aforesaid practices of Hindu devotees, once told Sai Baba at midnight while Sai Baba was sleeping in the *chavadi,* that he was being spoilt and led astray by his Hindu devotees. And he asked for Sai Baba's permission to massacre all the Hindus sleeping in the *chavadi.* Sai Baba replied, "If there is anybody to blame, it is I myself and not these Hindu devotees. So slit my throat and kill me." But the Pathan did not dare to do this mad act and so the Hindus sleeping in the *chavadi* were saved that night!

Thereafter, in 1915, a Pathan who was called a *Rohilla* because of his rough and rowdy ways, came to Shirdi. He was attracted by Sai Baba's personality and power and called the latter Paigambar. However, his fundamentalist nature could not brook Sai Baba's worship by his Hindu devotees and in his anger he raised his *danda* to deal a lethal blow to Sai Baba. Sai Baba merely glanced at him and caught hold of his wrist. Immediately he became powerless and collapsed to the ground and could get up only on being supported by two persons. This experience gave him an idea of Sai Baba's divine powers, and he realised that it was not his business to judge Sai Baba.

All communities should exist peacefully with goodwill for each other, and instead of concentrating on differences of social customs and practices, similarities in human behaviour should be emphasized and efforts made to strengthen and enrich the society and the country. Implicit in every religion is the teaching of love of humanity. As a step in that direction, Gopalrao Gund and other prominent villagers of Shirdi asked Sai Baba whether and when an annual fair should be held in Shirdi, and Sai Baba said that it should be held on Ramanavami day. Both Hindu and Muslim devotees of Sai Baba would gather on that day. As a result, many a misunderstanding was removed, respect and regard developed for each other and the basic cause of clashes was done away with. The desired good effect of this was seen much later. Hindus would celebrate with gaiety and music the festival of Ramanavami in the *masjid,* and Muslims too gave up their objection to playing of music and started taking out *sandal* procession at night. Both are bound by a common sentiment - love of Sai Baba - and all differences between each other are forgotten. Both the communities are present for each other's festival and when Sai Baba's two devotees raise flags in the evening it appears as if it is the symbol of Hindu-Muslim unity. Blessed is this great soul who attracted these antagonistic communities, and helping them to transcend their differences, drew their attention to the principles uniting humanity, and planted in them seeds of love and cooperation.

Even after Sai Baba's passing away, his efforts to establish brotherhood continue unabated. On Tuesday, the tenth day of the bright lunar phase in the month of *Ashwin* in *Sake* year 1840 (October 15, 1918) after the noon *arati*, those devotees who normally took their meals in the *masjid* were sent away by Sai Baba to their respective abodes, and only a few of the local devotees like Lakshmibai Shinde, Bayaji Appa Kote, Bhagoji Lakshman Shimpi, Nanasaheb Nimonkar, Madhavrao Deshpande, etc., remained behind. At that time Sai Baba to Lakshmibai Shinde gave Rs. 9 and said, "I don't feel well here. Please take me to the Wada." Then sitting at his usual place in the *masjid* near the railing, he leaned on the body of Bayaji and gave up the ghost. Digging commenced in the Buti-Wada for Sai Baba's *samadhi*. In the meantime, the Fauzdar arrived. He agreed to the interring of the body in Buti-Wada. But next morning Muslim devotees arrived from Bombay. The Mamledar too arrived from Kopargaon. There was a difference of opinion between Hindu and Muslim devotees. The Muslims wanted his body to be buried in an open space and a tomb to be constructed over it. Double the number of Hindus desired that his body should be interred in Buti-Wada. The Mamledar, therefore, thought of referring the matter to the Collector, and Kakasaheb Dikshit got ready to leave for meeting the Collector. Seeing this, the Muslims decided to withdraw their demand conditionally. The condition was that they should have the same free access to the *masjid* and Buti-Wada as existed in Sai Baba's lifetime. The Hindus accepted this condition willingly. In the circumstances, it was unanimously agreed that Sai Baba's body should be interred in Buti-Wada, and an edifice should be constructed over it, and devotees of all communities should have the freedom of worship.

So Sai Baba's body was interred in Buti-Wada and a *Samadhi Mandir* thus came into existence. And Hindus, Muslims, Christians and Parsis, irrespective of their social standing and position, have freedom of *darshan*. The objective that Sai Baba placed before himself has taken a permanent form. Saints take birth for the welfare of the world. They restrain and control their bodies and regulate their activities in the interest of society. Because of differences of opinion between the two communities, his body lay there for twenty-two hours, unattended. The body was thus put to trouble, but even though it lay there it was neither disfigured nor did it. become heavy. The radiant figure remained unaffected. Only when the mouth was opened for offering *tambul* (roll of the leaf of Piper betel, with areca nut, lime, cardamoms, etc.) a little blood appeared to ooze in the neck. Even so the body put up with all the trouble in order that a *Samadhi Mandir*, useful to all, may come into existence.

Notes

1. *Adhyatmic, Adhibautik* and *Adhidaivik*, i.e., psychical or corporeal (as sorrow, sickness, etc.), physical or material (as earthquake, conflagration, inundation or storm), from the gods, devils or fate (as injury from lightning, pestilence, blight, etc.).
2. Preface of Hari Sitaram Dikshit to *Sainath Bhajanmala* (Marathi) by Raghunath Vitthal Tendulkar and Savitri Raghunath Tendulkar, 1915; *Shri Sai-Sat-Charita*, XII, pp. 151-173.
3. *Shri Sai-Sat-Charita*, XII, pp. 85-150.
4. Ibid., XXVIII, pp. 117-214.
5. Ibid., Chap. XXIX, pp. 2-93.

6. *Shri Sai Leela, Sake* year 1847, issue 2-3, p. 337; see the letter
    dated 21-4-1925 of the doctor.
7. *Shri Sai-Sat-Charita,* Chap. XXXVI, pp. 16-60.
8. Ibid., Chap. XXX, pp. 29-91.
9. Ibid., Chap. XXVI, pp. 57-112.
10. *Shri Sai Leela,* Vol. III, *Shravan Sake* year 1847, issue 5, 363.
11. *Shri Sai-Sat-Charita,* Chap. XIV, pp. 64-89, 159-200.
12. *Devotees' Experiences of Sri Sai Baba,* Part I, p. 125.
13. This biography in Gujarati was written by Swami Sai Sharan
    Anand in 1946 and describes the conditions then prevailing.
14. *Devotees' Experiences of Sri Sai Baba,* Part I, p. 121.

6. SUPERNATURAL POWERS

Riddhi-siddhis (Affluence and supernatural powers)
are our maidservants and we have the *Kamadhenu*
(wish-giving cow),
Yet we have not a *bhakri* (loaf of bread) to eat.   (1)

Beds, mattresses and bolsters and all other comforts
are at our disposal
Yet we do not have a *langoti* to wear.   (2)

If ye must know, we are residents of Vaikunth
Yet we have no place to rest our heads - we are
homeless.   (3)

Tuka[1] says we are kings of the three worlds
But we are neither deficient nor filled (i.e., God takes
care of all our meagre wants).   (4)

Tukaram

For those who regard use of supernatural powers as
obstacles on the spiritual path, it is necessary to remind
them of the thoughts of experienced saints on this
subject. When a devotee strives diligently for the
realisation of God, he gets supernatural powers which try
their utmost to entangle him in the web of temptation.
But if one remains singularly steady in the intense
meditation of God, he is rewarded with the state of
godhead. After that state is attained no *karma* can stain
him. But if supernatural powers are used before and
without attaining this state, they harm the user and the
state of godhead recedes and ever remains a dream. It is

difficult to fathom the state of him who is one with the Brahman. Sai Baba always used to be in a state of *sahaj samadhi*, ever in tune with the Divine. So if in this present account there is a description or narration of miracles know that the following observation of Sai Baba about Tukaram and other eminent saints explains this mystery. For the welfare of the world, all these operations have to be undertaken by incarnations of godhead with the divine purpose. Or in other words, they are the instruments through which these happen. They never do anything for themselves or for their kin.

In the days before Sai Baba's fame had spread far and wide, he was fond of burning lights in the *masjid* (Dwarakamayi) and other *mandirs*. But for the oil in the *pantis*, he depended on the generosity of the grocers in Shirdi. He had made it a rule to light *pantis* in the *masjid* every evening and he would visit grocers' shops for the required oil, though for the lights in the *mandirs* he had made no such rule as above. The grocers tired of giving him oil free. So, once when Sai Baba went to ask them for oil, acting in concert, they told him that they had no stock of oil. But as he had made a rule to light a certain number of lights in the *masjid,* how would he cease to act on his rule just because of the grocers' refusal? He returned quietly to the *masjid,* filled the *pantis* with water instead of oil and lighted the *pantis* as usual. The grocers were waiting to see the fun! But when they saw that the *pantis* were not only lighted with water but they burnt the whole night, they were aghast and were highly embarrassed. Then they went to Sai Baba and craved his pardon for telling him a lie. Sai Baba said, "If you wish to say no, say so plainly without telling a lie. The Lord is displeased by such lies. God acts according to the word of his devotees who speak the truth." Sai Baba performed this *leela* to drive home this lesson.

Once, harvesting in Shirdi had been completed and the foodgrains of the whole village had been stored in a yard. The summer was on. One afternoon Sai Baba said to Kondaji Sutar, "Go, your field is on fire." Kondaji ran to his field and found nothing. He came back running and informed Sai Baba, "There is no fire anywhere in my field. You unnecessarily made me run in the heat of the sun." Sai Baba replied, "Turn back and see." Kondaji then noticed that a stack of sheaves had caught fire and smoke was emerging out of it. In the meantime a strong wind began to blow and people began to run helter-skelter. All the foodgrains of the village had been stacked in the yard where one stack of sheaves had caught fire. People were now frightened and on coming to Sai Baba appealed to him to extinguish the fire to save them from the impending ruin. Thereupon, Sai Baba went to the yard, sprinkled some water round the stack of sheaves on fire and said, "Only this stack will burn and fire will not touch the neighbouring stacks." And so it happened.

Once in the afternoon, the fire of the *dhuni* in the *masjid* suddenly flared up and touched the ceiling. People wondered whether the *masjid* would be consumed by fire! But nobody dared to sprinkle water to put out the fire as everyone was afraid that Sai Baba would get angry. Sai Baba did not leave his seat and behaved as if nothing had happened. When his attention was drawn to the fire, Sai Baba lifted his baton and struck blows on the wooden post opposite him. With every blow the flames began to subside and the fire died out.

Sometimes Sai Baba would cook *prasad* in a *handi* (metal vessel) for distribution, or prepare a decoction for purge. However, he would never use a ladle to stir the boiling food or decoction in the *handi*, but would roll up the sleeve of his *kafni*, insert his hand in the *handi* and stir the boiling food or decoction. Yet his hand was never scalded. Both the above examples show the power he possessed over fire.

In the days when Sai Baba was not much known outside Shirdi, he was once partaking of the alms and two or three devotees were seated by him. Suddenly he exclaimed, "Stop!" No one understood the meaning or significance thereof. After he had finished his repast, Sai Baba got all the articles in the *masjid,* such as pitchers, tumbler, chillum, tobacco pouch, removed outside. As soon as this operation was completed the plaster of the roof over Sai Baba's seat came down with a thud. Then the devotees seated near Sai Baba understood the implication of the word 'stop' uttered by him and wondered how his control extended even over lifeless matter!

Varuna and Indra also respected Sai Baba's word. Once a gale was blowing in Shirdi, accompanied by heavy showers and lightning. All low-lying areas were soon flooded and the villagers and cattle took refuge in the *masjid.* The villagers narrated their woes to Sai Baba and he, leaving his seat, stood on the edge of the raised foundation and cried aloud to the heavens. The gods were evidently concerned and the gale and thunder subsided and the showers also ceased. The sky became clear, the moon and stars appeared in the firmament and all hearts were gladdened.

Similarly, once Rao Bahadur Moreshwar Pradhan with his wife came for Sai Baba's *darshan*. On the day of their departure to Bombay there was a storm and it began raining heavily. Pradhan came to take leave of Sai Baba. Sai Baba looked at the sky and exclaimed, "Oh Allah, let the rain cease. My children are going home. Let them go peacefully." The storm immediately ceased, the rain turned into a drizzle and the Pradhans were able to reach their destination safely.

In the beginning there were no basic facilities in Shirdi. There was a well only in name for it had no natural spring of water, and if ever there was one, it had dried up. People would fetch water for use from a distance. When Sai Baba gave permission to hold a fair on Ramanavami day in Shirdi, the big problem before the organisers was one of water supply. So the organisers requested Sai Baba to provide the well with plentiful supply of water. Sai Baba took the platter of leaves on which consecrated food was placed, put some *bhakri-bhaji* obtained in alms on it, and after tasting some part of it told the organisers to drop the platter along with its contents in the well and assured them that all would be well. Surprisingly, after the platter was dropped into the well, the well began to fill up and when the fair was held, it was full of water.

Sai Baba had invisibly held up a small girl, as soon as she remembered him, as she fell into the water. This shows that he held sway over the element water. Shanta, the three-year-old daughter of a poor man called Baba Kirwandikar, was very fond of Sai Baba. She would say, "I am Sai Baba's sister." Sai Baba would also indulge her. Once, while playing she fell into a well and people thought that she was drowned. But when they peeped into the well they found that Shanta was suspended in mid-space. When she was taken out she said that Sai Baba had held her aloft. As she was not injured in any way the above incident can be appreciated only in the light of the girl's explanation.

Sai Baba had also saved a child older than Shanta in a miraculous way. Once a child was running in a narrow lane in Shirdi on a slushy road. At the end of the lane was a five-foot-deep foundation dug up for construction of a house, which was full of water. The child fell into the pit but nobody noticed it. Yet the child came out of the pit. He did not know swimming. So when asked how he had managed to get out, he said that he had climbed the steps which Sai Baba had shown in the water.[2]

Besides the above experiences, Sai Baba's devotee, Das Ganu, once had an unforgettable experience of Sai Baba's control over the element water. He asked Sai

Baba on a festive occasion for permission to bathe at a place called Singba on the banks of the Godavari (to which Sai Baba would refer as 'Ganga'). Sai Baba not only refused permission but told Das Ganu that the Godavari was at his own feet. Das Ganu was vexed. He knew that the Ganga had its rise from the feet of Lord Narayana, but his faith was not so deep that the joy he would derive from the actual bath in Ganga would be had from the word of his *guru*. Sai Baba, who knew the inner thoughts and intents of the heart, immediately understood the limitation of his faith. So, in order to give Das Ganu direct experience of the dictum that the feet of the *Sadguru* are the embodiment of all the merit obtained by bathing at centres of pilgimage and holy rivers, Sai Baba said to him, "Come near me and hold the hollow of your palms at my feet." As soon as Das Ganu did so, water flowed out of the two big toes of Sai Baba's feet and filled the hollow of Das Ganu's palms in no time. Then Das Ganu was convinced that the flow emerging out of Sai Baba's feet was of Ganga water. Delightedly, he sprinkled some of the water collected in his palms on himself and gave it as *tirtha* to other devotees.[3] Being a poet of no mean order, overcome with emotion of joy, he was inspired to compose on the spur of the moment a *pada* (poetical composition) in Marathi which is translated below:

THE SONG OF DAS GANU[4]

Oh, Supreme Sadguru, boundless is your power and marvellous your deeds;
You are the ship transporting the ignorant across the ocean of life. (*Refrain*)

You became Veni Madhav himself and made your feet Prayag;
And manifested the Ganga and the Yamuna from your two toes.   (1)

You are Brahma, Vishnu and Shiva, the quintessence
of the three gunas;
And on this earth, You manifest as Sai, the
Powerful. (2)

In the early morning you become Brahma and
spiritual knowledge flows from you;
And sometimes resorting to the quality of Tamas, you
assume the terrible form of Shiva. (3)

Sometimes like Shri Krishna, you indulge in childlike
pranks;
And at times you become the fabled swan in the lake
of your devotees' minds. (4)

Considering your fondness for *gandha* (mark of
sandal-paste), how can you be called a Muslim?
And yet if you are a Hindu, how do you dwell happily
in a mosque? (5)

If rich, why should you go asking for alms?
And yet how can you be called a *fakir*, when you put
Kuber (god of wealth) to shame with your
generosity? (6)

If your house be a mosque, why does it have the
sacred fire (of the Hindus)
Burning continually in the *dhuni* which produces the
udi (sacred ashes)? (7)

From morning, devotees in their simplicity worship
you;
At noon, when the sun comes overhead, your *arati* is
performed. (8)

Devotees stand all around you like attendants of
gods;
And holding *chowrie, chamar* (emblems of eminence),
wave them over you. (9)

Trumpets, *dhols* (large sort of drum) *pipani, shahnai*
(wind instruments) and bells resound;
And *chopdars* (attendants in uniform) wearing belts
proclaim your glory at the gates.   (10)

At *arati* time on your divine seat you look like Lord
Vishnu (Kamalavar);
And at dusk as you sit before the *dhuni*, you appear
as Shankara (The destroyer of Cupid).   (11)

Such *leelas* of the Trinity (Brahma, Vishnu, Mahesh)
manifested in you,
Are experienced by us daily, Oh, Baba Sai!   (12)

Even so my mind wanders idly;
Oh steady it, I implore you.   (13)

Vilest of the vile, and a great sinner, I take refuge at
your feet;
Oh, Supreme Guru, ward off the threefold afflictions
of your devotee Das Ganu.   (14)

Sai Baba had the power to appear in dreams of his
devotees and actually give them material things which
the devotees found in their bed on waking up. From this
they would realise that their dream was real! To a
childless woman, Sai Baba gave in her dream a coconut
with his blessings and said to her, " Partake of this
coconut and you will get a son." This was narrated by the
woman when she had come during Ramanavami fair at
Shirdi with her newborn for Sai Baba's *darshan*.

Another experience of this kind was given to Fakir
Amiruddin, former *murshid* of Abdul, Sai Baba's
personal attendant. Sai Baba appeared in Amiruddin's
dream and said, "Take these two mangoes, hand them
over to Abdul and instruct him to come to Shirdi." On
waking up Amiruddin found the two mangoes in his bed.
As per Sai Baba's instructions, he gave them to Abdul
and asked the latter to proceed to Shirdi. The third

instance is that of Megha Marwadi Brahmin from Kheda whose story was narrated in the previous chapter. Even though the door of Megha's room was bolted from within, Sai Baba entered the room, gave him *darshan*, threw *akshata* (consecrated rice) on him and directed him to trace a *trishul*. Megha found the *akshatas* in his bed on waking up. It may be recalled that Sai Baba had clarified later to Megha that what he experienced was not a mere appearance but the actuality!

There are many instances of Sai Baba having given *darshan*, saved from calamity, and of having given an experience of his powers, to many of his devotees who had come to Shirdi from long distances. Some of them will be described at the appropriate places. These incomparable experiences had been given in order to create or strengthen in his devotees faith in and love of God.

That Sai Baba possessed the *annapurna-siddhi* is clear from the distribution among twenty-five persons of *prasad* from 2-4 pieces of almonds and candy offered to him by Nanasaheb Chandorkar in his first meeting with Sai Baba, an acoount of which has appeared ealier in this biography. Another telling instance of this *siddhi* of Sai Baba is seen in the story of Purandare, another devotee of his. Purandare once went on Good Friday to Shirdi when Sai Baba said to him, "I will come to your place for a meal." Purandare replied, "I am blessed. What shall I prepare for the meal?" Sai Baba said, "Some rice, a little *khichri, shira* and one or two vegetables, for two-three fakirs, you and I." Accordingly, Purandare made purchases in the bazaar and asked his wife to cook. His wife made all the preparations. After the noon *arati* was over, Purandare returned to his place when the meal was ready for serving. Now five *fakirs* came and said many more would follow. The Purandares were concerned about how the quantities cooked would suffice if twenty-five guests were to lunch instead of five. So it was decided to cook an additional quantity of rice. After the five *fakirs* had their lunch twenty more *fakirs* came and sat down for meals. All of them had their fill and yet the food cooked was not exhausted! Thereafter another batch of ten *fakirs* arrived and they too were fed without any loss of the quanitity of the food cooked. The additional quantity of rice cooked remained untouched. Then Purandare went to fetch Sai Baba for his meal. But before he could say anything Sai Baba remarked, "I have had my fill. Oh, this gentleman got frightened!" Purandare offered *vida* (a roll of the leaf of Piper-betel with Arecanut, cloves, lime, etc., enclosed in it) and *dakshina* to Sai Baba, who said to him, "Go, have your meal now and also feed Bala Shimpi with whom you are staying." Purandare returned to his place and all family members of Purandare and Bala Shimpi had their lunch. But the food that remained after all this sufficed Purandare for two more days and part of it he carried to Bombay as Sai Baba's *prasad.*

Sai Baba performed a similar *leela* at the place of his devotee, Balaji Nevaskar. All the members of Nevaskar family were devotees of Sai Baba. Once there was a *shraddha* ceremony at Nevaskar's and as three times the number of guests expected turned up for meals Nevaskar's wife was frightened. She spoke of her anxiety to Nevaskar's mother. Nevaskar's mother did not lose her equanimity. She prayed sincerely to Sai Baba and put his *udi* in the cooked food and covered it with a piece of cloth. Sai Baba did not fail his devotee. Everything went off well without a hitch and yet food remained! What can be said of the *siddhi* of one by whose remembrance Annapurna herself is propitiated?

There are many experiences of Sai Baba's power of speech or resolution. We will narrate one out of them here. A couple who were true devotees of Sai Baba used to reside at Bandra, a suburb of Bombay. They both had great love for Sai Baba. The eldest son of Raghunathrao Tendulkar and Savitribai Tendulkar, named Babu, was studying for medicine. An astrologer who examined Babu's horoscope told him that the stars were so unfavourable to him that he would not be successful in his examination that year. Babu was disappointed and did not study as he ought to have. At that time Savitribai had occasion to go to Shirdi. She told Sai Baba about the predicament of her son Babu and asked for his guidance. Sai Baba immediately replied, "Tell Babu to keep aside the horoscope and have faith in me. Ask him to appear for the examination with a calm mind and he will undoubtedly succeed." Accordingly, Babu appeared for the examination. His answers were also proper but somehow he had the feeling that his answers were inadequate and he would fail. So when the oral examination commenced he stayed away. The first day passed off uneventfully. On the second day, when Babu sat down for lunch, a friend of his who dropped in told him that the oral-examiner was concerned at his absence and had enquired why Tendulkar was not present the day before. The friend informed the oral-examiner that Tendulkar was not present as he was under the impression that he had fared poorly in the written examination. Thereupon the oral-examiner had asked him to inform Tendulkar that he had passed in the written examination. On hearing this Babu was delighted and presented himself for oral examination. He was declared successful in the examination in that year. The Tendulkar couple and their son had the feeling that the credit for Babu's success was due to Sai Baba by whose blessing sympathy was aroused in the oral-examiner who had sent for Tendulkar.

On the other hand, there are many instances of people who have come to grief because they disregarded Sai Baba or his word. From these it becomes clear that

Sai Baba always spoke the truth and his authority was unparalleled in the three worlds. There is a maxim to the effect that God may excuse disobedience of his own word but will not tolerate his devotees being treated scornfully. The strange condition to which Durvasa reduced himself as a result of harassing Ambarish is well known. These experiences also show how effortlessly Sai Baba exercised his powers. These experiences primarily comprise cases of those who acted in spite of the refusal by Sai Baba to grant permission to depart, in defiance of his word and came to grief. Ignoring Sai Baba's warning that he would be troubled by rain, Aurangabadkar, seeing the clear sky, trusted his own eyes instead, and left, but was lashed by rain on the way—in spite of Sai Baba's warning, "What work is so important that you must go? You will break your bones!"

Tatya Kote went by bullock cart which overturned on the way, but he was narrowly saved by Sai Baba's grace. 'There is plenty of time for the train to arrive; have your meal and then go,' was the advice of Sai Baba to the *keertankar*, who, disobeying him, left for the station and had to remain hungry. As per Sai Baba's advice, Nanasaheb Chandorkar left after having his meals and when he arrived at the station he found the *keertankar* who was waiting for the train, and was hungry. Only then did the *keertankar* realised the value of Sai Baba's word.

Adbul Rahim Shamsuddin Rangari left against Sai Baba's order and on the way a wheel of the tonga broke, and for two hours at night he had to wait. Had Sai Baba out of his kindness not sent another tonga at night, Rangari would have had to pass the whole night along with his wife in great discomfort.

Even though there was plenty of time for the train to arrive, Behare, who left, on Sai Baba's advice, immediately by tonga was saved from being looted on the

way by dacoits. Those who are parties to court
proceedings have to remain present in the court on the
appointed day. But such persons who stayed back on Sai
Baba's advice were not only saved the trouble of the
journey but never experienced any harm or impediment.
Rao Bahadur Sathe, Rao Bahadur Dhumal, Kakasaheb
Dikshit and others had repeated experiences of such
kind.

'Be content with half a loaf of bread that you get here,
do not go away out of greed for more', was the advice of
Sai Baba to Tukaram Barku who left Shirdi and went to
Karaji, twenty miles away, for work on the road. There
Barku began to get fever and suffered from it for two
months. It was only when he returned to Shirdi that with
Sai Baba's *udi* he was restored to normal health.

Kavaji Patil of Andheri desired to construct a temple
in memory of his father. He asked permission of Sai Baba
to build a temple of Vanidevi at a certain place. Sai Baba
said 'no' once. When Kavaji asked him again Sai Baba
again said 'no'. When even thereafter Kavaji began
pestering Sai Baba he said, "In spite of my saying 'no'
repeatedly, as you still pester me, do what you like and
suffer the consequences." In the meanwhile Kavaji
continued his preparations for Vanidevi's temple on the
advice of a quack. When Kavaji brought the quack to his
place, plague broke out in the vicinity and some people
died thereof. So Kavaji lost faith in the quack and gave
up the idea of installing Vanidevi's idol. Sai Baba had
advised him from the beginning to install his family
deity. Kavaji was still not convinced about the soundness
of Sai Baba's advice, and in his own wisdom he
established the idol of another goddess. Thereafter, for
two years he lingered on under sickness and was barely
saved from death by Sai Baba's grace. It was only after
undergoing great suffering that he developed faith in Sai
Baba. And when he went for Sai Baba's *darshan*, the

latter repeated his earlier advice and said, "Install the family deity of your ancestors and remove the idol of the other goddess from the temple." By obeying Sai Baba's advice Kavaji was saved from any further harm and obtained peace of mind. Kavaji Patil then composed a *keertan* in poetical form (in Marathi) on this incident which was published in *Shri Sai Leela*.

A Sai devotee went on a pilgrimage of Shri Rameshwar with his wife and wife's sister. Their first halt was at Madras in a Gujarati *dharamshala*. The sister-in-law of the devotee, who was particular about observing pollution taboos, began grumbling; so her sister told her, "Even though the arrangements here are good you are grumbling. Then what will you do at Shirdi? There even orthodox persons, particular about pollution taboos, place their heads on Sai Baba's feet without any reservation. The sister-in-law replied, "If that is so, my prostration to your Sai Baba is from here only!" This ironical speech must not have gone well with Shri Rameshwar, for in the evening she got such shooting pain in her limbs that in spite of massage, fomentation, etc., there was no relief and she could not get up from her bed. They had to start next morning for Rameshwar as per their rail reservations. Since there was no improvement in the sister-in-law's condition till night, it was decided to leave her behind in the *dharamshala* at Madras for which proper arrangements were made with the authorities. The two sisters could not sleep at night and began discussing how suddenly this obstacle had developed. The wife of the devotee remarked jokingly to her sister, "Since in the afternoon you said to Sai Baba 'My prostration to you is from here only', you got the shooting pain and you are missing Rameshwar. Sai Baba is God. You salute him from here. So Shri Rameshwar also says, 'Salute me only from there'." This conversation was no doubt in humorous vein, but it did make some impression on the sister-in-law for she said, groaning, "I am sorry. I withdraw my words and apologise. If my shooting pain stops by the morning and I am able to complete the Rameshwar pilgrimage, I will immediately go to Shirdi for Sai Baba's *darshan*." After a few hours she began to feel better and by morning the pains had ceased and she was able to proceed to Rameshwar. The moral is that Shri Rameshwar also could not suffer the insult to Sai Baba, and as soon as the sister-in-law of the devotee was repentant he was pleased and his doors which were earlier closed to her had been opened.

The newly married wife of Aba Samant invited the wrath of fire by her insult to Sai Baba. One day Samant bought a sari and gave it to his wife saying, "This sari has been given to you by Sai Baba." Samant's wife had no faith in Sai Baba. She said, "What has Sai Baba got to do with this sari? You worked and earned money and out of your earning bought this sari." So saying she kept the sari on a box and made preparation for dinner. After dinner she said to her husband, "Now let me see the sari," and went to pick it up. What did she find? The packing was as it was, but the sari inside was charred to pieces. Samant's wife was now full of anguish for having shown lack of faith in Sai Baba. Yet a doubt was still lingering in her mind. So she prayed to Sai Baba, "If I get a new sari tomorrow I will know that the sari was burnt because of the expression of my lack of faith in you." The surprising thing was that a person who owed Samant some money for work done earlier, himself came to Samant the next day unexpectedly, and gave him Rs. 10 from which Samant bought a sari for his wife. His wife now admitted her mistake and also came to have faith in Sai Baba.

Once Sai Baba performed a miracle before which all other supernatural powers pale into insignificance. This was to revive the dead. The daughter of the maternal aunt of Vasudeo Sitaram Ratanjanakar, who had come to

Shirdi, had this experience. Tuberculosis had developed
out of low fever the daughter was getting. As treatment
of doctors and *vaidyas* had proved ineffective, she was
being given only *udi* of Sai Baba (nedicine). She also
began saying that unless she haᴏ the *darshan* of Sai
Baba she would not get well. Though the girl's condition
was delicate, Ratanjanakar brought her to Shirdi and
took her for Sai Baba's *darshan*. Baba let off a volley of
abuses and said, "Let her lie on the *kambal* (coarse
blanket) and keep her on water." Accordingly, she was
given only water for seven days and on the eighth day the
girl died in the morning when it was the time for Sai
Baba to wake up. That morning Sai Baba was in *chavadi*
but he did not get up at the usual time. It was eight
o'clock and yet Sai Baba was asleep! It was the first time
in the history of Shirdi for Sai Baba to wake up so late.
People began attending to the arrangements for the
funeral of the girl. The girl's mother and Ratanjanakar's
mother were weeping and other devotees were trying to
pacify them. Just then the girl made some movement,
yawned and looked around bewildered. All were
gladdened on seeing this. Then the girl narrated the
following account: A black man was forcibly taking her
away when she called out to Sai Baba. Immediately Sai
Baba belaboured the man with his staff, rescued her and
took her to the *chavadi*. The girl had not seen the *chavadi*
but she described it vividly. While all this was happening
in Dikshitwada where Ratanjanakars were staying,
people were discussing animatedly why Sai Baba was
still asleep. Suddenly Sai Baba got up in *chavadi*,
shouting loudly, and striking his staff on the ground, ran
in the direction of Dikshitwada. There was excitement all
round, and the hearts of the *bhaktas* were filled with joy
and wonder at the miracle Sai Baba performed in this
mortal world.

Notes

1. `Tukaram, the saint of Maharashtra.
2. *Shri Sai Leela*, 1951, p. 16.
3. About this incident Das Ganu has observed in his statement (*Devotees' Experiences of Sai Baba*, Part II, p. 42 and p. 53) as under:

   Once for Mahashivaratri I was at Shirdi and wanted to have *Gangasnan* (a dip in the river Godavari) at Singaba (three miles off Shirdi) that day. Megha brought that water daily for sprinkling or pouring (*abhisheka*) over Baba - as Ganga must naturally fall on Mahadeva's head. But Baba did not allow me to go. He said, "Ganga is here at my feet. Do not go." I felt a bit depressed. Theoretically I knew that he was God Narayana and that Ganga flowed from Narayana's feet. But that was a poor, weak faith, insufficient to give my heart the pleasure which a tangible Ganges bath would give me. Baba knew my mentality and asked me to approach his feet and hold my palms near his feet. Then at once water began to flow from both his feet. It was not a few drops like perspiration. It was rather a slow and thin current. In a short time, say a few minutes, I had collected a palmful of that water. Here was Ganga and I was delighted. I bathed, i.e., sprinkled the water over my head. I did not drink this water. Usually I do not drink the *tirtha* offered at Baba's *arati*. On one occasion Jog complained to Baba about it. Baba then said that I should abide by my own convictions and *sampradaya*, and that Jog should not trouble me.

   As observed by Narasimhaswami in his *Life of Sai Baba*, Das Ganu was an orthodox Brahmin who believed that Sai Baba's body was Muslim while his soul was pure, and, because of this belief in pollution taboos, Das Ganu did not drink the water which flowed from Sai Baba's feet.
4. *Shri Sai-Sat-Charita*, Chap. IV.

7. SON TO THE SONLESS

In the beginning there was the Self, one and sole. He thought: "Let me have a wife that I may have children; let me have wealth that I may do something in the world."

Brihadaranyaka Upanishad, 1, 4, 7

A householder, be he rich or poor, attached or detached, *rajasic* or *sattvic*, irrespective of whatever class or strata to which he belongs, wishes in his inner being to have a son, an heir. There are many sayings in the *shastras* in support of the desire for a son. Among the Hindus there has been a belief from ancient times that to continue the family line and to offer an oblation to the deceased for one's own emancipation it is necessary to have a son. And there are many instances of vows, *tapas* and charity (*daan*) having been practised to get a son. The *tapas* that King Dasharatha practised for getting a son like Shri Rama is well known. In the *Puranas* too, there are many tales of having got a son by such vows. Even the rich, who have amassed wealth with great effort, desire to have a son to inherit their wealth and if this desire is not fulfilled they may exercise the right of adoption given to them by law.

Man is a social creature. It is rare to find a person who does not long for a son. Naturally, in the lifetime of Sai Baba, many persons used to come to him for receiving his blessings for a son and even now many visit his *samadhi* with the same objective.

Babasaheb Dengle of Nimgaon was a devotee of Sai Baba. His brother, Nanasaheb Dengle, had no son. As his first wife bore him no son he married again. But even through his second wife he had no son. So on the advice of his brother Babasaheb he went for Sai Baba's *darshan.* By Sai Baba's blessings he got a son and he came to have faith in him. As Nanasaheb Dengle had many friends among government officials, the Collector's Personal Assistant and others began visiting Sai Baba. One such official was the Circle Inspector, Gopalrao Gund. He had three wives but no son. He came for Sai Baba's *darshan* and through the latter's blessings begot a son. Out of gratitude to Sai Baba he wanted to repair the dilapidated *masjid* (Dwarakamayi). Sai Baba did not grant him permission to repair the *masjid* but got the adjacent Hanuman temple repaired by him. On Gund's suggestion an annual fair was first held on Ramanavami day in Shirdi in 1897 which practice is being continued even now.

Damodar Savalaram Rasane, a bangle merchant of Ahmednagar, had no son even though he had two wives. He was a devotee of Sai Baba for many years. In 1900 a devotee sent to Sai Baba a parcel of quality mangoes from Goa. Sai Baba picked out eight mangoes from them and distributed the remaining among children. The children asked Sai Baba to distribute even those eight mangoes, but Sai Baba said, "I have to give them to Damya." The children said, "He is not here," but Sai Baba told them that he would soon arrive. Actually, Rasane was on his way to Shirdi and had reached Kopargaon. The naughty children stole four out of the eight mangoes when Sai Baba was not paying attention to them. Then Rasane came, and went to see Sai Baba. Sai Baba said, "Take these mangoes which I have kept for you and die." As Rasane did not understand the meaning of Sai Baba's words, he was frightened. So Sai Baba said, "Do not eat the mangoes yourself but give them to your second wife.

Thereby you will have sons. Name the first one Daulatshah and the second one Thanashah." Rasane took away the mangoes and his second wife partook of the *prasad*. After a year she gave birth to a son. After another year and a half, another son was born to her. In all she had eight sons, out of whom four survived. As we have seen earlier, two flags are hoisted at the time of annual fair in the *masjid* (Dwarkamayi), out of which one is on behalf of Damodar Rasane and the other on behalf of Nanasaheb Nimonkar.

The thread ceremony of Daulatshah, the eldest son of Rasane, was performed in Shirdi. Daulatshah had offers of marriage from three or four rich parents of marriageable daughters, but on Sai Baba's advice he married a poor man's daughter. Daulatshah had one son but he died shortly due to a fit of epilepsy. His wife was also not keeping good health. Daulatshah was dejected because of his son's death. He went to Shirdi and after taking *darshan* of Sai Baba's *samadhi* prayed to him: "Please give me only one son who will live long instead of many who will die soon." Sai Baba came into his dream and said, "I took away your son because of the unfavourable stars in his case - he was born in *Mool Nakshatra* (one of the 27 asterisms in the moon's path). I will give you a good son. Do not worry." Daulatshah returned from Shirdi and examined his dead son's horoscope, and found that what Sai Baba had told him in his dream was correct. Then he had another son who lived long.

Rao Bahadur Hari Vinayak Sathe became a widower in 1900. Then he was forty-five years old and had two daughters. His relations pressed him to remarry, but he told them that he would marry again only if a holy person assured him that he would get a son by his second marriage. In 1904 Sathe was transferred to Ahmednagar District and he went for Sai Baba's *darshan*. After having *darshan* he took leave of Sai Baba and stood in silence

before him. Then a *mamledar* accompanying him told Sai
Baba that Sathe had no son. Sai Baba replied that if
Sathe were to remarry by God's grace he would get a son.
Sathe married a second time and had three issues of
whom the first two were daughters, and the third was a
son.

Shantaram Balwant Nachane went for Sai Baba's
darshan in 1915 with his wife. All the children who were
born to her till then had died young. Nachane's wife
offered a coconut to Sai Baba which he put in her *oti*
(cavity formed with the end of sari over the shoulder).
While doing so Sai Baba's heart was softened and his
eyes were filled with tears. In 1919, a son was born to
Nachane's wife. He was born under the constellation
Moola (Moola Nakshatra). When the son was two years
old (1921) his mother passed away. As the son was born
after Baba's *nirvana*, he was named Kaluram. When he
attained the age of five, like a yogi whose spiritual
practices were interrupted in his preceding birth, he
would retire into solitude, gaze at the sky and go into
samadhi. He had written the mantra 'Rama Hare Rama'
on paper more than a *lakh* times. Standing before Sai
Baba's picture he would perform *arati*, listen to the
reading of a religious work like Hari-Vijay and say
'Krishna comes to play with me'. Gadge Baba had come to
visit him in 1924.

Once the boy faulted his father for not meditating on
Sai Baba and, pointing to the picture of a dog on a
gramophone record of His Master's Voice, asked his
father to listen to Sai Baba's voice with the same intense
concentration as the said dog listened to the music of the
Ustad (Master Musician). He died of abdominal dropsy at
the age of eight. When his end approached, Kaluram
called his father to his bedside, asked for *Jnaneshwari*,
opened it at Canto 13 and asked him to read it. When his
father started crying Kaluram cheered him and said,
"What is there to cry for? Read the 13th Canto aloud for

me. I am going today." Now we know why Sai Baba's eyes
moistened when he placed the coconut in the *oti* of
Nachane's wife - he had foreseen that the *sattvic* child
would be short-lived, that its mother would pass away
shortly and the father would have to bear the pangs of
separation from his son. Nachane now married a second
time, a girl whom Sai Baba had approved of in Nachane's
mother's dream and three sons were born of this
marriage who were doing well.

Govind Narayan Shinde of Harda had seven
daughters and no son. On the suggestion of a friend he
had vowed before the *padukas* at Gangapur, that if he got
a son through the grace of Dattatreya he would get his
newborn son for *darshan* of Dattatreya at Gangapur. He
got a son within a year but he did not fulfil his vow. Seven
years thus elapsed. Later, Shinde along with the friend
at whose suggestion he had taken the vow, had an
occasion to go to Shirdi. Then Sai Baba rebuked Shinde
thus: "How have you become so arrogant? Don't you
know that you were not destined to get a son? Out of my
own body I have given you a son." So saying he looked at
Shinde's friend and asked, "Isn't this true?" Shinde
apologised to Sai Baba and fulfilled his vow. In this way
Sai Baba not only showed his oneness with all chosen
deities, but also suggested that those whose vows are
unfulfilled are likely to come to grief; so when they come
to Shirdi, by helping them to discharge their vows, he
leads them onto the path conducive to their welfare.

Chhotubai, wife of Rao Bahadur Moreshwar
Pradhan, had once been to Shirdi along with her
husband's sister. Looking at Chhotubai, Sai Baba said in
the presence of all, "She is going to be the mother of my
Babu." Some of those present, thinking that the blessing
was for Pradhan's sister, sought clarification from Sai
Baba. Then, pointing at Chhotubai, he said, "No, no, she
will be my Babu's mother." At that time Chhotubai was
not pregnant but within a year she gave birth to a son

who was named Babu. At the age of four, Babu had a
serious illness. A Telangi Brahmin, named Madhav
Bhatt, was staying with Pradhan. For the welfare of the
Pradhan family he used to perform *puja, japa,* etc. He
was deeply concerned with the sickness of Babu and had
a suspicion that Pradhan had invited this calamity upon
himself by serving a Muslim *fakir* (Sai Baba). But Bhatt
had no courage to give expression to his view.

One night Madhav Bhatt had a dream in which he
saw Sai Baba sitting on the stairs with a staff in his
hand. He said to Madhav Bhatt, "What do you think? I
am the owner of this house." Bhatt did not reveal his
dream to anyone. Then Babu's illness became acute.
Madhav Bhatt got frightened and going up to Sai Baba's
photograph he said loudly, "If by 4 p.m. Babu's condition
improves sufficiently to take him down to the ground
floor, I will admit that you are Dattatreya." After this
prayer the fever began coming down and at 4 p.m. Babu
asked to be taken to the ground floor for playing. Thereby
Madhav Bhatt was convinced that Sai Baba was
Dattatreya, and in his joy he offered Sai Baba Rs 120 as
dakshina. Recognising that Sai Baba was a *Kalpataru*
(wish-fulfilling tree) he vowed that he would give Sai
Baba *dakshina* of Rs 108 if he got a son. And on begetting
a son he discharged his vow by giving Sai Baba Rs 108 as
dakshina.[1]

Sapatnekar, a *vakil* (pleader) of Akkalkot, had a
similar experience. When he was reading law, he first
heard of Sai Baba from a co-student, Shevade. After the
examination was over, while exchanging notes in
Sapatnekar's room about the answers to questions in
examination papers with co-students including Shevade,
Sapatnekar found that Shevade's answers were wrong.
Shevade's co-students including Sapatnekar made fun of
him and said, "How will you ever become an LL.B.?"
Shevade replied with self-assurance, "My Sai Baba has
told me that I will fail this time but will pass at the

second attempt. I have full confidence that as told by Sai
Baba I will surely pass at the second trial." After all other
co-students had departed Sapatnekar asked Shevade,
"Who is this Sai Baba? Where does he reside?" and
gathered all the necessary information. When Shevade
said once again that he would definitely pass as per Sai
Baba's word, Sapatnekar, who had no faith again, poked
fun at him. Thereafter Shevade and Sapatnekar parted.
Later, Shevade passed as assured by Sai Baba, and
became a *vakil* and Sapatnekar came to know this.

Ten years had passed since the above incident. In the
meanwhile Sapatnekar had married and had started
legal practice. He begot a son but he died of inflammation
of the glands of the neck (scrofula). So Sapatnekar was
very unhappy and had lost interest in life. It is said that a
man remembers God only in his misfortune, and
Sapatnekar was reminded of what Shevade had told him
about Sai Baba. Moreover, a person who was considered
to be slow-witted had passed. Thinking that he might get
peace of mind if he approached Sai Baba, Sapatnekar
went to Shirdi along with his wife and brother. All of
them offered a coconut to Sai Baba and prostrated before
him. When Sapatnekar saluted him Sai Baba exclaimed,
"*Chal Hat*" (Get away), and every time Sapatnekar
saluted him during his first visit to Shirdi he met with
the same response from Sai Baba. So he was
disheartened. Finally he went for Sai Baba's *darshan* in
the company of Bala Shimpi, an old devotee of Sai Baba.
Yet he met with the same response as before and Sai
Baba added, "Go away immediately from here." After this
order of Sai Baba, who would dare to stay there? So
Sapatnekar and his wife returned home.

Even after one year thereafter Sapatnekar's mind
was not at rest. So he went on a pilgrimage to Gangapur
and also thought of going to Varanasi. However, two days
before the appointed day of departure Sapatnekar's wife
had a dream in which she saw that while she was going

to fetch water she saw a *fakir* with a piece of cloth tied around his head, sitting under a neem tree. He said to her, "Dear girl, why do you labour in vain? I will get your *ghagar* (brass or copper vessel) filled with clean water." Fearing the *fakir* she retreated but the *fakir* was following her. Just then she awoke and the Sapatnekar couple decided to go to Shirdi instead of Varanasi. When they reached Shirdi, Baba had gone to the *Lendi* (stream), so both of them sat waiting for him. After sometime Sai Baba returned to the *masjid* and took his seat. Sapatnekar's wife then went up the steps of the *masjid* and had Sai Baba's *darshan*. Seeing her humility Sai Baba was pleased, and said to a woman devotee sitting by him, "My hands and feet, stomach and waist have been aching much for last many days. I have tried several remedies but to no avail. But I am surprised that after coming here my ache has suddenly vanished." Sapatnekar's wife was astonished on hearing this, for it was a recital of her ailment. When she was cured of her ailment after two months' stay in Shirdi, she came to have faith in Sai Baba. In order to rid himself of his sorrow Sapatnekar too prostrated before Sai Baba, but once again the latter said, *"Chal Hat"* (Get away). Sapatnekar had already repented for having shown lack of faith in Sai Baba. Finally he decided that when Sai Baba was alone he would hold fast the latter's feet until he secured his blessings. When he approached Sai Baba with this resolve, the latter blessed him by placing his hand over Sapatnekar's head. Then Sapatnekar sat doing *charan seva* (pressing the legs of Sai Baba). In the meantime a shepherd woman arrived. She commenced her usual *seva* of Sai Baba - pressing his back and Sai Baba conversed with her. Sai Baba was telling her a story while she nodded. The tale related to Sapatnekar and his lost son. Sai Baba narrated the whole story from the child's birth till its death. Sapatnekar was amazed. Then, pointing to Sapatnekar, Sai Baba said, "He accuses

me of having killed his son. Why does he come to the
masjid and bewail that I strike down others' children? All
right, I will now see that he gets back his son." On
hearing this Sapatnekar rose, glanced at Sai Baba and
prostrated. Sai Baba assured him and said, "These feet
(of mine) are very ancient. Have complete trust in me. Do
not worry. Your wish will be fulfilled." Sapatnekar was
overjoyed and stayed on in Shirdi for many days. When
the time came for him to take leave Sai Baba asked him
for *dakshina* of two rupees which Sapatnekar had
already decided in his mind to offer. Then Sai Baba
placed a coconut in the *oti* of Sapatnekar's wife. She
delivered a son a year thereafter and Sapatnekar came
with his wife and son for Sai Baba's *darshan*. Sapatnekar
was now a changed man. His cynicism was replaced by
faith in Sai Baba. He begot two more sons later.

The reader may wonder how he can get Sai Baba's
help now that Sai Baba is no more in his physical frame.
The answer is partially found in the foregoing account of
Daulatshah Rasane who, after the *darshan* of Sai Baba's
samadhi, had a dream in which Sai Baba promised to
give him a son within a year and fulfilled his promise. In
his lifetime Sai Baba would often say 'After I pass away
my *samadhi* will protect you'. Devotees get experiences
even now in keeping with this assurance. One woman
devotee vowed that she would go for the *darshan* of Sai
Baba's *samadhi* if she got a son of her choice. When she
got a son as she wished she went for the *samadhi-
darshan* and in discharge of her vow offered a coconut
and a gold bead at the *samadhi*. Even by worshipping
Baba with faith or by partaking of his *udi* and *samadhi-
darshan*, many have begotten children.

Narayanrao Angre of Thana was treated by many
doctors but did not have progeny. With devotion to Sai
Baba he begot a son within four years.[2] P.R. Joshi of
Poona conveyed by his letters dated 10 October 1949 and
15 November 1949 to the author of this biography that

his wife was ill since nine years and had no progeny. By calling out to Sai Baba with love and devotion his wife's condition improved and she gave birth to a son.[3] Similarly, Baburao Ingle of Worli, Bombay, begot a son through devotion of Sai Baba.[4] Godavaribai, wife of Shripad Hari Kulkarni, whom doctors had advised that she could not deliver without an operation as the foetus in her womb was upside down, delivered a son naturally and safely without an operation as a result of *Sai-bhakti*.[5] Smt. Prela Uparkar of Dadar who had no issue for twelve years also got a son as a result of Sai-devotion.[6]

Notes

1. When Madhav Bhatt took Babu to Shirdi for Sai Baba's *darshan*, Sai Baba took Babu in his lap and said, "Well Babu, isn't our house ready? Haven't you come for five years to your father and for five years to your mother?" So saying he gave Babu back to him. As told by Sai Baba, Babu died at the age of ten and Pradhan's bungalow was constructed in the meanwhile. Pradhan's two sons and one daughter are alive. (*Shri Sai Leela* 1952, *Punyatithi* issue, pp. 52-53).
2. *Shri Sai Leela,* (1948) Vol. 25, issue 2, p. 9.
3. Ibid., (1949) Vol. 26, issue 4, p. 12.
4. Ibid., (1949) Vol. 26, issue 5, p. 18.
5. Ibid., (1952) Vol. 29, issue 4, p. 49.
6. Ibid., (1953) Vol. 30, issue 1, pp. 14-16.

8. KNOWLEDGE OF PREVIOUS BIRTHS

You and I Arjuna,
Have lived many lives,
I remember them all:
You do not remember.

Bhagavad Gita, IV, 5
(translated by Swami Prabhavananda & Christopher
Isherwood)

As said, toward the end of Chapter Seven, referring to
Chhotubai, wife of Rao Bahadur M.W. Pradhan, Sai
Baba had said that she was going to be the mother of his
Babu. Readers would be curious to know who this Babu
was. He was a young devotee dear to Sai Baba. Sai Baba
loved him deeply. Babu was the nephew of Ganesh D.
Kelkar, father-in-law of Rao Bahadur H.V. Sathe. He
was employed as a clerk at Kopargaon and Yewale under
Limaye, assistant to Rao Bahadur Sathe. Pursuant to a
dream, Babu left home and came on foot to Shirdi for Sai
Baba's *darshan*. He would serve Sai Baba in many ways
and was thus dear to Sai Baba. He paid more attention to
the service of Sai Baba than his clerical duties. So Sathe
would complain to his father-in-law about it.

Whatever sweetmeats Sai Baba received as *naivedya*
(consecrated food) he would give to Babu, would feed him,
and, knowing that the latter's end was near, would tell
Ganesh Kelkar whenever he brought the complaint of his
son-in-law to his notice, "Let it be. Let him serve me."

Babu would eat to his heart's content mangoes from the mango baskets received by Sai Baba as offerings. In 1910, Sai Baba asked Ganesh Kelkar to look after Babu - in a few days he had high fever and when his end approached Sai Baba merely asked Ganesh Kelkar, "Is he still alive?" Babu died at Shirdi at the age of twenty-two, leaving behind a childless widow. As predicted by Sai Baba that Chhotubai, wife of Pradhan, would bear him, she gave birth to a son who was named Babu. That child was brought to Sai Baba when it was four months old. Sai Baba fondled it and said, "Babu, where had you been? Were you tired of me?"

Ganapatrao Narke was a Professor in Poona Engineering College. In 1913-1914, he stayed at Shirdi for some length of time. Once in his dream Narke had Baba's *darshan* and saw a person looking like a labourer standing near himself. Pointing to the latter Sai Baba said, "See this friend of your last birth! One's condition changes according to his *karma*." A few days after this dream Narke was sitting beside Sai Baba in the morning when a labourer carrying a load of firewood on his head came to the *masjid*. Looking at him Narke felt that he resembled the labourer he had seen in his dream and wondered whether he was the friend of his last birth! Immediately Sai Baba said to him. "Go and give your friend two rupees for the load of firewood." Why so much for the load was the doubt that arose in Narke's mind. At once Sai Baba said, "This is the one known to us in our preceding birth, isn't it?" The chain of thought in Narke's mind about the labourer instantly ceased and he was convinced that the person who brought firewood was the labourer introduced to him in the dream as his friend. The present writer had also a similar experience. In his dream he saw a woman blind in one eye. Later, when he was sitting near Sai Baba, a woman resembling the person in his dream came to the *masjid*. Sai Baba gave her two rupees from his pocket, suggesting that she was the person known to the author in his preceding life.

On one occasion, Sai Baba expressed his knowledge of the preceding birth of two she-goats. Once, in the morning, while returning from *lendi* he bought two she-goats at the rate of rupees sixteen per goat. Tatya Kote and Madhavrao Deshpande did not approve of the transaction as the price paid for them was excessive. The average market price for a she-goat was rupees two and the maximum rupees four. They could not understand why Sai Baba paid such a high price and blamed him for being too generous. Sai Baba did not reply to their arguments but merely remarked, "Buy two seers of pulse from the grocer, feed one seer to each of the two goats and return them to the shepherd." This strange behaviour of Sai Baba perplexed Tatya Kote and Madhavrao. Then Sai Baba narrated the story of the preceding births of the two goats: "In their preceding birth they were human beings. They were two brothers with whom I was well acquainted. Initially, they were affectionate to each other. They lived and moved together. By the quirk of destiny an enmity developed between the two of them. The elder brother was lazy while the younger one was hard-working. The younger brother thus acquired considerable wealth. The elder one became envious of his younger brother's wealth and devised a plot to do away with him and appropriate his wealth. When the plot came to light, the younger brother understood the crooked stratagem of his elder brother. An altercation ensued and one of them struck a blow with a stick on the head of the other, as a result of which the latter collapsed. In retaliation, the latter hit the former with a hatchet. Both of them died a few days later, due to the injuries sustained by them, and by their *karma* were born as goats. Seeing the two brothers in this form, I was overcome with pity and wanted to shelter them. So, at my own expense, I fed them with pulse but the constraints of *karma* (destiny) interfered through your agency. No doubt, I am full of compassion for the goats but on your importuning me I agreed to return them to the shepherd."

The effects of greed for money, mutual hatred and enmity, Sai Baba once described through a story of past birth. He said: "Once after my breakfast at eight-o'clock I sauntered out. I walked quite a distance, felt tired and came to the bank of a river. I bathed in the river and was delighted with the prospect around. The bed of the river was narrow but it was full of water. There was a thick growth of trees along the bank and a tender breeze was blowing. I sat quietly in the cool shade of the thicket and, thinking of having a smoke, went to the water to wet the cloth over the *chillum*. There I heard the croaking of the frog. It was the natural habitat for a frog. With the help of a flint and steel, I struck fire and lighted my *chillum*. Just then a passerby came, greeted me and sat down. I handed him the *chillum* which he took respectfully and said, 'How is it that you have wandered so far? The sun will be overhead by the time you return to the *masjid*. Yonder is my house. Have a smoke, partake of some food, rest for a while and when the heat of the sun is less you may go back. I will also accompany you.' So saying the passerby lighted the *chillum*.

The frog was croaking piteously and the passerby enquired what the matter was. I replied, 'A frog is in danger and his *karma* is following him. Listen. Just as you sow in your past birth, so you reap in the present birth. What is the use of crying now?' Hearing this the passerby humbly handed the *chillum* to me and said, 'I will go and see personally what is happening.' Knowing his curiosity I said, 'Go and see for yourself. A frog which is caught in the mouth of a serpent is croaking. Both are wicked. Both have committed great sins and are born to suffer.'

The passerby went near and saw that a ferocious serpent had caught a frog. The passerby was frightened and coming to me said, 'The serpent is big and fierce and the frog is hideous but it is on its last legs and in no time will be swallowed up by the serpent.' Then I said to him, 'How dare the serpent swallow the frog? Will I, his father, who has come and sat here be a helpless witness to this? See how I save the frog from the clutches of the serpent. Thereafter we shall leave. Go and fill the *chillum*. Let us see what the serpent will do.' The passerby made the *chillum* ready. I had one or two puffs at it and taking the passerby with me made my way through the rush-like grass to the specific spot. The passerby got frightened at the terrible form of the serpent and pleaded with me not to venture farther as according to him it was dangerous to do so. Then I went near the serpent and said, 'Oh Veerbhadrappa, this enemy of yours, Chanbasappa, has become a frog and in order to pay off old scores you have been born a serpent but will you not forget even now the enmity? Aren't you ashamed? Give up your hostility and be quiet.' Just as these words came out of my mouth, the serpent dropped the frog and entering deep waters vanished from sight. The frog too, as soon as he was released, hopped and hid himself in the thicket. Seeing this the passerby was astonished and said to me, 'Who among these is Veerbhadrappa and who Chanbasappa? Tell me their story.' I said, 'Let us return to the shade of the tree and smoke the *chillum*. Then I will satisfy your curiosity.' Sitting there while puffing away at the *chillum*, I told him the following tale."

He began his tale. "Five to six miles from my place was a holy shrine of Mahadev which was in a state of disrepair. With the intention of renovating the temple, all the devotees collected a large sum of money. A *sowcar* of that town was requested to look after the task and was given all the collection. The *sowcar* was honest and he kept the collection separately. But being a born miser he would not apply any part of his funds to the operation. The work of repair started and some progress was made but there was a shortage of resources. Then the devotees said to the *sowcar*: 'What is the use of your moneylending business? If you do not help monetarily how will the work progress further? We will coax the people to contribute once again but please see the completion of the task through.' Some more collection was again made but the *sowcar* sat quiet without utillising the money collected. After some days the *sowcar's* wife had a dream in which she was directed to arise and construct the dome and was assured that Shiva would give her hundred times the amount of expenditure incurred. Next morning she apprised her husband of her dream but he belittled her and paid no attention whatsoever. However, he resumed the work of repair but the work would come to a stop as soon as the collection handed to him was exhausted. The *sowcar* would not spend a pice of his own on repairs. After several days the *sowcar's* wife had a dream again — Out of your *streedhan* donate whatever you wish to. As you have faith a pice given by you willingly is worth a lakh. — Hearing this the wife decided to complete her task by selling the ornaments given to her by her father and informed her husband about it. The *sowcar* was confused but he thought of a way out. A helpless woman had mortgaged her land with the *sowcar* for a loan of Rs. 200. It was a piece of uncultivated wasteland. So valuing the ornaments of his wife as Rs 1000 he purchased the ornaments himself and instead of giving her cash decided to transfer the land in his wife's name. He said to her, 'Take this land worth Rs 1000. Donate it to Shankar so that he may be pleased with you.' The *sowcar's* wife agreed and donated that land to Shiva temple. After some years during the constellation of *Kruttika* (third of the lunar asterism) it rained heavily. There was a storm and the *sowcar's* house was struck by lightning. The whole structure sank in and the *sowcar*, his wife and the woman who had mortgaged the land died after a few years.

"The *sowcar's* wife was born as the daughter of the Pujari at Shankar's temple and was named Gauri. The woman who had mortgaged the land was blessed with a son by the Gurav of Shankar's temple and she named him as Chanbasappa. The *sowcar* was born in a Brahmin household in Mathura and was named Veerbhadrappa. I had great affection for Gauri's father, the priest at Shankar's temple. He would always visit me and we would talk of many things far into the night. He would also bring Gauri with him and she was devoted to me. When Gauri reached the marriageable age her father made all efforts to find her a husband but something or other came in the way. So her father was worried. I would assure him that a spouse would come to her door on his own.

"Now let us turn to Veerbhadrappa. As Veerbhadrappa was born in a poor family, he decided to leave his home to seek his fortune. He wandered and supported himself by asking for alms or by doing physical labour. In the course of wandering he arrived at the household of Shankar Pujari. He was liked by all and with my consent the Pujari gave his daughter in marriage to Veerbhadrappa. Veerbhadrappa stayed in his father-in-law's house and improved in his health after his marriage.

"When the Pujari passed away he bequeathed the land to his dear daughter Gauri. By God's grace the land appreciated in value. A purchaser agreed to pay Rs one lakh for the land, of which he paid half on the spot and the balance was due to be paid in annual instalments of Rs 2000 plus interest over twenty-five years. The deal was approved by all except Chanbasappa. He said that as

Gurav, he had the first claim over the money received by Shankar and as such he should receive half the annual interest. Veerbhadrappa flatly declined Chanbasappa's demand. The two had a heated argument and the dispute came to me for arbitration. I told them both that the real owner of the land was Shankar. The land ought not to be utilised for any other purpose. It was therefore necessary that neither of them should covet the land. It was for Gauri to decide. If they acted according to her wishes they would be happy. Veerbhadrappa had also no authority to act independently. Hearing this Veerbhadrappa called me names and alleged that by declaring Gauri as the owner I wished to establish my hold over the land. I was stunned at this accusation.

"The same night Gauri had a dream in which Shankar appeared and instructed her: 'All this money is yours. Don't give anything to anyone. As regards the permanent arrangements, do as I tell you. For the temple expenditure Chanbasappa's wishes may be respected as I have full trust in him in this regard. For other things do nothing without consulting the Baba in the *masjid.*' Gauri apprised me of her dream and sought my counsel. So I said to her: 'Keep your capital to yourself. Give half the annual interest to Chanbasappa according to divine guidance.' While we were thus conversing, Veerbhadrappa and Chanbasappa came there quarrelling. In spite of being told about the divine guidance in Gauri's dream it had no effect on Veerbhadrappa. He abused the opposite party to his heart's content. Then he had spasms and in supervening delirium he would gabble and rave and say often to Chanbasappa, 'When I get you alone I will mince you to pieces.' In fright Chanbasappa would hold my feet and I would assure him. Later Veerbhadrappa died and due to his enmity in his previous birth he was born as a serpent. Chanbasappa was my devotee but he shrank in terror and died of shock. So he was born a frog. In the form of serpent, Veerbhadrappa chased Chanbasappa who was in the form of a frog and caught hold of him. And hearing the latter's call for succour, pursuant to my assurance I came here and saved Chanbasappa. That the principle of *karma* is relentless in its operation thus becomes clear. So greed, hatred, enmity and fear should not be entertained."

In the foregoing account of Nanasaheb Chandorkar (Chapter Three) Sai Baba had clarified in his reply to Nanasaheb: "Well, there are any number of men in this world, but instead of calling them when I call you, there must be a reason for it. There is a relationship between us going back as far as four births. You are not aware of it but I am." Sai Baba would say many times, "I will willy-nilly drag anyone who is my man, here, even if he is hiding in the seventh nether world."

When Balakram Mankar and the present writer were once sitting by Sai Baba, the latter remarked, "This Balakram and this (writer) were at one time residing in caves opposite to each other and doing penance." In the open *durbar* Sai Baba once said about the present writer, "I have known him from very early times." When I made enquiries at home I came to know that as a child I was weak and often falling sick. When my father was employed in government service at Dharasana, in my infancy I once suffered from irregular state of the bowels-costiveness alternately with diarrhoea, vomits, etc., and everyone lost hope of my life. At that time my mother was sitting in the evening in the courtyard sighing. Suddenly, a *fakir* arrived there and said to her: "This kid is very fortunate. Look, on his right side is a birthmark." Then my mother complained to him about my delicate state of health. Sai Baba who had appeared in the garb of a *fakir* gave her sacred ash and from that time my condition began improving. Similarly, Sai Baba's devotee Upasani was suffering from dreadful breathlessness and he had lost all hope of survival. Once when Upasani was going for a stroll Sai Baba met him in the garb of an old person and advised him to drink hot water by which he would be benefited. Similarly, he convinced Upasani by telling him many things about his childhood, his austerities, etc., that he (Sai Baba) was connected with his family since long. About Mrs Chandrabai Borkar who practised the vow of *Kokilavrata*, Sai Baba had said, 'Wherever I go she comes in search of me. She is a sister of mine of seven births." Similarly, the story of a she-buffalo in Shirdi whose desire was gratified through the agency of Mrs Tai Jog and realeased from the birth of a beast will be narrated in detail later.

From all this, one comes to know that Sai Baba had knowledge of past births. But he would reveal this to a devotee only when it was absolutely necessary. Ordinarily otherwise he would keep mum. Though one with Brahman, outwardly he feigned to be an ignoramus.

9. REMOVAL OF OTHERS' SORROWS

My honour, O God, is in Thy keeping;
Thou art ever my refuge,
For Thou art Protector of the weak.
It is Thy promise to listen to the wail of sinners;
I am sinner of old, help me
Thou to cross this ocean of darkness;
It is Thine to remove the sin
And the misery of mankind.
Be gracious to Tulsidas
And make him Thy devotee.

Tulsidas
(translation by Mahatma Gandhi)

How is it possible that Sai Baba would sit quiet when people of Shirdi or a devotee of his was threatened with calamity? When fire broke out in a yard in Shirdi where the foodgrains of the whole village had been stored, by his own power Sai Baba quelled the flames. When an epidemic of plague broke out in Shirdi, he took the *karmic* suffering upon himself and removed the danger to the lives of others.

Once the whole village was affected by an epidemic of cholera. To put an end to it he devised a marvellous remedy. In the *masjid* of Sai Baba there would always be a sack of wheat, a scuttle-basket and a quern. Many persons died of this disease. One day in the morning Sai Baba cleaned his teeth, washed his face and took out several measures of wheat from the wheat-sack and put into the scuttle-basket. He then spread an empty sack on the ground, put the quern on it and hammered its peg firmly into position. He then rolled up his sleeves, and spreading his legs began grinding wheat. Devotees watched him with surprise but dared not ask him what he was doing. When the news spread in the village men and women assembled and four of the women entered the mosque and snatched away the quern-peg from Sai Baba's hands. Sai Baba became angry and showered a volley of abuses. Not minding them the women began grinding at once; and grinding, sang of Sai Baba's playful deeds. Seeing their affection, Sai Baba's (feigned) anger subsided. Eight pounds of wheat were ground, emptying the scuttle-basket. Then, raising the quern, it was rested against a wall.

Then the women collected the flour and thought: 'Sai Baba has no house, no family, and no children. What will he do with so much flour? Let us carry it away.' So they divided the flour into four parts. Till then Sai Baba merely watched the scene with amusement and did not utter a word. But as they began carrying away their share he burst out, "Are you mad? Where are you carrying the flour to? Does it belong to your father? Go to the boundary of the village and cast it on the bank of the brook." The women fretted and felt ashamed of their greed, but proceeded to the boundary and cast the flour on the bank of the brook as directed by Sai Baba. Devotees from outside Shirdi had no idea why Sai Baba directed the flour to be cast on the bank of the brook. Therefore, villagers when asked said that whenever the village is threatened with the outbreak of an epidemic Sai Baba does so. At that time the village was affected by an epidemic of cholera. So this antidote was devised by Sai Baba. The city-bred educated devotees were a bit mystified. They could not see the connection between the wheat and the disease. But when they saw that after the scattering of the wheat there was not a single case of death due to cholera and the epidemic was ebbing, they were amazed and love surged in them.

The above incident reminds me of the strange ways in which Sai Baba saved his devotee, Gopalrao alias Bapusaheb Buti, twice when the latter was suffering from cholera. Buti was a disciple of the well-known saint of Berar, Gajanan Maharaj. He was a barrister and his business had branch offices at many centres. On the direction of Sai Baba, he had constructed a Wada of black stones and the oblong space forming the central portion of the Wada was left open. Buti was thinking of raising a temple therein. A beginning was also made, but artisans brought from outside fell sick and in the meanwhile Sai Baba breathed his last.

According to Sai Baba's wish, his body was taken to the Buti Wada. It was interred in the sanctum sanctorum of the central portion over which an edifice of his *samadhi* has come up. Actually the Wada was constructed by Buti for his personal use and residence but as Sai Baba passed away Buti's desire remained unfulfilled. He liked to serve holy persons. Earlier he wished to spend a large part of the year in the service of Gajanan Maharaj and later when he came to know Sai Baba he remained mostly in Shirdi.

After he had made his residence in Shirdi, Buti once suffered from diarrhoea and vomits. Many days passed thus and his daily visit to the *masjid* was interrupted. He did not get relief through medical treatment and he was frightened. Sai Baba sent for Buti and the latter reached the *masjid* with great difficulty and sat down. Sai Baba merely raised his fingers and said, "Mind you, from now onwards you will not go for evacuation of bowels and vomits." Buti was between the devil and the deep sea. On one side was his physical helplessness and on the other side was the sin of disobedience of the command of his Guru. But the power of Sai Baba's words was such that both motions and vomits stopped instantly!

On another occasion when cholera broke out in Shirdi, Buti was affected by it. Dr Pillay who was then in Shirdi treated him with many remedies but without success. So Dr. Pillay approached Sai Baba with concern and asked him what should be done in the circumstances. Sai Baba replied, "Feed him with *kheer* made of walnuts, almonds and pistachio and he will get well immediately." Both Barrister Buti and Dr. Pillay, a practising allopath, were stumped on hearing the remedy prescribed. But Buti was not a weak or raw disciple. He had firm faith in Sai Baba. He drank the *kheer* made of walnuts, almonds and pistachio. And, wonder of wonders! He was cured of cholera!

Bhimaji Patil of Narayangaon in Junnar *taluka,* Pune district, suffered from tuberculosis which became so acute that he vomited blood every five minutes. Sai Baba cured him by merely blessing him and without administering any medicine. Bhimaji Patil's condition had been worsening steadily. He began passing blood in vomits and foaming at the mouth. He gave up all hope of his life. As a last resort he wrote a detailed letter to Nanasaheb Chandorkar, apprising him of his condition. He stated in his letter that he had lost self-confidence and all hope of living and expressed his last desire to meet Nanasaheb.

Nanasaheb was touched by Bhimaji's letter. He had close ties with Bhimaji and appreciated his goodness. So he replied with feeling that there was only one way out and that was to take refuge in Sai Baba. Bhimaji trusted Nanasaheb fully. Consequently he went to Shirdi with two or three of his relations.

On reaching Shirdi, Bhimaji was most eager to have *darshan* of Sai Baba. He was in no condition to walk. Hence when the bullock cart arrived at the front entrance, he was bodily lifted and carried to the *masjid* and seated before Sai Baba. Nanasaheb Chandorkar and Madhavrao Deshpande were both present. Seeing

Bhimaji, Sai Baba said, "Oh Shama (Sai Baba would always address him thus), how many thieves will you bring and set upon me? Is this proper?" Bhimaji placed his head on the feet of Sai Baba and prayed, "Take care of this helpless man." Sai Baba was filled with compassion and immediately Bhimaji's sorrow was at an end. Sai Baba said with a smile, "Give up your mental anguish. There is no reason to worry. As soon as you put your foot in Shirdi your misery has ended. However deep the distress or calamity, one who enters this *masjid* is relieved. The *fakir* here is very kind. He is the Protector of all. Now retire to the house of Bhimabai and stay there. Within a day or two you will experience remission of your sickness." While Bhimaji sat with Sai Baba for an hour he did not have any vomits at all. He also felt energetic. Slowly, he made his way to Bhimabai's place where he was directed to stay.

In Bhimabai's house the floor had been just smeared over with mud and cowdung wash and it was damp. Bhimaji knew many others in Shirdi, and could easily have secured suitable accommodation in the village. But with firm faith in Sai Baba's word, he spread two sacks and bedding over it and went to sleep. The same night Bhimaji's childhood teacher came in his dream and caning him on the back got the following verse on *sati-dharma* memorised by him:

> To her stepping into another's house is like stepping on the head of a serpent,
> Her words are as scarce as the money coming from the hands of a miser.
> She likes only the company of her husband, however poor he may be;
> She is really a devoted wife who acts according to her husband's wish.

Soon he had another dream, stranger than the first one, in which a person came and sat over him and with his stone roller or muller, began levigating by using his chest as a slab. Due to caning in the first dream and levigating in the second, he panted and struggled under extreme pain. Now the dreams ended and he slept peacefully. When he awoke at daybreak he remembered the terrible dreams but he was full of joy on noticing that his disease had completely disappeared. He had neither spasms, nor vomits with blood nor foaming at the mouth. Seeing this marvel all were astonished. Slowly Bhimaji walked to the *masjid* with a cheerful face for Sai Baba's *darshan*. He prostrated himself before Sai Baba and expressed his gratitude. After staying in Shirdi for a month he returned home. Thereafter, he frequently came to Shirdi for Sai Baba's *darshan*.[1]

Bala Ganpat Shimpi used to stitch Sai Baba's *kafnis*. Once he was affected by malaria and was having high fever which would not come down to the normal temperature. So he went to the *masjid* and said to Sai Baba, "What sin have I committed that I should suffer thus? Please have mercy on me." Sai Baba had a great sense of humour and would joke with Bala Shimpi many times. Hearing Shimpi's request Sai Baba said to him, "There is a remedy but it's a little strange one. If you feed cooked rice and curds to a black dog near the Laxmidevi temple you will be cured of malaria." Shimpi wondered whether Sai Baba was joking or was seriously suggesting the remedy. He returned home, found some cooked rice and obtained some curds from a neighbour. His immediate worry was to find a black dog at the time of his visit to the Laxmidevi temple. But the fountain of mercy who suggests the remedy also supplies all the necessary constituents for the devotee. Shimpi approached the appointed place with anxiety, but found a black dog wagging its tail as if waiting for him. He fed the black dog with rice and curds as directed and found that malaria had left him!

Lakshmanrao alias Kaka Mahajani who had once been to Shirdi suffered there from *cholera morbus* (bilious disorder from overeating, etc.) and had severe diarrhoea. Believing that Sai Baba knew the innermost thoughts of his devotees, he neither informed Sai Baba about his condition nor did he take any medicine. He was anxious to be present in the *masjid* at the *arati* every time, but was having loose motions every five to ten minutes. So, while going to the *masjid* for *arati* he would carry a *lota* of water with him. Every time he had to answer nature's call he would have a wash thereafter. This continued for some days. Mahajani was tired but it was not as if his condition had not attracted Sai Baba's attention. But the time for treating Mahajani's complaint was brought about in a strange way and Mahajani was cured merely by Sai Baba's blessing. The occasion arose like this. It had been decided to make a paved flooring in the *sabhamandap* of the *masjid*. As soon as the digging started Sai Baba suddenly assumed a fierce form and frightened everybody away. While Mahajani was trying to make good his escape Sai Baba caught him by his hand, overawed him and asked, "Why are you running away? Stand here." And so saying took him to the *masjid*. Some devotees from Bombay, when they saw Sai Baba's fierce mood, left the *masjid* in great hurry, retired to the *wada* and in the process left behind a bag containing peanuts. Putting his hand in the bag, Sai Baba went on taking out peanuts and feeding them to Mahajani. In between he would also eat a few himself. This way approximately one seer peanuts in the bag got exhausted. Then Sai Baba said to Mahajani, "I am thirsty, get some water." He drank some and also made Mahajani drink some. Thereafter he said to Mahajani, "Now you may go. You are cured of *cholera morbus*. Bring back the devotees who ran away. It is *arati* time." Mahajani's bilious disorder thus ended and he was all right once again.

Lakshmanrao Mahajani's brother, Gangadharpant, was affected by colic which was cured by Sai Baba by his mere blessing. Gangadharpant went to Shirdi and prayed to Sai Baba. Sai Baba saw him, touched his stomach, pressed it at a certain spot and asked, "Does it pain here?" When Gangadharpant replied in the affirmative, Sai Baba blessed him. Instantly the pain disappeared. Nanasaheb Chandorkar also once suffered from spasmodic griping pain in the belly and could not get sleep. Sai Baba made him eat a piece of *barfi* with ghee and thus cured him.

Here it is necessary to sound a note of caution that remedies such as peanuts, *barfi*, etc., which Sai Baba had used for curing old acute ailments are not safe infallible remedies for the aforesaid ailments. Faith in Sai Baba and the blessings that a devotee obtained from him as a result are the only infallible remedies. They are an indication of the power in Sai Baba's words. Madhavrao Deshpande had an experience of this kind. Once he was much troubled by piles and he approached Sai Baba with his complaint. Sai Baba asked Madhavrao to fetch many things from a grocer, prepared a decoction and administered it to Madhavrao who got immediate relief thereby. After two years the same complaint resurged. At that time, without consulting Sai Baba, Madhavrao prepared a decoction of the same constituents as before and drank it. However, instead of getting relief his condition worsened. When Madhavrao went to the *masjid* Sai Baba asked, "Well, Vaidyaraj, how are you feeling?" Realising the implication of this remark Madhavrao submitted to him and was relieved of his bodily ailment.

The importance and influence of Sai Baba's word was experienced by Madhavrao a second time. A poisonous snake once stung the small finger of Madhavrao at seven in the evening. That part turned black and he experienced unbearable pain. His whole body became red and he was frightened. His relations and friends gathered. Some suggested that he should be taken to

Viroba's temple but Nimonkar (Madhavrao's maternal uncle) came forward and said that he should be given Sai Baba's *udi* before doing anything further. Madhavrao then quietly made his way to the *masjid*. What did Sai Baba do? As soon as their eyes met Sai Baba shot out a volley of abuses. He did not allow Madhavrao to climb up the steps of the *masjid* and thundered, "Do not come up, Bhaturdya[2], mind if you ascend the steps, get down, away with you." Thinking that Sai Baba had poured out his anger on him and interpreting his words literally, Madhavrao was dismayed. He felt as if his only support was lost and he sat down mutely. When Sai Baba calmed down after some time, Madhavrao took courage, went up and sat down beside Sai Baba. Assuring him Sai Baba said. "Don't lose heart, the merciful Lord will protect you. Go and sit quietly at home. Have faith in me and do not fear." No sooner had Madhavrao reached home than Sai Baba sent Tatya Kote to him with a message: "Tell him *not* to sleep. Ask him to move about in the house. Ensure this much." Then turning to Dikshit Sai Baba said, "See that Madhavrao does not sleep." With this caution Madhavrao's suffering ended. He had a little burning sensation in his little finger but that too ceased after a few days. It was only then that Madhavrao realised that Sai Baba's outpouring was not directed at him but at the poisonous snake who had no option but to obey it.

The word of a saint is a warrant for all creatures in this universe. Bapusaheb Jog had an experience of this adage. Once a scorpion stung him at 8 p.m.. He immediately approached Sai Baba. As he stepped into the *masjid* Sai Baba asked him, "Bapusaheb, what is it?" Bapusaheb replied, "A scorpion has bit me." Sai Baba said, "Go, it will be all right." Bapusaheb turned back. No sooner he was out of the *sabhamandap* than his pain ceased.

Sai Baba cautioned a devotee about the forthcoming danger and saved him miraculously from snakebite.

Balsaheb Mirikar, son of Sirdar Kakasaheb Mirikar of
Ahmednagar, was a *mamledar* of Kopargaon. While he
was on a tour of Chithali he came for Sai Baba's *darshan*.
When he went to the *masjid,* Sai Baba enquired about his
well-being. Thereafter he asked Mirikar, "Do you know
our Dwarakamai?" When Mirikar did not understand the
allusion, Sai Baba said, "Oh, Dwarakamai is this very
masjid. She makes him who ascends her steps fearless.
This *masjidmai* is very kind. He who comes to her
reaches the goal." Mirikar bowed to Sai Baba and got up
to leave when Sai Baba asked him, "Do you know the
long *bawa?*" Then holding his right elbow by the palm of
his left hand, he turned his fist and remarked, "He is so
fierce. But how can he hurt the children of Dwarakamai?
What can he do before the Protector?" No one knew why
Sai Baba was making this clarification then and no one
dared to ask him.

Madhavrao was sitting there at that time. Sai Baba
said to him, "Shama, you also go to Chothali with him
(Mirikar)." So Madhavrao went up to Mirikar and said,
"Sai Baba has directed me to accompany you." Mirikar
asked, "What's the use of your going as far as Chithali?
Why do you take the trouble?" Madhavrao turned back
and told Sai Baba what had happened. Sai Baba
remarked, "What do we lose? Whatever is destined will
happen." Now Mirikar had second thoughts and feeling
that Sai Baba's word must be respected, he beckoned
Madhavrao and with Sai Baba's permission, left for
Chithali. At Chithali Mirikar learnt that his superior
officer who was to come had not arrived. So both rested
and retired to Maruti-temple where they were to halt for
the night. At nightfall the peon spread the bedding for
them. Madhavrao and Mirikar chatted for a while and
then Mirikar started reading the newspaper in the light
of the lantern. In the meanwhile no one noticed a big
snake which was creeping up. Mirikar had a *uparna*[3] on
his body. One end thereof was on his waist where the

snake lay quietly curled up. When the snake crept up, there was a whizzing sound but neither Madhavrao nor Mirikar suspected the presence of a snake. Mirikar was engrossed in reading the newspaper. But the peon had a doubt and brought the lantern. When he saw a snake he cried sofly, "Oh! a snake!" Mirikar shivered and Madhavrao too was surprised. The people around got hold of sticks to kill the snake. The snake now slipped along the waist and as it got to the ground blows of sticks fell on it and it was killed. Seeing the manner in which a calamity was averted, Mirikar was overcome with emotion.

Gopalrao Buti was fond of astrology and he himself had made a study thereof. Nanasaheb Dengle, an astrologer, once told Buti in the morning, "This day is bad for you. According to the stars, your life may be in danger." Buti was worried and waited for the day to be over. At the usual time he went for Sai Baba's *darshan*, and sat by him. Just then Sai Baba asked, "What does Nana (Dengle) say? Is he planning to kill you? How dare he do that! There is no need to fear." In the evening, as Buti went for evacuation of bowels, a snake entered the lavatory. Immediately Buti came out. Buti's servant thought of killing the snake with a stone and was about to lift one but Buti told him, "Go and get a stick. Impulsiveness is of no use in such matters." The servant went to fetch a stick. In the meantime, the snake crept up the wall but in doing so slipped to the ground and made good his escape through a hole. So there was no need to kill the snake. Thus Buti realised that this was Sai Baba's way of averting the impending danger.

Amir Shakkar also had an experience of having been protected by Sai Baba. Once while he was sleeping in the *chavadi*, a snake was hanging from the ceiling. To draw his attention to the danger, Sai Baba began striking his baton on the ground loudly. Amir woke up and realising that Sai Baba must be calling his attention to something sent for a lantern in the light of which he saw the snake over his head and thus saved himself. Ambedkar was a well-to-do devotee who had fallen on evil days and come to Shirdi. As he did not see any sign of improvement in his monetary condition, he decided to commit suicide and was sitting opposite Sathewada waiting for the crowd to thin out. How Sai Baba dissuaded him from committing suicide by jumping in a well, through indirect instruction, will be narrated in the chapter on the Ways of Instructing.

Shantaram Balwant Nachane, a first clerk to the Shirastedar of Kurla, was a devotee of Sai Baba. In 1913, when he was at Shirdi, Sai Baba said to him. "Beware of a mad man." Nachane did not understand the significance of the caution at that time. Later in 1914, when Nachane was engaged in performing daily *puja* at home, an insane person was standing at some distance from him. Though deranged, the aforesaid person was thought to be harmless. So no one took notice of him. Suddenly, the madman entered the room of worship and grasping Nachane's neck with both his hands and shouting, 'I will drink your blood', he tried to throttle him and bite his neck. With a quick reflex action, Nachane thrust the bowl end of the small ladle used in *puja* and his fingers of one hand into the madman's mouth. Though the ladle stuck in his throat the madman was biting away Nachane's fingers with his teeth. With his other hand Nachane struggled to extricate his neck from the clasp of the madman. Other family members ran to Nachane's rescue and separated him, but in the meanwhile Nachane had lost consciousness. After some first aid he recovered his consciousness. When Nachane went to Shirdi next time, pointing at him, Sai Baba said to Anna Chinchnikar sitting nearby, "Anna, if I had delayed an instant, this man would have indeed perished. The madman had seized his (Nachane's) throat with his own hands. But I extricated him. What is to be

done? If I do not save my own children, who else will?"
Similarly, Sai Baba had saved Nanasaheb Chandorkar
from a fatal accident. Once Nanasaheb was riding in a
tonga in Poona when the horses ran away wildly, and
jumping on their hind legs overturned the *tonga*.
Nanasaheb and his companion fell down but did not
sustain any injury. At the very time the accident
happened in Poona Sai Baba was heard to exclaim in
Shirdi, "Oh, Nana was about to die. But how will I permit
him to die?" Many days later when Nanasaheb visited
Shirdi, he came to know how he had survived the
accident by Sai Baba's grace.

Sai Baba similarly protected Hari Sitaram alias
Kakasaheb Dikshit's seven-year-old daughter from a
serious accident while she was playing with her toys at
her residence in Ville Parle. Dikshit was then in Shirdi.
When Dikshit went in the morning for Sai Baba's
darshan as usual, Sai Baba said to him, "Kaka, why
should you worry? I will bear all your burden." Dikshit
nodded his head to signify his assent. However, he did
not understand why Sai Baba uttered these words only
on that day when he had said nothing of the kind earlier.
After some days when he returned home he realised that
on that particular day on which Sai Baba had uttered
those words of assurance, his daughter was involved in
an accident. She had been playing with her toys near the
cupboard containing them. Suddenly the cupboard came
down on her but the wonder was that she was not hurt.
Only her bangles broke, she had scratches on her hand
but did not feel the weight of the cupboard at all.
Moreover, the toys in the cupboard fell on one side of her.
This was one of Sai Baba's *leelas*.

A woman in Bombay and her son were good devotees
of Sai Baba. While in Shirdi they went to the *masjid*. Sai
Baba seated the boy near him on a *chatai* (mat of
bamboo/borassus) and told him not to get up without his
permission. Exactly at 3 p.m., a huge, ugly, hideous

woman jumped over the fence and straightaway entered the *masjid,* saying, "I want to take away this boy." Sai Baba prohibited her. But not heeding him as she attempted to catch hold of the boy, Sai Baba kicked her so hard that she ran screaming and vanished. Sai Baba later said that she was the goddess of cholera and he had extricated the boy from her clutches. The ugly hideous woman was visible to the boy but as his limbs were benumbed he could not hear anything.

More wonderful than this was the experience of an educated woman who was freed from demoniac possession by Sai Baba. Six months after her marriage Sushilabai, wife of Babasaheb Sakharam Sule, fell sick in March 1951. Her jaw would remain rigidly closed up and she would lose consciousness. Many persons said that it was an evil occasioned by the fiends but the educated couple paid no heed to this talk. But the ailment grew worse and Sushilabai would lose consciousness for eighteen hours at a time. Ultimately, on the advice of the father of Babasaheb Sule, on 25 October 1952, Sushilabai was taken to Shirdi for the *darshan* of Sai Baba's *samadhi.* At *arati* time Sushilabai was taken forcibly for two days and after putting *tirtha* (holy water) and *udi* (holy ash) in her mouth, was made to circumambulate the *samadhi.* On 26 October evening, after the *arati* was over, Sushilabai collapsed. On the suggestion of devotees, *tirtha* and *udi* were repeatedly administered to her and Sushilabai started talking. One Shri Pradhan interrogated her and she answered the questions. The gist of these answers was that while returning from her parents' place Sushilabai was possessed by the spirit of a Bhil woman inhabiting a big tree near Belapur stand (S.T.). But the spirit was overwhelmed by Sai Baba's *samadhi-darshan* and *tirtha-udi,* and agreed to leave Sushilabai for good. Then Sushilabai was made to prostrate with her whole body before the *samadhi* and her husband sprinkled a lot of *tirtha-udi* on her. Now Sushilabai on her own circumambulated the *samadhi*, and from that day the demoniac possession left her. This example shows that even the evil of demoniac possession disappears by Sai Baba's *samadhi-darshan* and partaking of his *tirtha-udi*.

Once Sai Baba pulled the son of his devotee, Raoji Balkrishna Upasani, out of the jaws of death. In March 1913, the son had high fever for six days continuously and doctors gave up hope. The doctor and Upasani sat near the bed of the patient the whole night as they thought that his end was near. At 2 a.m. Upasani came out, sat in the verandah, dozed off, and had a dream in which he saw Sai Baba applying *udi* to his son and standing before Upasani. Sai Baba said, "Now don't worry. He will perspire after two hours and his condition will improve. After he gets well bring him to Shirdi for my *darshan*." Upasani woke up and so it happened that after two hours his son perspired and felt better. The doctor was surprised. Two to three days after this Upasani received a letter from Madhavrao Deshpande from Shirdi in which it was stated, "I had not written to you so far as I had no direction from Sai Baba to do so, but now on Sai Baba's order, I am doing so. Sai Baba said to me: 'I had been to your friend's place in Dhulia.' I asked him who that friend of mine was. Upasani Bahalkar Raoji was his clear reply. He added, 'I go to his place often. Write to him.' So I am penning this letter."

Fifteen days after Upasani's son was restored to good health, Upasani started along with his wife and son for Sai Baba's *darshan*. In the morning he got off at Kopargaon and fixed up a tonga for going to Shirdi. On the way they bathed in Godavari's waters with the intention of remaining present for Sai Baba's *arati*. However, the tongawala came late and Upasani was doubtful whether he would reach in time to attend the *arati*. In Shirdi everything was made ready for *arati* at the usual time but Sai Baba said, "Wait, your relation from Dhulia is to arrive." So the *arati* was delayed and it took place only after Upasani arrived. After Upasani had *darshan*, Sai Baba hugged the young son with affection and said, "Do you know that when you were sick I had visited Dhulia?" Everyone was surprised at this remark and Upasani's faith in Sai Baba was confirmed.

Just by *darshan* or vowing to visit Shirdi for *darshan*, old acute ailments of the following devotees have been known to be cured. Nine-year-old bilious vomiting of Krishnaji Narayan alias Chhotubhaiyya Paralkar, Honorary Magistrate at Harda, ceased the day he had *darshan* of Sai Baba. Madhavrao Deshpande's sister-in-law had high fever and two buboes on account of plague. Sai Baba was informed of her condition in the evening but in one night by Sai Baba's blessings the fever as well as the buboes subsided.[4] A two-year-old ailment of the nephew of Govindrao Gadre of Nagpur vanished by his vowing to visit Shirdi for *darshan*. A headache of the wife of Ramachandra Atmaram Turkhud disappeared merely by Sai Baba's *darshan*. Epileptic fits of Harischandra Pitale's son stopped by mere *darshan* of Sai Baba for the first time. The health of Sakharam Krishna Pangarkar who suffered from an acute liver complaint, who couldn't bathe for months and had great difficulty digesting food, began improving from the day he started for Shirdi, and he was completely cured after eight days' stay in Shirdi. The six-year-old asthma of Balaram Dhurandhar, Principal of Law College, Bombay, ceased at the time of his first visit to Shirdi for Sai Baba's *darshan* after he had a puff at the chillum handed over to him by Sai Baba. Later, it was as if Sai Baba desired to send a signal of his passing away to Dhurandhar, for on the day of Sai Baba's *mahasamadhi*, Dhurandhar had a mild paroxysm. After he received a letter from Shirdi telling him of Sai Baba's *nirvana*, the asthma never troubled him again. The month-old pain in the heel of a friend of Kaka Mahajani stopped after Sai Baba's *darshan*. The wife of Abdul

Rahim Shamsuddin Rangari, inhabitant of Mahagiri in Thana district, could not eat due to the swelling of her neck. Hence, she proceeded to Shirdi and on the way at Igatpuri, felt better. After Sai Baba's *darshan* the next day, she was able to eat normally. The eyes of the wife of R.A. Tarkhad smarted and watered. In this condition of hers she was sitting near Sai Baba. The latter glanced at her and as a result her eyes stopped secreting tears, and tears started flowing from Sai Baba's eyes which also stopped in a short time.

Baburao Ingle had wet eczema on his face and legs which could not be cured by medical treatment. He went to Shirdi on the advice of a Sai devotee, had a bath with *samadhi-tirtha* and circumambulated the holy neem tree 108 times. With this he was cured of eczema.[5] On 16 January 1935, Dr. Keshav B. Gavankar had fever and became unconscious. He passed fifteen days in this condition. When his wife vowed to take him to Shirdi, the fever came down the next day.[6]

C. M. Dave, resident of Kandivli, a suburb of Bombay, who suffered from hydrocele, was cured without removing the serous fluid, by vowing in 1949 to go for *darshan* of Sai Baba's *samadhi*. He also had asthma of which he was cured. The brother-in-law of Keshav Narayan Shete, Nandgaon, District Nasik, was saved from severe illness by vowing to go for *darshan* of Sai Baba's *samadhi* on five Thursdays.[7] Dattoba Vishnu Vani, a car driver of Baramati, Pune District, had a long-standing desire to start an independent business which was not only realised, but his business also flourished.[8] Lakshman Ganpat Yadav, retired Havildar, Ankai Ambewadi, Yeole taluka, had a fistula which was cured by vowing to go for Sai Baba's *samadhi-darshan*.[9]

Dr. Mohiniraj Ganesh Kathe and his wife Kumudini of Nasik district, had a similar experience in the case of their son Vijay. Since Vijay was two years old he had stopped drinking milk and had developed a stone in his kidneys. The treatment of the best doctors in Nasik proved of no avail. So they desired to try out other remedies. They decided to visit their family deity Shri Bhairavnath at Kasara. When they alighted at Kopergaon railway station seeing the rush of Shirdi-bound pilgrims they too changed their earlier plan and instead of directly going to Kasara they thought of visiting Shirdi on the way. They reached Shirdi around 2 p.m. and went straight to the Sai Baba Sansthan office. They were informed there that since they had come from a distance they should first take *prasad* and later have *darshan*. So they sat down for meals with their son Vijay and asked him to eat the meal (Sai's *prasad*) with his own hands. Prior to this he would never eat with his own hands but now he started eating with his own hands, and what he ate he retained in his stomach and did not vomit it out. From that time he began to eat with his own hands. He had still to take *darshan* but now he came to have faith in Sai Baba, and all was well later.

The *karmic* suffering of Ribatibai of Nimgaon was taken upon himself by Sai Baba, and she was relieved of the pain. When her delivery pains started Sai Baba began complaining of stomach-ache and his stomach was fastened so tightly by a turban that Ribatibai's labour pains ceased. Parshuram Appaji Nachane of Dahanu had violent fever with delirium and syncope. Dr. Vaidya and others lost all hope. At such time just by vowing to go for Sai Baba's *darshan*, he was relieved of his trouble.

Some devotees' sorrows did not cease at once but only after service of Sai Baba for a specified number of days. The severe eye complaint of Bapusaheb Jog's wife disappeared within a short time after taking medicine prescribed in confidence by Sai Baba. Annasaheb Dabholkar's pregnant daughter, who was deranged, recovered by Sai Baba's blessings. Amir Shakkar of Korhale in Kopergaon taluka, who was a broker in Bandra, suffered from rheumatism in the joints. After he stayed for nine months as per Sai Baba's instructions in the open damp *chavadi*, he became fit. Mrs Chhotubai Pradhan's pains vanished on her sister's calling out to Sai Baba with fervour for succour and the child suffocating in the womb came out, and Chhotubai was saved. The breathing of Chhotubai's one-year-old son once became heavy due to high fever and cough. Shankar-devotee Telangi Brahmin, staying with the Pradhan family, prayed to Sai Baba for showing his prowess and within five minutes the son's fever came down, the coughing stopped, the breathing became normal and he was cured.

Some experiences of devotees who were cured by Sai Baba by giving *darshan*, assurance and suggestions, are as follows. When Hari Sitaram, alias Kakasaheb, Dikshit's brother, suddenly fell ill, Sai Baba groaned as if he was suffering the pain thereof, and Dikshit could not understand why Sai Baba had groaned. Next day Sai Baba asked Dikshit to leave for Bombay, whereupon, getting to know that his brother was ill, Dikshit left for Nagpur. At Nagpur Dikshit came to know that on the day on which Sai Baba had groaned in Shirdi, Sai Baba had appeared to his brother in Nagpur and assured him that he would soon get well and he did get well. The breathing of Upasani of Sakori had become irregular due to mortification of his body. Sai Baba appeared to him in the garb of an old man and advised him to drink warm water whereby his breathing became normal.

There are many instances of Sai Baba having saved his devotees by his omnipresence. Nagesh Atmaram Savant, a devotee of Sai Baba and Police Inspector, stayed on the upper storey of the police station. One day, while he was working in the police station, he heard the sound of someone falling. Savant thought that perhaps his child might have fallen on the stairs, so he came out of his office and noticed that his child was playing on the first step of the stairs. Before he could ask his child to go in, the child slipped and Savant stretching out his arms caught him. Had he not come out of his office his child would have had fatal injuries. To Savant Sai Baba appeared through the medium of sound.

For another devotee Sai Baba had assumed the form of a cat. A Bombay merchant named Hansraj, an asthma patient, went and stayed in Shirdi. Sai Baba had prohibited Hansraj from taking any medicine and also had asked him to avoid things producing phlegm, and especially curds in his diet. But disobeying Sai Baba's orders he would take medicine. His ailment would thereby get worse, and so, being disgusted, he stopped intake of medicines. However, he could not overcome his fondness for curds. He would ask his wife to warm the milk and add a wee bit of curd the previous night so that the curd would set for the noon meal the next day. She pleaded with him to avoid taking curds but he would not listen. Therefore, his wife would set curd in a vessel daily placed in a wire basket and suspended at a height. Both Hansraj and his wife would go for Sai Baba's noon *arati*, and have their meal after coming back. They would find on their return that someone had polished off the curd from the vessel. In spite of all the precautions there would be no curds in the vessel every time they returned from the *arati*. Thus Hansraj controlled himself for two months.

One day he lost his patience and said to his wife that she should go alone for *arati* and he would wait and catch the thief red-handed. As usual a cat came in and Hansraj saw her but sat quietly watching her. As the wire basket containing the curd vessel was suspended at a height, he thought the cat could never get at it. Yet the cat gently approached and jumped into the wire basket, removed the lid of the vessel and lapped up the curds. Hansraj was waiting at the door with a staff in readiness to punish the cat. As soon as the cat emerged and was running away through the open door, Hansraj struck a blow with his staff on the cat's back which left a weal behind. Around 4 p.m., after his meals and rest, Hansraj went to the *masjid* for Sai Baba's *darshan*. After bowing to Sai Baba, he sat by him. Then pointing a finger at him, Sai Baba said, "I had been to this obstinate mulish person's house today and all I got there was a blow!" Saying so, Baba bared his back and showed the weal on his back. Hansraj now realised that Sai Baba had assumed the form of a cat to eat the curds and felt ashamed of his behaviour. Thereafter, Hansraj overcame his weakness for curds and he was cured of his asthma after some time.

Shantaram of Turbhe in Thana District was suffering from bone-sore for seven to eight years. Sai Baba appeared in his dream and asked him to apply a strong-smelling resin, the produce of *Gardenia gummifera,* over the sore and he was cured by its application. A nephew of a doctor from Malegaon suffered from the same ailment. He was brought to Shirdi and merely by Sai Baba's blessings he was cured.[10]

Dr. Chidambaram Pillai had unbearable pains due to guinea-worms. Sai Baba caused a devotee's foot to fall over the ankle of Dr Pillai and the wound opened so that on the tenth day seven guinea-worms came out and the ailment was cured.[11] The pain in the waist of a devotee, Lala Laksmichand, was removed by feeding him *prasad* made from semolina.[12] When Police Inspector Somnath Shankar Deshpande of Poona went for Sai Baba's *darshan*, Sai Baba made him aware of how Sai Baba took care of his devotees. After *darshan*, Sai Baba blessed him and said, "Take care of the child." Deshpande thought this caution was with regard to his two-year-old son. So he administered *udi* given by Sai Baba to his son and then went to his village of Nimon. There he found that his nephew was at the doorstep of death. Deshpande realised that the caution given to him by Sai Baba was not concerning his son but about his small nephew. He took his nephew in his lap and prayed fervently to Sai Baba and within a short time his nephew recovered.

A Muslim devotee of Sai Baba came to Shirdi and prayed to Sai Baba that the sentence of death by hanging pronounced against his Brahmin friend should be set aside. Sai Baba blessed him and detained him in Shirdi for a few days. During his stay the Muslim devotee received intimation that his Brahmin friend was acquitted in appeal and the death sentence against him set aside.

The experiences that devotees got when Sai Baba was in his mortal case, one gets even after his *mahasamadhi*. Here are some cases of the latter type. Satyabhamabai, wife of Vasudeo Sitaram Ratanjankar, who was dying, was saved from pneumonia while the latter's son escaped the plague in 1921-22 by remembering Sai Baba.

In 1926-27, Sai Baba saved a woman miraculously from a railway accident. The facts are as follows. Many devotees of Sai Baba who had gathered in Shirdi for Ramanavami were returning to Bombay by train. This woman devotee got down at Thana station to fill her brass vessel with water. As she ascended the step to enter the compartment the train started. Her foot slipped and she fell in the space between the platform and the train. The co-passengers shouted and stopped the train (by pulling the chain) only after the train had gone somewhat further. People thought that the woman involved in the accident must have been crushed. But wonder of wonders, they saw her standing! They were astonished and asked her how she had managed to survive. She said, "While I was falling I called out to Sai Baba. Immediately Sai Baba was beside me and he pressed me to the platform wall! Thereby I did not sustain any injury. Obviously there was not enough space between the platform side wall and the train for a person to stand. But what is impossible for Sai Baba? Of course, no one except myself saw Sai Baba standing." This is not the result of *siddhi*; a yogi can get out of his gross body and assuming a suitable form or in an invisible manner save his devotee. It is the time-old immemorial way of divine love that when a devotee is in danger, even before calling upon Him, He responds and saves His devotee.

In 1927, Sadashiva Tarkhad stayed in Shirdi with his whole family. At that time his wife, Tarabai, was in the family way. While they were in Shirdi, the foetus in the womb died, Mrs Tarkhad's face turned intensely black and her system was poisoned. As there was no doctor, midwife or nurse available in Shirdi, some medicine was brought from Ahmednagar but it was of no avail. Then Mrs Tarkhad lost consciousness but in that state began giving instructions for abortion of the foetus. On these instructions being followed, Mrs Tarkhad was saved. Thus Sai Baba made Mrs Tarkhad her own doctor in her state of unconsicousness or semi-consciousness and pulled her out of the jaws of death.

Eleven years after Sai Baba's *samadhi*, i.e., in 1929, Sai Baba saved his devotee, police sub-inspector Nagesh Atmaram Savant in a strange way. One day Savant was on duty at Parel. He had a high temperature and a headache. In the meanwhile, his superior, a European, paid a visit to the police station for inspection. Looking at Savant's condition, he asked Savant to go home and said that he would remain in the police station until an alternative arrangement was made. Savant returned home. Then within an hour a riot broke out in Parel in which the European unfortunately lost his life.

There is a railway station named Asavali near Nasik. Mrs Chandrabai R. Borkar was staying there with her husband. One day Mr Borkar got high fever after returning from his employment. There was no one in their house besides the couple and they had no medicine except Sai Baba's *udi*. At 2 a.m. Borkar dozed off, Chandrabai also lay near her husband's bed. She had a dream at about 3 a.m. in which she saw a fakir wearing a *kafni*, who came up to her and said, "Bai, do not be

frightened. Your husband will perspire shortly. Apply the
udi and don't allow your husband to leave the house
before 11 a.m." Chandrabai got up and noticed that her
husband was perspiring. She wiped the perspiration on
her husband's body and narrated the dream to him. But
he had not much faith in Sai Baba and disregarding
Chandrabai's objection he went to the station. At that
time the Mail from Manmad and the Passenger from
Bombay to Manmad were moving in opposite directions.
As Borkar reached the station the Passenger arrived on
the platform. Standing on the Mail track Borkar was
chatting with the officer who alighted from the
Passenger, but being off his guard he did not notice the
Mail. Just then the Mail steamed in and Borkar was
jolted and thrown off on the third track. Chandrabai,
standing in the courtyard, saw the accident taking place
and loudly screaming out 'Baba' became unconscious. In
the meantime, the railway porter came and after
Chandrabai became conscious told her that her husband
had sustained a severe injury in his leg. Chandrabai
brought her husband home and placed him on his bed.
His leg bone was badly injured. Chandrabai prepared a
paste of marking nut and Sai Baba's *udi*, applied it over
the injured leg and bandaged it. She also applied *udi* to
other parts of her husband's body. After a short while
Borkar came to consciousness, and asked, "Where am I?
Our house is pervaded by a *fakir*." Chandrabai said,
"Don't be afraid. He is our Sai Baba. Sai Baba had
instructed you, through me, not to venture out but you
disobeyed. Even then he has saved you. Take courage.
Our Sai Baba will cure you." Next day the railway doctor
came and after applying some medicine bandaged the
leg. But the pain increased for the leg had been fractured.
At 11 p.m. Chandrabai dreamt she saw the same *fakir*
again. He asked, "What, you want the leg to be damaged
permanently? Apply a mixture of coconut, dough and *udi*
over the leg and bandage it. Then foment it with a

mixture of leaves (of some medicinal plant), salt, turmeric and *jowar*." Chandrabai carried out the instructions faithfully and diligently and the bone of the leg was healed up. Thereafter, Borkar came to have faith in Sai Baba and to deeply appreciate Sai Baba's disinterested love for them.

In 1942, Sai Baba cured Aba Samant's wife without her having to undergo a complicated operation which was advised medically. In 1943, a poor woman from Madras came to Shirdi for Sai Baba's blessings for her son who had been hospitalised. At night when she was sleeping on the platform outside the *samadhi mandir*, Sai Baba appeared to her in a dream, with a lantern and assured her that her son had been operated upon and was progressing well. The dream over, Sai Baba vanished and she fell off the platform. Hearing the sound of someone falling, devotees gathered round her. The old woman narrated to them her dream and said that as Sai Baba had stroked her body, she was feeling no pain in her body after the fall.

Ramchandra Babaji Salaskar was down with typhoid in 1953. On the 14th of May, he became unconscious. On the advice of Dr. Gavankar, Salaskar's parents prayed to Sai Baba fervently. Sai Baba gave them *darshan* and Salaskar's condition began improving that day. After he recovered he went to Shirdi for *samadhi-darshan*. The son of G. L Talavadekar had a fleshy lump near his navel from the time of his birth. The lump grew in size day by day. Doctors advised an operation but Talavadekar hesitated. The son was now seven years old and willy-nilly it was decided to go in for an operation. According to the surgeon without a cut in the stomach it was not feasible to remove the fleshy growth. The Talavadekar couple were frightened and prayed to Sai Baba. As a result when their son was taken to the operation theatre, another idea suggested itself to the surgeon by which he could remove the fleshy growth without a cut in the stomach.

Rajabhau Malhar Sardeshmukh of Sholapur was suffering from malarial fever in 1942-43 and in spite of treatment for about one and a half to two years the fever continued. Finally in 1943, Rajabhau's father took him to Shirdi and prayed fervently before Sai Baba's *samadhi*. The same night Rajabhau had a dream and he felt that strength was being poured into him. After a few days the fever left him.

Nanda, the son of Sadashiv Dattatreya Joshi of Chitalenagar, Sholapur District, was suffering from skin diseases like the itch, sores, etc., due to impurities in his blood. In spite of penicillin injections, there was no improvement in his condition. So, on a Thursday, he was taken to Shirdi for *samadhi-darshan*. There he was treated with *tirtha* and *udi* and he was cured in seven days. Mrs Surajbai Kasaliwal Jain of Khamgaon, Berar, went on a pilgrimage of Mahavira but instead of Mahavira's *darshan* she had Sai Baba's *darshan*. From that day she came to depend on Sai Baba. In her dream she was instructed by Sai Baba to stop the financial transactions with a certain party and was thus saved from impending losses. By her fervent prayer her husband was also cured of his sickness. In 1952-53, Sai Baba saved Mahendraprasad G. Derasari from colossal losses by sending a person, gentlemanly in external appearance but really a crook, to jail on the day on which Derasari was to enter into partnership with the latter. Dattatreya Ramachandra Patil writes in his letter dated 5 October 1951 to the author that due to his long illness his power to sing had been weakened, his voice had lost its tenor and he had not been able to sing for months. On a friend's suggestion he went to Shirdi and sang before Sai Baba's *samadhi* with devotion, as a result of which he recouped his voice and was able to give performances as before.

In the month of Bhadrapad (August-September) of *samvat* year 1999, i.e., 1943, a devotee of Sri Sai Baba, Pushpavati, residing at Dakor, had been on a pilgrimage and while bathing in the Jamuna River was drawn into a whirlpool and was about to be drowned. She struggled hard to come out and at that very moment she felt some invisible form had pulled her towards the bank. She was convinced that this form was none other than her chosen deity, Sai Baba. Once at 5 a.m. she went for a swim in the river at Vrindavan and while returning missed her way. It was dark and there was jungle around; she could not find the road. In her predicament she remembered Sai Baba and a *sadhu* appeared from nowhere, and on being requested by Pushpavati to show her the way, he accompanied her home and then disappeared. Later, she searched for that *sadhu* but could not find him anywhere. Inscrutable are the ways of Providence.

In 1911, Shankarlal Keshavram Bhatt of Bombay, a devotee of Shankar, slipped and fell down, and as a result had a limp in his gait. Hearing Sai Baba's fame he went to Shirdi, had Sai Baba's *darshan*, stayed there for a day or two and taking leave of Sai Baba started for Kopergaon by a tonga. It was the rainy season and the river Godavari could be crossed only by a ferry. So, getting down from the tonga, he was limping toward the ferry when he felt that the nerve which had been strained by the fall was suddenly released. And he was able to walk the remaining distance without a limp. His limp vanished permanently which he attributed to Sai Baba's grace.

In 1956, the only son of a widow-teacher in Sholapur who appeared for the matriculation examination came home on the last day of the examination, suffering from high fever. By medical treatment his fever abated but the lower half of his body below the waist was paralysed. He could not walk and had to be carried. Hearing the fame of the shrine of Sai Baba, his mother took him to Shirdi.

While in Shirdi, she would go alone to the *samadhi-mandir* and pray to Sai Baba. Feeling ashamed to be seen carried, the son would not accompany her. On the third and the last day of his stay in Shirdi, while his mother had gone to the *samadhi-mandir* for *arati*, Sai Baba gave him *darshan*, bucked him up and taking him by his hand led him to the *samadhi-mandir* and made him stand against the support of a column. The mother prayed fervently to Sai Baba to cure her son and was about to leave the *samadhi-mandir* when she was astonished to see her son leaning against a column! She asked him how he had managed to get there. She could not believe him when he narrated what had happened. But the proof of it was before her eyes and she was naturally overjoyed. Within a month of this incident the boy was restored to health.[13]

The grandfather of Vitthal Yeshwantrao Deshpande was blind. He was a devotee of Sai Baba who had got back his sight merely by *darshan* of Sai Baba. Accompanied by his grandson Vitthal, he proceeded to Shirdi and directly went for Sai Baba's *darshan* with Vitthal. While taking *darshan* the grandfather said to Sai Baba with a sad heart, "Sai Baba, I cannot see." Sai Baba replied, "You will be able to see," and wonder of wonders, his sight was restored! The grandfather's blindness vanished but Vitthal had to pass through an amusing situation. The grandfather was so happy that without waiting for Vitthal, whom he had despatched to get *dakshina*, he emerged from the *masjid* and went straight to Dikshitwada. Vitthal brought the *dakshina*, offered it to Sai Baba and then went out looking for his grandfather. Finally he found him in Dikshitwada but wondered how he got there. His grandfather told him that he had got back his vision. Vitthal did not believe him and thought that this was a device of his grandfather to keep him in check from acting irresponsibly in a strange place. While returning home Vitthal lost his cap in the moving train and was afraid of what his father would say about the loss of the cap. Both of them alighted from the train on reaching their destination. Vitthal was nervous about going home without a cap, and did not notice his grandfather who met a friend of his and got lost in the crowd. Vitthal was now doubly worried. He was so scared that as soon as he saw his house he howled. Thinking that Vitthal was crying loudly because some harm had come to his grandfather, his father called him and asked him what had happened. As Vitthal's father approached him, Vitthal, being afraid of being beaten, started shying away. In the meanwhile, the grandfather arrived from the bazaar with a new cap for Vitthal. When they noticed the grandfather all of them were delighted, and more so Vitthal who saw the new cap in his grandfather's hand.

Another blind devotee came for Sai Baba's *darshan*, and said to him, "I do not particularly need vision but I wish to see your form with these eyes of mine for such time that I may be able to store it in my mental eye." So saying he saluted Sai Baba and sat by him. Instantly he could see and he took Sai Baba's *darshan*. As soon as he was satisfied, he reverted to his previous condition.

Betwen 1912 and 1915, a blind man would stand before Sai Baba in the *sabhamandap* and perform *bhajan*. His blindness slowly became less until it totally disappeared. On obtaining sight he put it to good use. He memorised the whole of the *Bhagavad Gita*, and Jnaneshwar's *Anubhavamrit* and sitting in Sai Baba's *masjid* would recite them. He was to be seen there until 1952.

In February 1917, Dr. D.M. Mulki was conducting a forceps delivery and some fluid from the decomposed operated part flew into his left eye which he did not realise until it was too late. The left eye was swollen. He treated himself but as he did not get any relief consulted the Civil Surgeon, who opined that he would lose the vision of his left eye. Once earlier, when he had suffered from typhoid, Sai Baba had appeared to him in a dream and saved him after taking a promise from him that he would visit Shirdi. However, he had failed to keep up his promise. As a last resort he now surrendered himself to Sai Baba and prayed to him fervently. Thereby his left eye was cured in a week's time. Later, he paid a visit to Shirdi in fulfilment of his earlier promise.

A dumb girl got back her power of speech. She was injured in a car accident and was hospitalised. Though her wounds healed she lost her speech. In spite of treatment for nine months there was no change in her condition. When *udi* touched by Sai Baba was administered to her she recovered her speech and she could talk without any defect.

Rajalakshmi, daughter of T.R.S. Mani of Kumbhakonam, was born dumb and until she was nine years old there was no change in her condition. Her father then began praying to Sai Baba and he was ordered to go to Shirdi with his daughter. Accordingly, on 28 March 1942, after she had *darshan* of Sai Baba's *samadhi*, she got back her speech. The first words she uttered were, "Sai Baba, Sai Baba." Slowly her speech improved and she was able to attend a school.[14]

Such have been the experiences of devotees. And devotees continue to get them without interruption. So we are reminded here of the following lines of a very great devotee of Lord Sri Krishna, Saint Surdas:

Bow at the feet of Shri Hari which are the source of happiness;

When His Grace descends the disabled climbs a mountain and the blind sees everything around him;

The deaf hears, the dumb speaks and a poor wretch walks with a large and lofty parasol of silk held over his head;

Oh Compassionate Lord, Surdas bows at Your Feet again and again.

Notes

1. *Shri Sai-Sat-Charita*, XIII, pp. 31-84; 158-179.
2. A contemptuous term for a Brahmin.
3. A small single cloth worn loosely over the shoulders as a part of the outfit, now out of fashion.
4. In *Shri Sai-Sat-Charita*, XXXIV, 92-131, it has been stated that the cure was the result of Sai Baba's *udi*.
5. *Shri Sai Leela*, 1948, issue No. 2.
6. Ibid.
7. Ibid., December, 1952, p. 44.
8. Ibid., March, 1953, pp. 11-12.
9. Ibid., March, 1956, p. 9.
10. In *Shri Sai Sat-Charita*, XXXIV, 31, it is stated that the cure was the result of *udi* and Sai Baba's begign glance.
11. *Shri Sai-Sat-Charita*, XXXIV, pp. 48-90.
12. Ibid., XXVIII, pp. 23-98.
13. *Shri Sai Leela*, July, 1956, p. 7.
14. *Shri Sai Sudha*, December, 1944, p. 4.

10. WARDING OFF FINANCIAL DIFFICULTIES

The Poet tormented by poverty says in disgust:
    May my pride of caste sink to the lowest of the seven
    nether worlds, my virtues sink even lower than that,
    my character fall off the cliff, my birth in a good
    family gets burnt by fire, my bravery be struck by the
    thunderbolt of Indra; may we enjoy forever wealth,
    that single thing, without which all our virtues are
    reduced to straw.

Bhartruhari's *Neetishatak*, 73

Utterance of a once rich man reduced to pauperism:
    All the limbs are the same, *karma* the same, intellect
    the same (literally, unarrested), speech the same; yet
    how strange that deprived of the warmth of money, in
    less than a moment, the same man appears so
    different (to the world).

Bhartruhari's *Neetishatak*, 74

Manu has said that one's old parents, faithful wife,
son, and an infant should be supported even by
performing a hundred bad actions.
But if a man will worship me, and meditate upon me
with an undistracted mind, devoting every moment to
me, I shall supply all his needs and protect his
possessions from loss.

Bhagavad Gita IX, 22
(translation by Swami Prabhavananda and
Christopher Isherwood)

> But to those who adore me with a pure oneness of
> soul, to those who are ever in harmony, I increase
> what they have and I give them what they have not.
>
> *Bhagavad Gita* IX, 22
> (translation by Juan Mascaro)

Bhartruhari has aptly depicted in two stanzas the
emotions that well up in the heart of a poor wretch. In the
third stanza Manu has spoken of the duty of every man.
Every constituent of a nation or society should strive to
ensure that his own or his family's burden does not fall on
others. A sensible person knows that it is better to starve
than to beg. Saints and mahatmas teach the same lesson
in their discourses and by example. Tukaram says, "Fie
on that shameful life which resorts to begging." Out of
the four ends of the existence of man, one is pursuit of
wealth and two others, acquisition of merit by pious or
virtuous acts and enjoyment of the pleasures of senses,
are both dependent on wealth. It is clearly stated in the
Smriti that if honest means of livelihood are not
available and there is no other way out except performing
actions which one ought not to do, then in such
circumstances one's old parents, a faithful wife, son, and
an infant should be supported by performing a hundred
bad actions. It may also be remembered that it being
God's covenant to supply all the needs of His devotee, He
will as far as possible, protect him from the sin of
committing bad actions. He will also surely save the
devotee who carries out his individual, social and civic
duties. To be concerned about earning for one's living or
reputation is natural for a human being. He alone who
has suffered the mental anguish of this kind knows what
it is. Generous good-hearted persons who can imagine
what it is, actively sympathise in removal of poverty. In
this golden land of ours when there is scarcity due to
famine, we cannot be blind to it. Then how will Sai Baba,
who has incarnated to remove the woes of his devotees,

disregard their fervent prayers? Let us examine some such experiences of the devotees.

Rao Bahadur S.B. Dhumal, B.A. LL.B, Pleader, Nasik, was a staunch devotee of Sai Baba who did not take any important step without consulting the latter. He states, "I was holding the office of Revenue Member of the Dewas State from 1 September 1930 to 9 April 1932, and I was the Karbhari of the Surgana State from the end of 1932 to August 1933. Each time I returned to Nasik I resumed my practice and got on as well as I did before, without having to wait idly even for a day. Baba's kind help on the financial side was manifested in a peculiar incident while I was in the latter State. One day I was seated at my meal and the Chief of that State walked into my room. I apologised for my inability to leave the table and accord him a proper reception or even to offer him a fitting chair or seat. But he quickly walked into the next room, gazed a while at the portrait of Sai Baba that was hanging on the wall, and returned to my dining room. He at once announced to me that from that time, I should have an increase of Rs. 50 in my salary. I had never asked for this increase. This grant of an increase in my salary within a fortnight of my appointment and without any motion on my part, can only be explained by his having been with Baba in my pooja room. I had not asked for the increase. Evidently 'the child's welfare was the concern of mother Baba'."

Every advocate works hard at his brief to win the case and get on in the profession. Dhumal was not an exception to this. But the difference between him and the others was that as Sai Baba was his all-in-all, he relied not on his own egoistic effort. On the other hand, he depended on the efforts based on his faith in Sai Baba. So, even in cases in which eminent lawyers gave little hope of success, Dhumal would succeed. In 1911-12 there was a criminal case from Shirdi. Raghu, a servitor of Sai Baba, and five others were arraigned on a charge of outraging the modesty of a Marwadi woman. There have always been party feelings and factions at Shirdi as in most villages. On the direct evidence of a 'number of eye-witnesses', they were convicted and sentenced to six months, or less, of imprisonment. Tatya Kote Patil's sympathies were on the side of the accused. He took up a copy of the judgment and the case papers to eminent lawyers like the Hon. G.S. Khaparde, H.S. Dikshit and retired Magistrate Rao Bahadur H.V. Sathe. They found the judgment to be strong and gave little hope of success in case an appeal were preferred. Tatya Kote went to Sai Baba who simply told him to go to Dhumal with the case papers. Tatya Kote accordingly came to Nasik and showed Dhumal the case papers. As the judgment was based on direct evidence of a number of eye-witnesses, Dhumal asked Tatya Kote to engage counsel from Bombay or a prominent lawyer from Ahmednagar where the appeal had to be filed. But Tatya Kote told him that Sai Baba's order was to go to him. So Dhumal felt that he had neither option nor responsibility on his shoulders.

He wrote out an appeal memo after studying the papers and took it to the District Magistrate at his residence. On the basis of Dhumal's answers to all the questions put to him by the Magistrate, the latter remarked that it looked like a strong case and asked Dhumal what he had to say. Dhumal stated that the case and its number of witnesses were due to factions in the village. "Do you think so?" asked the Magistrate, to which Dhumal replied, "Think! I am more than sure of it." The Magistrate pronounced judgment at once, orally acquitting all the appellants, and immediately taking up the appeal memo wrote on it his judgment mentioning the facts relied upon by Dhumal. As soon as this was over he asked Dhumal, "How is your Sai Baba of Shirdi? Is he a Moslem or a Hindu? What does he teach you?" Dhumal replied that Sai Baba was neither a Hindu nor a Moslem but above both, and that he could not state what his teachings were - to know which he must go in person to Shirdi. Dhumal then started for Shirdi. While he was on his way to Shirdi, Sai Baba remarked to the devotees sitting near him, "I will show you some *chamatkar* (miracle)." But the devotees went away to attend the cremation of H.S. Dikshit's daughter who had died that day. Shortly thereafter, Dhumal returned from Ahmednagar with news of the acquittal of the accused. Then they found what the '*chamatkar*' referred to by Sai Baba was. Dhumal was, of course, convinced that it was only because of Sai Baba's help that he had succeeded in the case.

There was another criminal appeal in which Dhumal got success which he attributed to Sai Baba's kindness. There was a charge against and conviction of three brothers for grievous hurt by breaking a bone of one of the opponents. The injured man had been treated by a medical man, who was not a qualified or certified doctor, for over twenty days in his private nursing home. Dhumal who was engaged for the accused appellants filed an appeal memo and a bail application. The Sessions Judge, who was a senior European officer, remarked on hearing Dhumal, that the case against the appellants was strong and he was not going to allow bail. Dhumal at once thought of Sai Baba and turning to the Judge told him that the evidence for a bone being broken was that of a quack and that the prosecution evidence was interested and unreliable.

The three appellants were agriculturists and if they were to remain in jail, the agricultural work would suffer in their absence. On the other hand if their sentence were confirmed, they could be sent to jail finally. At once the Judge allowed bail. When the case came up for argument Dhumal argued for a reversal but wound up with a prayer for reduction of the sentence. The Judge stated that if he were merely asking for the mercy of the court, he need not have taken so much time to contest the conviction. But inscrutable are Sai Baba's ways and Dhumal won. When the Public Prosecutor was arguing, the Judge wanted to know how he made out a case for grievous hurt as the opinion of an unqualified man, a quack, could not be accepted as to the breakage of the bone. The Public Prosecutor replied that the injured man had been in a nursing home for twenty days. The Judge reacted sharply and remarked, "That is an argument which you can advance before a Third Class Magistrate. Remember, you are arguing before a Sessions Judge." On receiving this snub the Public Prosecutor was silenced and the appellants were acquitted.[1]

It is the experience of Chinubhai Vadilal Shah and Harshadbhai P. Mehta, advocates of Ahmedabad and Baroda, respectively, that they receive help from Sai Baba both in civil and criminal cases by remembering him.

Experiences of Sadashivrao Tarkhad and Sadashivrao Dikshit testify that devotees who had been tested by Sai Baba as regards their faith and had come up to his expectations had been provided with highly paid jobs.

In 1915 Sadashivrao Tarkhad lost his job and for quite some time he was unemployed as managerial positions were not easily to be had. It was then that he came to Shirdi and stayed there. When the time came for him to take leave of Sai Baba, the latter said to him, "Go to Bombay via Poona." As the railway fare to Bombay via Poona was more than for the direct route from Manmad to Bombay, Mrs Tarkhad was hesitating as her husband had been out of a job. But Sai Baba's order was clear. Secondly, as their faith in Sai Baba was firm, they proceeded to Poona and halted for a night at a friend's place. There they learnt that a mill-owner wanted for his mills a manager who was experienced in handling labour. Tarkhad met the mill-owner and he was immediately appointed as the manager of Raja Bahadur

Mills. This naturally strengthened the faith of Tarkhad in Sai Baba.

Hari Sitaram alias Kakasaheb Dikshit's younger brother, Sadashiv, B.A. LL.B. tried his hand at practice at Nagpur and Khandwa with disheartening results. Then Kakasaheb cast lots before Sai Baba, and as per Sai Baba's decision Sadashiv began practising in Bombay. As he did not make much headway, again,by casting lots Kakasaheb kept him in his own solicitor's firm. As the result was even then unsatisfactory. Sadashiv desired to return to Khandwa. Kakasaheb wondered how, in spite of Sai Baba's approval, the step should prove to be utterly futile. As Sadashiv was getting restless, Kakasaheb asked him to wait until Diwali, to which the former agreed. In between things took a strange turn. A friend of Kakasaheb came to him and said that the Kutch State required a highly reliable officer for their Bank, with a knowledge of Gujarati. At once Kakasaheb asked him if Sadashiv would suit. The friend was very glad to have Sadashiv (whom he believed not to be available) and recommended him to the State. As a result Sadashiv was appointed on a salary of Rs. 1,000 a month and he served until his retirement.[2]

Another person who had faith in Sai Baba, obeyed his orders and obtained a good job was Prof. Narke, who was the son-in-law of Gopalrao Buti, Malgujar of Nagpur. Narke was a scholar from Central Province and Berar having passed his M.A. in 1905. During 1907-09 he was at Calcutta for being trained in Geological Survey. He was sent in 1909 by the Government of India to Manchester University, from whence he got his M.Sc. in Geology and Mining, and returned in August 1912. Being trained in Natural Sciences, Narke naturally believed in knowledge based on verification. He had carried Jnaneshwari with him during his studies abroad from which he would read regularly. His faith in Sai Baba grew gradually by his own experiences and he would abide by his advice, whether in temporal or spiritual matters. As a Geologist and Mining Engineer he would get prospecting jobs intermittently. Sometimes he got a number of offers at the same time, and he would approach Sai Baba each time, relying on the latter's foresight and wisdom to guide him. Sai Baba would always say, "Go to such and such place and Poona," adding Poona every time he made the selection. In 1916, Narke had to choose between an offer from Benares of a Professorship and a prospecting job in Burma. Sai Baba told him, "Go to Burma and Poona." Narke would laugh within himself at the addition of Poona every time as he was a Mining Engineer and Poona held no prospect for him.

It was in 1917 that an announcement was made that a Professor of Geology was wanted for the College of Engineering at Poona. Sai Baba asked Narke to apply. There were many applicants for the post and some of them had the backing of influential personages. By Sai Baba's blessings, Narke secured the appointment in 1918 in which he was confirmed in 1919. Now he understood why Sai Baba always added 'Poona' every time to whatever he chose for Narke out of a number of options. He settled down and constructed a house of his own in Poona. Even in April 1913 when Narke first went to Shirdi, Sai Baba could see his permanent appointment in Poona and, in fact, the entire future of his career.[3]

The worldly cares and ambitions, whether of the higher or lower income groups, are similar. Cholkar, belonging to the lower middle class, could not secure a permanent appointment without passing a departmental examination. He vowed to go to Shirdi for Sai Baba's *darshan* if he were successful and worked hard. By Sai Baba's grace he passed the examination and secured the job. His salary being low, he could not save enough to go to Shirdi. So he decided to abjure sugar from his diet until his vow was fulfilled. After some months when he had laid by a sufficient sum, he proceeded to Shirdi and after taking Sai Baba's *darshan*, sat near him. Bapusaheb Jog was then present. Sai Baba said to Jog, "Take him home and serve him many cups of highly sugared tea." Thus Cholkar had an experience of Sai Baba's inner vision and his love for the devotees. When Cholkar was asked why he was to be served highly sugared tea he narrated his account. Govind Dhondo Pansare of Sholapur, who had vowed to go for Sai Baba's *darshan* if he passed the Vernacular final examination, the prescribed qualification for appointment as a primary teacher, had a similar experience. He passed the examination and got the job. At the first meeting itself, Sai Baba asked him, "What do you do?" "The job of a teacher which you gave me," was his respectful reply. Everyone around appreciated his simple faith in Sai Baba by means of which he had secured a job.

In 1913 the new Headmaster of the primary school at Shirdi, Daji Waman Chitambar, was concerned about the low standard and attitude of the pupils and complained to Kakasaheb Dikshit that the reputation earned by him over the years would be lost at Shirdi! The pupils were lazy, they did not study and said that it was not necessary for them to do so as they would pass in the examination by Sai Baba's *udi*. Dikshit advised him to be patient and to wait for the result as Sai Baba would be concerned about the pupils and him personally. The Deputy Inspector came at the time of the examination. On that day all the pupils went for Sai Baba's *darshan* and got his *udi*. The final results showed that not a single pupil had failed. In his whole career the Headmaster had never seen cent per cent results. He then became a devotee of Sai Baba and when pensioned off, settled down at Shirdi.

Dr. Tendulkar's father, Raghunathrao, and mother, Savitribai, were both devotees of Sai Baba. They had published a book of songs on Sai Baba in Marathi,

entitled *Raghunath-Savitri Bhajanmala.* Due to
advancing age Raghunathrao's sight had become weak.
He was already suffering fits of epilepsy. So he applied for
long leave preparatory to retirement from the Graham
Trading Co. where he had served for many years. The
last salary drawn by him was Rs.150 per month, and he
was worried whether he would get a pension at all.
Moreover, if a pension were sanctioned it would not
exceed Rs.75 per month from which it would be difficult
to meet living expenses. According to the dictum that God
has to take care of his devotees, Sai Baba did take care of
his loving devotees. Raghunathrao's boss was a kind-
hearted man. After he had applied for a pension, fifteen
days before an order was expected to be passed Sai Baba
came into Savitribai's dream and asked her, "I intend
giving Rs. 100 as pension, is that all right?" Savitribai
replied, "What is this you ask us? You are our sole refuge.
You will do what is proper." Fifteen days later an order
was passed on Raghunathrao's application sanctioning
him a monthly pension of Rs 110. Raghunathrao and
Savitribai were thus relieved of their anxiety and they
devoted themselves with increasing zest to singing
praises of God.[4]

Rao Bahadur Hari Vinayak Sathe was dissatisfied at
not getting promotion in his official career. He conveyed
his dissatisfaction to Sai Baba and told him that he
would even resign on that account. But Sai Baba forbade
his resignation from Government service and said that
he would get promotion. Sometime later, he was
promoted over the head of some seniors in service and got
an increase of Rs. 100 in pay and eventually a higher
pension than those seniors.

Though Sai Baba, either out of humility or out of
policy, ascribed all beneficent things done for his visitors
and devotees to God, he disclosed in some cases his own
authorship by his words. An instance of this is the case of
Daji Hari Lele, District Inspector of Land Records at

Nasik, who was proceeding to Shirdi to see Sai Baba. On the way he went to the library at Kopargaon and saw the Gazette. Therein he discovered that he had received a raise of Rs. 25 in his salary. Then he came to Shirdi and bowed to Baba. Sai Baba told him, "Bring me Rs. 15." The man said he had no money. Baba retorted, "It is only yesterday I gave you Rs. 25. Go and bring the money (*dakshina*)." Lele then came to Sathe, informed him of all the facts and borrowed the money to pay Sai Baba. Another instance of this kind was that of Somnath Shankar Deshpande, son of Nanasaheb Nimonkar, a great devotee of Sai Baba. Somnath was a Police Sub-Inspector at Kopargaon and Shirdi was within his jurisdiction. As soon as he got his pay he would send Rs. 2 every month by money order to Sai Baba. That was his father's order and possibly his vow. When Somnath once went down to Shirdi in the company of his father, Sai Baba asked him for a *dakshina* of 10 rupees, which he paid. It appeared to have no significance at that time. But about six months later, he got the order that his pay had been increased by Rs. 10 from that date (i.e., the date of his paying the *dakshina*).

It is not as if Sai Baba advised everyone to take up employment. Naranlal Motiram Jani, an employee of Sai devotee Ramachandra Waman Modak, along with his mother had come for Sai Baba's *darshan* a few days before the latter's *mahasamadhi*. Sai Baba then said to Jani's mother, "We do not have to serve anymore, we have to do independent business." Thereafter, in a short time, Jani left his job and started a Lodging-Boarding House in Nasik by the name of Anandashram which flourished due to Sai Baba's grace.[5]

Ramachandra Sitaram alias Balabhau Deo, an assistant teacher in a local board school, also did the work of a stamp vendor which interfered with his teaching. Knowing Deo's bright future Sai Baba would detain him in Shirdi beyond vacation periods. So Deo had to give up his post. Then he was able to stay in Shirdi as he liked and only attended to stamp-vending by which he could earn as much as Rs. 20-25 per day. When he became old he got his licence of stamp-vending transferred in the name of his son and his son's well-being was ensured by Sai Baba's grace.[6]

Janardan Moreshwar, alias Haribhau Phanse of Dahanu, had an amusing and pleasant experience of how Sai Baba looks after the maintenance and protection of him who takes refuge in him and puts all his burden on him. Being exasperated by the burden of the family, with his mother's consent, Phanse left on a pilgrimage of Rameshwar. But due to meritorious deeds in his past birth, he got a desire to meet a holy person. Therefore, he went to Shirdi, had Sai Baba's *darshan*, bowed to him and stayed there for seven days. Then Sai Baba said to him, "Go, go home, for Rameshwar is starving for the last seven days. If you don't go, you will intend doing one thing and something else will happen." So he returned home and seeing his mother starving remained at home quietly. He administered Sai Baba's *udi* to a patient in his town who was suffering from cholera, and he got well. Thereby Phanse's reputation as a *vaid* spread in the town. Now his stock of *udi* was exhausted and he was concerned how he should treat a case of cholera referred to him. But in the meantime, with Sai Baba's grace, there were no more cases of cholera in the town.

Once he had to go to a Marwadi in a neighbouring village called Bhopali. That Marwadi's brother was very sick. The Government doctor's medicine had no effect on him. Seeing a devotee of Sai Baba visiting him, the Marwadi said to Phanse, "I hear you do Sai Baba's *bhajan*. Well, if my brother is cured at your hands I will admit that Sai Baba is powerful, not otherwise." Phanse saw the patient whose condition was none too good. He did not relish the idea of staying at Marwadi's place but as it was dark by then, he had no choice. After dinner, the patient not only did all the preparation for the *bhajan*, but sat gazing at Sai Baba's picture until the *bhajan* was over. The patient himself as well as others were astonished and the Marwadi himself declared that from then on he would take only Phanse's medicine. Poor Phanse was troubled in his mind as he was really not a *vaid*. But with faith in Sai Baba he quietly went to sleep. At night, Phanse had a dream in which Sai Baba told him about the patient's ailment and the medicine for it. Sai Baba also appeared to the Marwadi in his dream and asked him to administer only Phanse's medicine to his ailing brother. To escape from his predicament, Phanse demanded a high fee of Rs. 200 from the Marwadi for treating his brother but the Marwadi agreed to pay Phanse's fees, gave the medicine with full faith to his brother who was completely cured. As agreed the Marwadi offered Rs. 200 to Phanse but the latter did not accept the money. Saying, "I did nothing, my *guru* did everything," he returned home.

The Marwadi was sad and once, seeing that Phanse was not at home, left a costly *zari*-turban at his residence. Phanse thought of wearing the turban and sending an equivalent amount of money to Sai Baba. In the meantime, Sai Baba passed away. One Thursday while doing *bhajan* Phanse was sorry at the thought of his poverty. After *bhajan* he dozed off. Appearing to him in his dream, Sai Baba said, "Currently there is famine. Sell your *zari*-turban, buy rice with the money realised and continue trading. It will be profitable. Thereby you will be able to meet your living expenses and will not be required to accept employment." By carrying out Sai Baba's instructions he was able to achieve a turnover of Rs. 50,000 to 60,000 and earn a profit of Rs. 10,000-20,000. This is a standing example of how, by directing his ignorant devotee on the path of welfare, Sai Baba benefits him.

V.C. Chitnis had also benefited by the *darshan* of Sai Baba's *samadhi*. His services had been terminated. On the advice of S.B. Nachane, he went to Shirdi and had *samadhi-darshan*. A few days thereafter he was reinstated in employment.

Fauzdar Joseph of 45 Turner Road, Bandra, had a very difficult criminal case to detect. He prayed for help. Sai Baba came to him in a dream and gave him directions on how he was to proceed. Acting on those directions he was successful in detection of the crime.

Baburao Boravke, of Saswad near Poona, had also a very pleasant experience. His parents died when he was but a child. Taking advantage of his position his uncle and other relations misappropriated his father's property and Boravke had to give up schooling to take up employment. One of his maternal uncles who lived in Shirdi cultivated sugar cane in his farms and made jaggery out of it. The said maternal uncle had become a devotee of Sai Baba. Boravke heard the fame of Sai Baba from his maternal uncle and became eager to see him. He somehow arranged to buy a railway ticket up to Kopargaon and decided en-route at Ahmednagar station not to take food until he had Sai Baba's *darshan*. Alighting at Kopargaon station he travelled three miles by tonga up to the banks of Godavari and had only three annas left in his pocket. Shirdi was eight miles further up and he realised that he did not have sufficient money for the tonga fare. So he decided to foot the distance. His maternal uncle's farm was on the way. The maternal uncle's wife asked him to have his meal before going for Sai Baba's *darshan*, but Boravke told her that he would have his meal after returning from Sai Baba's *darshan*. At the *lendi* near Shirdi he met his maternal uncle who also pressed him to have his meal before going for the *darshan*. Boravke also gave him the same reply. So the maternal uncle gave him a rupee. Thus with a rupee in his pocket Boravke proceeded to the *masjid*.

After the *darshan* Sai Baba enquired after Boravke and asked him for *dakshina*. When Boravke expressed his helplessness Sai Baba asked him to look into his pocket. Boravke was amazed and taking out the rupee from his pocket offered it to Sai Baba.

After some days Boravke abandoned the idea of taking up employment and stayed on in Shirdi with his maternal uncle. His daily routine now was to work in the farm and to take Sai Baba's *darshan* regularly.

After some days a friend from Kopargaon called on him. Seeing the improvement in his farm the friend asked him, "Who has so transformed the face of your farm?" The maternal uncle replied, "My nephew." The maternal uncle's friend was so pleased with Boravke that he expressed a desire to take the latter as his partner to which the maternal uncle consented. From that time Boravke began attending to the farms of both his maternal uncle and his friend. The production of jaggery increased considerably and fetched a good price and hence good profits. Boravke, who came with three annas for the *darshan* of Sai Baba, now earned Rs. one lakh as his share after the accounts for two years were made up. In the firm belief that he had prospered due to Sai Baba's blessing Boravke bought some land one mile away from Shirdi on the way to Rahata, constructed a bungalow on it and began residing there so that he could have the *darshan* of Sai Baba daily.

Vithoba Mhadba Fand, through his faith in Sai Baba even after the latter's *mahasamadhi*, was able to get a job. Fand had some formal education. He applied for a job addressing to the Railway Engineer but it was of no avail. His maternal uncle, Kashinath Dube, who was a devotee of Sai Baba, asked him to worship Sai Baba's picture. He agreed to do so on condition that he should get an experience of Sai Baba's prowess within two months. A month after he commenced the *puja* a vacancy arose in the Railway Engineer's office. Fand applied

again. In the meantime, a new officer had been put in
charge of the office. Fand was recommended by a devotee
who knew the new officer well. In all there were three
applicants including Fand. One applicant was an ex-
employee with ten years' service and the second was the
son of the *avval karkoon* (the first among the clerks). The
ex-employee's application for re-employment was
rejected. The two remaining candidates had to appear for
an examination. As Fand was not much educated he was
apprehensive but his maternal uncle advised him to have
faith in Sai Baba and to apply his *udi* before going into
the examination hall. There it so happened that the son
of the head clerk, who was better educated, was confused
and could not write correct answers. On the other hand,
Fand's answers turned out to be correct and by Sai
Baba's grace he got the job.

Nagesh Atmaram Sawant learnt of Sai Baba in
December 1922 by reading *Sai Leela* magazine. His *leelas*
drew his attention. In January 1924, he went to Nasik for
training at the Police school. His studies did not attract
him. He was often thinking of Sai Baba and hoped he
would save him. Sawant often prayed to him. He got a
picture of Sai Baba for worship from his friend. He failed
in his departmental examination at Nasik. Trainees who
fail are not given a chance of becoming sub-inspector.
Sawant continued as acting sub-inspector for about five
years. He was unwilling to go to Nasik again as it was
financially ruinous and he was confident that Sai Baba
would make him permanent sub-inspector without
passing the examination. From 1924 he began his
regular annual visits to Shirdi for each *punyatithi* on
Dusshera day. In July 1929, as a special case, he was
exempted from examination and given a permanent
appointment as sub-inspector.

There are many instances of how, by acting on Sai
Baba's advice, many devotees had earned money or were
saved from incurring losses, and how, by disregarding his

advice, had suffered losses. We will now examine some of these experiences.

Damuanna Kasar of Ahmednagar was one of the two persons who hoisted a flag on Dwarakamai on Ramanavami day. One of his friends in Bombay wrote to him inviting him to join in forward trading in cotton. Damuanna wrote to Sai Baba for his advice. Sai Baba exclaimed, "Sheth (Damuanna) is unhinged. He should be satisfied with what he is getting. Ask him not to run after a lakh of rupees." Sai Baba's advice was conveyed to Damuanna who was disappointed on reading it. Cotton prices were shooting up day by day. Therefore Damuanna personally went to Shirdi. He bowed to Sai Baba and sat down to perform *charan-seva* (press the legs). While doing so, a thought arose in his mind that if he were to offer a percentage of the profits to Sai Baba, perhaps Sai Baba would give his consent. No sooner did this thought arise than Sai Baba, who had the inner vision and was intent on the welfare of his devotees, said, "Bapu, I am not in any of your transactions." Damuanna was thus shamed and he gave up the idea of trading in cotton. His friend blamed him for going after a mad *fakir*, and thus losing a good opportunity. But all of a sudden the market crashed and his friend was put to great loss. Then Damuanna was able to appreciate the wisdom behind Sai Baba's advice.[7]

Bayaji Appaji Patil of Shirdi was a devotee who, during the last fourteen years of his life, used to get four rupees every day from Sai Baba from which he purchased 84 acres of land. Once he disregarded the advice of Sai Baba and came to grief. Sai Baba had advised him not to plant sugarcane on his lands as others had done. However, yielding to temptation he planted it and not only sustained the loss of Rs. 300, but had also to go without the supply of dry crops he would have got on the land.

Mangesh Shivaji Satam, resident of Bagtalavde in Deogad *taluka* of Ratnagiri district, heard of the fame of Sai Baba after the latter's *samadhi*. He brought a photo of Sai Baba and started worshipping it. Whenever he had to make any important transactions in business he would seek Sai Baba's direction by casting lots before him. In 1921, he thus sought direction on the question whether he should trade with the same party with whom he was dealing for many years past, and the answer was 'No'. Yet because of his long-standing connection with the party he disregarded Sai Baba's advice. As a result he was faced with many hurdles and the particular transaction could be completed only with great difficulty. Moreover, a sum of Rs. 1,200 was outstanding with that party at the end of one year. Satam was required to deposit a particular sum in the court within a specified period. He could not do so on account of financial stringency. He was fazed but finally he craved pardon of Sai Baba for disregarding his advice, and resolved to send Rs. 5 to Shirdi for his error. As a result the time for depositing the particular sum was extended by six months.

Maintaining accounts and exchanging goods or services are a part of our everyday life. Earning or spending money, lending or borrowing money on interest are very common operations. Earning money gives pleasure while spending money may cause satisfaction or dissatisfaction or loss of hope. Whoever may be the individual, if his hard-earned money is forcibly taken away, he may feel pain or unhappiness - he dislikes it intensely. If the money lent on interest is not repaid, generally it causes pain or dissatisfaction and may lead to loss of friendship. If the money borrowed is not repaid, the creditor may press persistently or the property may be auctioned, leading to the loss of reputation. Even if the creditor does not resort to such tactics, every man with a conscience feels troubled in his heart for not having repaid the debt. Sai Baba has helped his devotees even in such situations and saved their reputation. Let us examine such instances.

Vaman Chintamanrao Mule, Pleader, a devotee of Sai Baba, residing in Pimpalgaon in Niphad *taluka* of Nasik district, was staying in his farmhouse when an epidemic of plague was raging. One day, after midnight, thieves made a big hole in the northern wall of the house. One thief entered the house and others stood outside. Mule's father was sleeping on a bedstead under which was a small box containing notes of Rs. 200 and promissory notes of Rs. 4,000. The thief who entered the house handed over the box to his companions outside. Opposite the picture of Sai Baba hanging on the wall was a trunk which attracted the attention of the thief. The trunk contained silver vessels valued approximately at Rs.3,500 and ornaments worth Rs. 6,500. The thief was about to lift the trunk when the sister-in-law of Mule woke up and shouted "Thief, thief"! Mule was in deep sleep and did not hear the shouts. In the meanwhile Sai Baba appeared to Mule in his dream and said, "Your trunk is gone, get up." Hearing this, he woke up in fright and taking hold of a stick began shouting, "Beat him!" and he raised a hue and cry. The thief inside the house hurriedly escaped through the hole. All the inmates of the house woke up. The theft was reported to the police who came for inspection. During investigation it was discovered that the small box was missing and a written complaint to that effect was given to the police. After sunrise a villager came to the police station with the missing small box. On opening the box everything in it was found to be in order from which it was surmised that as the theives could not open the box, they had dropped the box and run away. Thus by Sai Baba's grace, Mule was saved from a serious loss of property.

In 1914, a devotee by the name of Ganpat Dhond Kadam was protected by Sai Baba from robbers. Kadam was travelling with his family by train to Manmad. As the train left Nasik station, a number of dark-skinned Bhils jumped into his compartment and sat by him. At that time Kadam was engaged in reading *Bhaktimargpradeep* by Lakshman Ramachandra Pangarkar. Seeing the group of Bhils around him Kadam innocently imagined that they might have got in to listen to the *bhajans* from the book. And so he began singing them loudly. The Bhils sat in the compartment for about five minutes and then they jumped off from the moving train one by one. Kadam went to the door of the compartment to find out what the mystery was. And what did he see? He noticed that all the Bhils were running like mad as if someone was chasing them. Then he turned back to resume his seat and saw an old *fakir* sitting opposite him. Kadam thought to himself, 'There was no one before in this compartment. How come that the *fakir* is now here?' In a moment the *fakir* vanished from sight. To Kadam this was a miracle and he was perplexed. When he reached Shirdi and was sitting near Sai Baba, the latter asked him, "Well, did you travel safely?" Then it dawned on Kadam that the group of Bhils was a gang of robbers and the *fakir* was none other than Sai Baba who appeared in the compartment to protect him from danger.

Sai Baba had similarly protected the telegraph-master of Veena railway station in Kapadvanj *taluka* of Nadiad district, Ratanlal Ganpatlal Dave, from thieves. As Dave was transferred from Veena to Nadiad, the day before his departure, he was feted by his friends and the Dave couple retired to bed late that night. After midnight, a thief entered their railway-quarter and in order to see what ornaments were worn by Mrs Dave threw a torch light on her. Mrs Dave awoke and for a moment she and the thief eyed each other. Only twenty years old, she was frightened and could neither move from her bed nor shout. By Sai Baba's inscrutable *leela*, her child began to cry. The thief was startled and stumbled against a bucket which caused a sound. Mr Dave got up in the meanwhile and tried to chase the thief, but the latter made good his escape. On inspection of his belongings, Dave found that nothing was stolen or lost. He attributed his good luck to Sai Baba's grace.

In the fifth chapter, we saw that two persons from Goa had come for Sai Baba's *darshan* and Sai Baba had asked for *dakshina* of Rs. 15 from one of them who had vowed to make such offering. The circumstances leading to the said person's visit to Shirdi are as follows. This person had a Brahmin in his employment for 35 years. Yet the Brahmin succumbed to temptation, and making a hole to the safe in the wall, stole notes worth Rs 30,000 belonging to his employer. When the employer discovered this he was broken-hearted, for all his life's savings had been lost. The thief could not be detected - enquiries about his whereabouts were of no avail.

Once while the employer was sitting on the verandah in a dejected mood, a *fakir* passed his house, to whom he told of his loss. The *fakir* advised him to vow to visit the *avaliya* Sai Baba of Shirdi if he recovered the stolen money and to give up an item of food of his liking until his vow was fulfilled. He did as he was advised by the *fakir* and after fifteen days his former Brahmin servant repented and voluntarily coming to him returned the stolen property and begged him for his forgiveness. The employer pardoned him and after sometime set out to travel by boat. The officer on the ship would not permit him to board but on the intervention of the attendant (who was none other than Sai!) he was admitted. Seeing all these *leelas* of Sai Baba he was astounded. Not only had he been enabled to get back his lost money but also to fulfil his vow in a strange way.

Dr. Madhar Ramchandra Tagare of Dashrathwadi had a strange experience on 14 May 1952. His war bonds worth Rs. 2,500 had matured and the money was due from the post office. He placed the war bond certificates along with other papers in his bag and set out for Kopargaon by a bullock cart. While he was engaged in conversation with another person in the cart, he did not notice the bag which fell out from the cart. When they were crossing Naradi river he found that his bag was missing. Therefore, he got down from the cart and walked back two miles in search of his bag but could not find it. While walking back he saw a cart with barrels of kerosene standing. He saw the cartman getting down from the cart, picking up something and placing it in the cart. However, it did not occur to him to ask the cartman about his missing bag.

He returned home late at night and tried to sleep. But his mind was agitated and till midnight he was awake. He thought of reporting his loss to the police but he could not remember where he had kept the record of the distinct serial numbers of the war bond certificates. At midnight, with a troubled mind, he sat near Sai Baba's photograph amd prayed to him. He dozed off in his seat and felt someone telling him, "Don't worry."

In the morning he left with the overseer of the workshop in search of the missing bag. He enquired in the vicinity but without any success. On the suggestion of one Mr Patel's suggestion, as a last resort, he went to a particular locality for a search. There he saw the daughter of the kerosene cartman standing but he did not ask her anything. Then he went to enquire about a friend of his in the locality who was not well. After giving him medicine he spoke to him of his missing bag. At that time the daughter of the cartman was standing there. She felt respect for Dr. Tagare and bringing the bag placed it before him and said, "We found it yesterday on the road." The bag was recovered but it was distorted out of shape. On inspection it was evident that the papers had been tampered with, but as nothing worth stealing was found in the bag, the war bond certificates had been left intact. Dr. Tagare was naturally overjoyed.[8]

Mrs Kamalabai Pednekar had a similar experience in October 1952. She was employed as a nurse in a big hospital. She misplaced currency notes worth Rs. 65 somewhere in the hospital. She searched for them but could not find them. The loss of this was a great hardship for her. In between she went on leave. On her return she picked up a register for daily entries from a table in the hospital and to her surprise found the missing notes in it. This could never have happened without Sai Baba's grace for the register was one of daily entries which had been handled by many persons in her absence. But the notes did not fall into the hands of anyone else but hers.

Kanoba Hari had gone to Shirdi to test whether Sai Baba was a saint or not. He arrived in Shirdi, wearing a new pair of sandals and with a *zari*-turban on his head. Before he entered the *masjid*, afraid that his new pair of sandals may be stolen, he put them away in a corner where they would not attract attention. After the *darshan* he could not find his sandals. He was sad but what could he do? Whom could he ask in an unknown place? With these thoughts he returned to his place of halt. Then he sat down for a meal, but the thought of the missing sandals troubled him. He could not enjoy his meal. His meal over, he was washing his hands when he noticed a boy with a pair of sandals held at one end of a stick across his shoulder going around with the cry *Hari ka Beta Zari ka Pheta*. Kanoba called him and claimed the sandals as belonging to him. But the boy said, "It is the order of Sai Baba that these sandals are to be given only to him who is the son of Hari and wears a turban of *zari*. Satisfy me about these two conditions and the sandals are yours." Kanoba who had worn a *zari*-turban at the time of *darshan* showed it to the boy and said that his father's name was Hari. Then the boy handed over the sandals to him. Kanoba was of course pleased to get back his sandals. More than that, however, he was astonished on seeing that his name which was not known to anyone in Shirdi was known to Sai Baba through his inner vision, and that his motive in visiting Shirdi had been revealed to him by Sai Baba in a skilful way.

A clerk in a well-known firm in Bombay embezzled funds of the employer and disappeared. In his peregrination the culprit arrived in Shirdi. A devotee of Sai Baba was the manager of the firm. The owner had got a warrant of arrest issued for serving on the clerk. A search was made at many places but it did not reveal the whereabouts of the culprit. So the manager thought of consulting Sai Baba on the way as to whether he should proceed with further search. When the manager arrived in Shirdi, he found the culprit sitting beside Sai Baba. The manager was worried - should he have the culprit arrested in Sai Baba's presence or allow him to escape, which course of action would amount to disloyalty to his employer! However, he was relieved when the culprit admitted his guilt to Sai Baba and sought his blessings. On Sai Baba's advice the culprit accompanied the manager and admitted his guilt before his employer. Thus the matter was satisfactorily resolved through the grace of Sai Baba.

A person may conduct himself carefully, may not spend in excess of his income, may eat moderately and may be a man of character, yet all his plans may go awry due to unexpected circumstances. Instead of profit there may be loss, expenditure may exceed income, suddenly a family member may fall ill and in such circumstances a person is duty bound to spend money and may have to take a loan for the purpose. With the best of intentions to pay off the loan he may not be able to do so due to hard circumstances. The possibility may then arise of loss of reputation, forfeiture or auction of property, etc. We will now see how Sai Baba saved his devotees in such circumstances.

The financial position of Hari Sitaram, alias Kakasaheb Dikshit, solicitor, deteriorated in the latter half of his life and he was indebted to the extent of Rs. 30,000. The creditor was pressing hard and the period for repayment of loan was expiring in four days. Yet no arrangement for repayment could be effected. That night Dikshit dreamt that the creditor demanded immediate repayment and he assured the creditor saying, "Do not fear that your loan will not be duly repaid. I have my resources. I know Sir Chimanlal Setalvad, Sir X and Sir Y. So you have no reason to fear." Shortly thereafter he woke up and remembered the dream. He was aghast at his stupidity on relying on the poor human support of Sir Chimanlal and others and failing to recognise that his only true sheet-anchor was Sai Baba. He repented for his folly, and with tear-filled eyes entreated Sai Baba to forgive him his grave lapse. Thereafter, he felt assured that Sai Baba alone would help him. And how could Sai Baba fail a devotee in the hour of his need? Yet as the day for repayment was nearing he could not see any money forthcoming. Now when only a day remained, the son of his deceased intimate friend called upon him and wanted his advice on how a sum of Rs. 30.000 that he had should be invested. On coming to know of Dikshit's financial difficulty, the friend's son pressed Dikshit to accept the deposit, and said that he would not be true to his father if he failed to help him with an accommodation at the time of need. Thus Dikshit paid his creditor on the due date with the help of the money received from his deceased friend's son.

A Muslim farmer was worried about paying off a loan of Rs. 500 which he had taken for the improvement of his farm. He decided to dig a well in his farm. While digging he came across a rock which needed blowing up, and he applied twice to the Collector for a permit for buying explosives. As both his applications were rejected he was disheartened and approached Sai Baba with his grievance. Sai Baba said, "Let Nana (Nanasaheb Chandorkar) come and I will tell him." During Nana's visit to Shirdi, when the farmer reminded Sai Baba, he said to Nana: "Give his application to the Collector with your recommendation so that his work will be done." Nana was aware of Baba's powers but he felt that the farmer's application would not be sanctioned.

Nanasaheb took the farmer to the Collector, placed the farmer's application before him and told him that two earlier applications had been rejected. The Collector then asked the farmer why he was insisting on using explosives in his farm. The farmer said to him, "Saheb, I have taken a loan of Rs. 500 from the Government. I wish to improve my farm and pay off the loan. Without a well I cannot improve the farm, and without explosives the well cannot be dug. If you do not grant the permit, how can the well be dug and how can I repay the loan?" The Collector was satisfied with the explanation and granted the permit. Nanasaheb had thus another experience of Sai Baba's powers, and the farmer was happy at the prospect of being free from his debt.

We suffer pain if our hard-earned money accumulates by denying ourselves pleasures of life, or that which is inherited, is stolen. Similar or greater pain is experienced if the money we have given on loan with interest is not repaid, or payment thereof is unduly delayed and we do not receive the money when we ourselves specially need it. Such experience is bitter and disturbs the peace of mind of even good devotees. We will cite here only two instances, though there are many, of how Sai Baba helped his devotees in such painful circumstances.

Dattoba Tulsiram Chavan, the grandson of Bapusaheb Shirsathe, had given a loan on interest to a person. Chavan was thinking of going to Shirdi and had some financial difficulty. By Sai Baba's grace the person himself came to Chavan and returned the money borrowed by him. Chavan was therefore not required to borrow money and his faith in Sai Baba increased.

The second experience is that of Bapusaheb Jog. When he was in service he had advanced a loan of Rs. 1,400 to a relation of his wife. About 12 to 14 years during which Jog was reminding the debtor through his letters about the amount due, not a pice of it was returned. Jog was earning about Rs. 200 a month when he was in employment and at that time did not feel the need of the money loaned. But after his retirement on pension he settled down in Shirdi and began experiencing the pinch. Finally, Jog told Sai Baba about his problem, and asked for permission to approach the debtor personally to demand the money or to recover it by filing a suit. Sai Baba said, "Oh, where will our money go? The money will come to your doorstep. Why are you in such a hurry?" Even after asking for permission many times, each time he got the same reply. Then Jog would grumble and in agitation say, "Twelve to fourteen years have passed and not a pice has been returned by him. What, will he now come to my doorstep with the money?" Even then Sai Baba would repeat what he had said earlier and refuse permission to Jog to leave Shirdi. Finally, Jog got tired of asking Sai Baba and satisfied himself thinking there was no prospect of his ever getting back the money.

After a few days, to his utter surprise, the debtor came to Shirdi with a couple of friends and put up at Jog's place. Jog was stunned and recollected Sai Baba's words. The debtor had brought only Rs. 1,400 with him and not the amount by way of interest. So entreating Jog's wife the debtor said, "Please persuade your husband to accept the principal and relieve me from the debt." Jog's wife first refused to intercede on his behalf but because of his pitiful pleading told Jog about it. Jog would not yield an inch. Even the companions of the debtor pressed Jog to forego the interest but he was unrelenting. At last both the debtor and Jog agreed to abide by Sai Baba's decision and the matter was referred to him. When asked how much amount should be paid to Jog by the debtor, Sai Baba said that Jog should accept Rs. 1,400 and free the debtor. As Jog had given up all hope of realising the money loaned and got back the principal without any legal proceedings by Sai Baba's grace, he considered himself fortunate and accepted Sai Baba's verdict. As per his rule, Jog offered the entire sum to Sai Baba who accepted a small amount therefrom and returned the balance to him. This experience further strengthened Jog's and his wife's affection for and trust in Sai Baba.

Notes

1. *Devotees' Experiences of Shri Sai Baba*, Part I, pp. 41-49. Statement of Shri S.B. Dhumal.
2. Ibid., p. 61. Statement of Shri S.B. Dhumal.
3. Ibid., p. 18. Statement of Professor Narke.
4. *Shri Sai-Sat-Charita* (Marathi), Chapter 29, verses 130-144.
5. Ibid., Chapter 33, verses 34-42.
6. *Devotees' Experiences of Shri Sai Baba*, Part II, p. 106.
7. *Shri Sai-Sat-Charita* (Marathi), Chapter 25, verses 18-85.
8. *Shree Sai Leela* (Marathi), September 1952, pp. 70-72.

11. UNRAVELLING TANGLES

Hari,
Thou didst remove the afflictions of Thy devotees.
Thou didst spare the shame of Draupadi
By continually lengthening her dress.
Thou didst assume the form of a Man-Lion
To save Thy devotee Prahlad.
Thou didst save the elephant from drowning.
Mira is the servant of Lal Giridhara:
He has removed all my afflictions.

The Devotional Poems of Mirabai, No 61
(translated by A. J. Alston)

Time and again in human life there occurs a combination of circumstances when a person is baffled and does not know how to meet them, how to unravel the tangled skein. He is unable to unravel them himself, and is not in a position to tell anyone else about them. If the circumstances take a favourable turn, by God's grace, then only a man is relieved of his anxiety. We will now examine instances of how Sai Baba gave a favourable turn to circumstances for his devotees.

The wife of Hari Vinayak Sathe was placed in an awkward situation when her husband and father gave conflicting directions to her. If she were to obey her father, she would have been a victim of her husband's wrath. Sai Baba saved her mysteriously from the lashes! On Sathe's instructions his father-in-law had bought land comprising 20 acres for a sum of Rs. 1,200 for Sathe. Once when Sathe was in Shirdi he felt a desire to visit his

land, but his father-in-law did not approve of it as he was
afraid that if the widow of his nephew got to know about
it she would demand a share in it. So he declined to
accompany Sathe. Sathe had called for the bullock cart of
Tatya Kote Patil and asked his wife to go along with him.
Earlier she had agreed but now on her father's direction
she changed her mind. Sathe was furious and taking the
whip from the cartman was about to flog her when
Megha suddenly came running to the Wada and told
Sathe that Sai Baba had summoned him immediately.
Sathe went to the *masjid* when Sai Baba said to him,
"What is it? What has happened?" Sathe realised that by
his inner vision Sai Baba had come to know everything,
and he hung his head in shame. Then Sai Baba added,
"Your land is where it is. What's the necessity of visiting
it?" Sathe calmed down, prostrated before Sai Baba and
thanked Sai Baba for saving him from inflicting cruelty
on his wife. How can the gratification of Sathe's wife and
father-in-law be described in words?

Sai Baba saved the wife of Nanasaheb Nimonkar
from disobedience of her husband's word. Nimonkar's son
at Belapur was ill. So Nimonkar asked his wife to visit
him for a day and return the next day and not linger on.
As the following day was *Amavasya* (the last day of the
dark phase of the moon), she knew that she would not be
permitted to leave and yet she did not want to stay on
against the wishes of her husband. After all preparations
were made to start she went to the *masjid* as Sai Baba
was about to go to the *lendi*. She placed her head on his
feet and asked for leave to go. Immediately Sai Baba
said, "Go, go soon and return after staying for four days
happily in calm enjoyment." Nimonkar, who was
standing near Sai Baba, understood and his wife was
pacified.

Parents in India experience great difficulty in finding
suitable spouses for their eligible daughters. The bitter
experiences through which they pass sometimes make

life unbearable for them. Those unfortunate parents who have had such experiences alone know the acuteness of the agony of this kind. We will now see instances of the succour which Sai Baba rendered in such situations through his wonderful suggestions out of concern and care for his devotees.

Govind Damodar Pant of Palaspe, Panvel *taluka*, Kolaba (now renamed 'Raigad') district, met parents of many eligible boys for his daughter but could not fix up her marriage. On the suggestion of one Sai devotee, Pant vowed to visit Shirdi for Sai Baba's *darshan* if his daughter was married in fifteen days. The result was that the son of one Hardikar from South Hyderabad on his own came to Palaspe in search of a suitable bride. Pant's daughter was soon married to him and Pant went to Shirdi in fulfilment of his vow.

Govind Narayan alias Baba Samant tried hard to fix up the marriage of his elder daughter but without any success. In such anxious state of his, he did not once get to sleep until 1:30 a.m. So he got up, lighted a lamp before Sai Baba's photograph and prayed fervently. Next day, by 5 p.m., Samant got detailed information about the eligible son of the late Bhaurao Dabholkar and marriage soon followed the engagement of his daughter to Dabholkar's son.

Sai Baba had also helped the *tahsildar* of Sunel in Holkar State, Keshav Rege Amin. His financial condition was so-so, but he desired that his daughter should get a good spouse. He tried hard in Indore, Ujjain, Bombay, Thane, etc., but was unsuccessful in fixing up her marriage. Then he went to Baroda and with his relation went to the houses of two prospective bridegrooms. At one of these places deceit was sought to be practised on him by substituting for the prospective weak bridegroom, a handsome healthy boy only for the purpose of fixing up the marriage! Fortunately, by Sai Baba's grace, the deceit was discovered in good time and the girl was saved from disaster. Then Sai Baba came into Tahsildar Amin's dream and asked him to proceed to Jirapur. Amin was baffled but in a few days' time he was transferred to Jirapur. After he left for Jirapur, he came to know that the son of Nabars of Soyat, 10-12 miles from Jirapur, was eligible for marriage. Amin went with his daughter to Soyat and by Sai Baba's grace her marriage was fixed up. She was married and Amin was relieved of his anxiety.

The experience of Gopal Ganesh Shriyan was that Sai Baba continues to take care of his devotees even after his *mahasamadhi*. There was an understanding since 7 to 8 years between Shriyan and the father of a prospective bridegroom that his son would marry Shriyan's elder daughter. Mutual relations of the two families were cordial. The boy had passed matriculation and was studying in a college. The boy's father became greedy and asked for a thumping dowry from Shriyan, and, as it was not forthcoming, communication between the two families stopped and the engagement was broken off. But Sai Baba is the refuge of his devotees. Shriyan prayed to Sai Baba who assured him that all would be well and his daughter would surely be married to the same boy. Then it came to Shriyan's ears that another party was prepared to offer a huge dowry to the boy's father. He was worried but Sai Baba again assured him in his dream and stated that his daughter would be married to him in two years' time. And it so happened that on completion of two years the boy's father came to Shriyan and persuaded him to fix up the marriage of their daughter with his son. Within a few days thereafter by Sai Baba's grace the marriage took place without any hitch.

Another Sai devotee, Chauhan's daughter's marriage, could not be fixed up in spite of her father's best efforts. In 1923, a person was vacillating with regard to marrying her. So Chauhan's wife was upset emotionally and approaching Sai Baba's photograph, she said, "You help all others by your mysterious power. Why then don't you give us some such experience? My daughter is still unmarried and I am anxious about her. If there be really prowess in you, then I should get a letter from that person by tomorrow." Notwithstanding her inconsiderate words, Sai Baba responded to the prayer of a mother with an ache in her heart. Next day, Chauhan received a letter from the man who was vacillating and their daughter's marriage was solemnised with him in a few days.

There is not as much anxiety for a son's marriage as much as that for a daughter. But for the sake of prestige in the community there is some anxiety all the same. Sai Baba helps his devotees even in such cases. Sai Baba's great devotee Abdul of Nanded had left home and served Sai Baba in Shirdi for forty-five years. He passed away in Shirdi on April 2, 1954. Abdul's mother was very eager to get her grandson married. Elders of one household conveyed in clear terms that they did not want to give their daughter in marriage to the son of a *fakir*. When Abdul's mother approached Sai Baba with a complaint, he assured her, "Do not be worried. The boy will get a good bride and everything will fall in its own place in good time." And so it happened. Once Abdul's mother and son went to a place where they met a person who was keen on his daughter's marriage with Abdul's son. Abdul's mother told him that the boy's father was a *fakir*. Yet the person offered the hand of his younger daughter who was married to Abdul's son, notwithstanding the fact that the person's elder daughter had not married till then.

Adam Dalal of Naopada, Bandra, was anxious to arrange for his son's marriage. He would talk to Sai Baba about it from time to time. Sai Baba would put off the discussion every time. After three years had thus passed, Sai Baba gave leave to his son to marry, and told the day on which the marriage was to take place. But from where was the money for the marriage to be obtained was the big question. By Sai Baba's grace, ten days before the marriage he got a job and an advance for it. Some other arrangement was also made possible and Adam's worry was removed.

Laxman Govind Munge of Main Road, Nasik, was engaged to a girl. As no arrangement could be made for the ornaments to be given to the would-be bride, Munge went to his maternal aunt's husband in Rahata in 1890 when Sai Baba was staying in Hanuman *mandir*. Munge went for Sai Baba's *darshan*. Sai Baba welcomed him and gave him a mango. Munge did *charanseva* and told Sai Baba the purpose of his visit. Sai Baba exclaimed, "Who is related to whom? No one is. No one helps in need. You may take Rs. 1,000 to 2,000 from me if you so desire." Then Munge went to his maternal aunt's husband who flatly expressed his inability to help. Dejected, he turned back, fearing that without any provision for ornaments, the engagement would be broken off. In the meanwhile, a friend of his arrived. When Munge told him of his difficulty he arranged from a Gujarati *sowcar* of Sinnar for a *chamki* (golden/diamond stud in the nose), *todas* (rings of gold or silver for the ankles) as well as thirty *tolas* of gold to be given on loan. The necessary ornaments from these were purchased. Thus through Munge's friend and the *sowcar* of Sinnar, all arrangements were made and Munge was able to get married.

Sai Baba had also helped Ramachandra Keshav Naik at the time of the latter's daughter's marriage by mysteriously providing Rs. 3,000 to him in a short time.

For the marriage of the niece of Gauriben of Bhatwadi, Umreth, negotiations took place with about four parties, but her marriage could not be fixed up. The niece of Gauriben was naturally dejected and shed tears before her aunt. Pointing to the picture of Sai Baba, Gauriben advised her niece to surrender to him. The niece prostrated before Sai Baba with her whole body touching the ground, took the *udi* and prayed: "Baba, unless you arrange for my marriage within a specified number of days I will have no faith in you." It was as if Sai Baba accepted her challenge. Her marriage was fixed up on the eighth day and the actual marriage soon followed. The girl's faith in Sai Baba was strengthened and her parents were relieved.

Many people in Ahmedabad also have experience of Sai Baba having removed difficulties in the way of the marriage of their daughters. The daughter of the present writer would be continually in attendance at Shri Sai Mandir of Ahmedabad. A proposal from a good family came for her on its own, and she was happily married. A lady devotee of Sai Baba, who would lovingly perform *bhajan*, was going unknowingly to be joined in marriage to a person which was not in her interest. Sai Baba alerted her in good time as a result of which she reversed her decision, and then her marriage was fixed up with a suitable person. Sai Baba appeared in the dream of a Parsi lady graduate and, by putting to her unerring questions, saved her from the clutches of a learned but cunning and unfaithful person. A graduate girl who was in love with a boy left her home and was staying separately. The girl's mother performed *parayana* of *Shri Saileelakhyana*, whereby her daughter was reconciled to her family. The opposition of the boy's father to the match was also neutralised, and the boy was married to the girl with the consent of the parents of both the parties. There are many other such instances but, due to limitation of space, they will not be cited here.

The remembrance of the separation of a missing son is pungently painful. Sai Baba showered grace on the pining parents of a missing son. There was no trace or news of the boy for many years. Hearing Sai Baba's fame the father of the boy came to Shirdi. Sai Baba told him that he would soon be united with his son. This person was a resident of Thane. At the time when the train by which he was travelling from Shirdi reached Thane, the local train from Bombay also arrived at Thane station. The boy alighted from the train and son and father met each other on the railway platform for the first time after many years.

The son of a Parsi merchant was missing. His father spent four to five thousand rupees in his search but to no avail. Finally he took refuge in Sai Baba and enquired through a letter when his missing son would be found. A reply was sent to him from Sai Baba that the boy had gone to the south, was happy and would return on his own. As told by Sai Baba the boy came back after a few days. When the matter had been referred to Sai Baba the son was actually staying happily in Madras.

Captain Dr. Hate of Gwalior was a staunch devotee of Sai Baba. One evening a person by the name of Savlaram came to him and said that both he and his wife were drowned in sorrow as their son had left the household, and was not traceable. Hate asked him to go to Shirdi for Sai Baba's *darshan*. Accordingly, Savlaram vowed that if his son was found he would go to Shirdi. After some days he received a letter from his son in Mesopotamia, saying that he had joined the Army without informing anyone and was now returning home. When this news was conveyed to Hate he said, "First go to Shirdi." Spurning Hate's advice Savlaram, along with his wife, proceeded to Bombay to receive their son. He, of course, met his son, but the latter was sick and weak. So he was brought to Gwalior for treatment by Dr. Hate. Hate reminded Savlaram that he had acted unwisely in not visiting Shirdi. Savlaram was willing to go to Shirdi and asked for a letter of introduction. Saying that no letter of introduction was necessary, Hate gave him a rupee and asked him to give it to Sai Baba. Though Hate had sent the rupee as offering to Sai Baba, he wished in his mind that Sai Baba would return it as *prasad* after touching it. But he did not speak about it to Savlaram. Savlaram accompanied by his wife and son went to Shirdi for Sai

Baba's *darshan*, after which he handed over Hate's rupee to Sai Baba. Sai Baba kept it in hand, looked at it and returned it saying it should be returned to its owner. After returning to Gwalior, Savlaram met Hate and said that he had good *darshan* and his son's health was satisfactory. He also returned to Hate his rupee, as per Sai Baba's instruction. On receiving the rupee as *prasad*, Hate was delighted and Savlaram was also happy that he had found his son and he was in good health.

A Parsi gentleman had a son who was insane. The son's condition was so pitiable that his father could not bear to see it and hence got him admitted to an asylum. Hearing the fame of Sai Baba, the gentleman came for Sai Baba's *darshan*. Sai Baba blessed him and said, "Go, your son will get well. Take him home." The gentleman was not sure whether the authorities of the asylum would agree to discharge his son from the asylum but when he arrived home from Shirdi, he found a letter from the authorities waiting to be opened. It was stated therein that as his son was losing weight it would be advisable to get him admitted elsewhere. So the gentleman was happy to bring his son home, as per Sai Baba's blessings. At home the son's condition improved rapidly and after some days he recovered completely and began assisting his father in his business.

Sakharam Hari, alias Bapusaheb Jog, who would attend to *arati* of Sai Baba, asked his permission to go to Nasik for performing obsequies after his mother's death. Sai Baba postponed giving permisssion. When Jog felt that the matter could not be delayed any longer he said to Sai Baba, "I must go to Nasik this afternoon," to which Sai Baba replied, "We will see in the afternoon." Jog was anxious because there was no Brahmin belonging to Jog's branch of Vedas in Shirdi. However, in the afternoon a learned Brahmin of Jog's branch of Veda arrived unexpectedly in Shirdi. Then Jog realised why Sai Baba had delayed giving permission. The obsequies were then performed in Shirdi at the hands of the learned Brahmin.

When Neelkanth Ramachandra Sahasrabuddhe first went to Shirdi, Sai Baba asked him for *dakshina* of Rs. 12-8 annas. Later, as Sahasrabuddhe offered to Sai Baba Rs. 5 received by Tatyasaheb Nulkar by money order from Ramachandra Waman Modak, Sai Baba told him: "Keep this money with you. You will require it for your expense." So he kept the money with himself. Then he was required to go to Jalgaon from Shirdi on his way back home, and he was falling short exactly by Rs. 5 for the rail fare, for which the money retained by him on Sai Baba's advice came in handy.[1] We shall now see instances of how Sai Baba continues to take care of his devotees even after his *mahasamadhi*.

A pensioned teacher, a devotee of Sai Baba, living at Chandoli in Ambegaon *taluka* of Pune District, used to grow potatoes and sell the crop to the Government. In 1945, as the potato crop in general was infested, no one was prepared to offer more than Rs. 200 for his crop. He had incurred an expense of Rs. 400 on growing the crop. So he worshipped Sai Baba thrice a day and vowed to go to Shirdi every Thursday. In the course of Government inspection his crop was adjudged as the best and was purchased for Rs. 600 by the Government. Thus he made a profit of Rs. 200 on it.

Bhikaji Mahadeo Bidwe, a peon of Shri Saibaba Sansthan of Shirdi, received Rs. 36 per month by way of salary. His sister Chhabutai was sick for about three months. Her condition took a serious turn on 5 December 1951. Therefore, Bhikaji wanted to get her examined by a good doctor. But how could he call a doctor for domiciliary visit on his meagre salary? So, putting his burden on Sai Baba and ever remembering him, he was doing his duty in the office when an old devotee, a doctor, came there for some enquiry. Bhikaji did not recognise him but strangely enough he did recognise Bhikaji. Bhikaji told the doctor of his sister's illness and requested him to examine her. The doctor gladly agreed and, after examining her, gave her medicine.[2]

Once Nanasaheb Chandorkar was restless as a seeming conflict between devotion to his father and devotion to his *guru* was raging in his mind, which resolved itself peacefully, for which he thanked Sai Baba in his heart. The facts regarding this seeming conflict are that, like Nanasaheb, his father Govindrao had been once a Deputy Collector. He owned a house in Kalyan and enjoyed a high standing in the town. Govindrao developed hostility towards some Muslims over some matter, as a result of which he gave instructions to members of his household not to have any truck with Muslims. At that time Nanasaheb was out of station on duty. On return he came to know about his father's instructions. So he was in a fix. For, while he was ready to sever relations with all other Muslims, as far as Sai Baba was concerned, though he was regarded by ignorant people as a Musalman, Nanasaheb was not willing to sever his relations with him. At the same time he did not wish to offend his father. Caught in such a dilemma, when Nanasaheb thought of speaking to his father about his mental conflict, omnipresent Sai Baba had already prepared his father's mind for dealing with such a matter. So when Nanasaheb told his father about his special relationship with Sai Baba, his father said, "Just as Sakharammaharaj is my *guru*, so Sai Baba is your *guru*. So even assuming he is really a Musalman, you should continue to visit him without any reservation." On hearing this Nanasaheb was delighted and his eyes were filled with tears.

Sai Baba was pledged to satisfying the desires of his devotees for the *darshan* of saints and God. Nanasaheb Chandorkar was convinced of this as a result of his following experience. Nanasaheb was then the Mamledar of a *taluka* near Pachora in East Khandesh. There is a shrine called Padmalaya about ten to twelve miles from Pachora. A realised soul named Govindbua stayed in the jungle at a distance of one and a half miles from the shrine. Govindbua would go into the temple early in the morning and, after attending to the worship of Gajanan, look after the visitors to the shrine and retire to his monastery at 10 p.m.. His intake of food consisted of only 18 tolas of tea per day. Nanasaheb felt a strong urge to have the *darshan* of Govindbua and told his friends about it.

The day for a visit to the shrine was fixed up. As his party missed the train by which they had planned to travel, they reached Pachora late in the evening. The road to Padmalaya passed through a forest. So, taking a guide, they set out on foot. It was a dark night and the road was uphill and down dale. After the morning meal none of them had eaten anything, and no snacks were taken with them. After covering about 6 miles Nanasaheb was very tired. He had no energy to go further and the party stopped for rest. What was to be done? By this time Pachora was well behind and it would be past 10 p.m. by the time they reached Padmalaya. Moreover, no one resided in Padmalaya. Govindbua would have retired to his monastery, in which case who was to provide them food and arrange for their lodging? Finally Nanasaheb got up and, remembering Sai Baba, he prayed fervently to him that, at whatever time they reached Padmalaya, if they were to get a gobletful of tea they would pass the night somehow. And, as nothing was impossible for Sai Baba, he should anyhow provide for them.

So praying and alternately walking and resting, the party reached Padmalaya after 10 p.m. As they arrived Govindbua came out of the shrine with a gobletful of steaming hot tea and asked, "Has Nana come?" Nanasaheb and others greeted him respectfully and wondered how he had stayed back in the shrine though it was past 10 p.m. Govindbua replied, "I received a message just sometime back from Sai Baba that Nana will be arriving here on foot from a long distance and in a tired condition. He will be hungry and so keep a gobletful of hot tea ready for him. So I have brought this tea for you." All members of the party drank tea to their heart's content, and yet some quantity of tea remained in the goblet. Appreciating Sai Baba's concern for his devotees, all of them rested for the night in the shrine while Govindbua retired to his monastery.

The next day they had a meal by way of *prasad* and then left the place for their destination.

During Christmas vacation of 1909, R.B. Modak thought of going to Khandesh via Shirdi. So he purchased railway tickets from Pune to Dhond and Dhond to Manmad. Then, taking baskets of fruits, flowers, etc., with them, they arrived at the station fifteen minutes before the departure of the train. Modak had the luggage weighed and then, leaving his wife and children in the women's compartment, was looking for a place for himself and the luggage when the guard sounded the whistle and waved the green flag. Modak requested the guard to charge him the difference between the second class and the third class fares and permit him to sit in a second class compartment. But the guard did not pay attention to him and the train started. Modak was dejected and remembered Sai Baba. Suddenly the station master was inspired to come there. He himself came to Modak and asked him what he wanted. On Modak's explaining to him his problem, the station master raised both his hands, stopped the train, made arrangements for Modak to get on to the train and got his porter to load Modak's luggage in the compartment.

Vasudev Narayan Desai had a similar experience after the *mahasamadhi* of Sai Baba. It was decided by Desai at short notice to go to Navasari with a party of 40-50 persons for his daughter's marriage. A compartment could not therefore be reserved in advance. The ticket collector told Desai before the train started that a compartment could not be provided for the party. Desai was in a fix. So, he prayed to Sai Baba fervently, and soon the Head Ticket Collector arrived there, and on Desai explaining his difficulty to him the latter got a compartment opened, reserved from Baroda, which was to go empty up to Baroda. Thereby Desai's entire party was accommodated. At Gholvad a *fakir* entered the compartment and with one leg placed across the other, sat like Sai Baba and said, "Well, you are all accommodated, isn't it?" Desai replied in the affirmative saying, "This is all Allahmia's doing." The *fakir* got down from the compartment and vanished.[3]

A clerk serving in the Port Trust was required to find several bills earlier returned by the customs office as they were called for again by the customs. Failure to produce the said bills would have resulted either in incurring the displeasure of his superior or even losing his job. The clerk was praying fervently to Sai Baba for help. The result was that the officer did not ask the clerk for the bills on that day, and on the second day the clerk found the bundle containing the bills on his table! The clerk had gone to the office before all the others on those two days. He tried to find out how the required bills came to be on his table, who placed them there, etc., but without any success. So the clerk believed legitimately that Sai Baba had answered his prayers.

The biggest calamity for a householder is to be charged with a criminal offence. Only the person who has undergone the bitter experience of a false criminal charge knows the agony of anxiety, mental torture and financial loss which he has to suffer. Many devotees of Sai Baba have been saved by him from such calamities. We will notice some of them here. A police officer was charged with the offence of extortion of money. He took refuge in Sai Baba and vowed to go to Shirdi for Sai

Baba's *darshan* if he were acquitted. After this vow he was exonerated and so on 8 December 1910 he visited Shirdi in fulfilment of his vow.[4]

Once, a Muslim doctor had come and stayed in Shirdi. In between somebody instituted a criminal case against him and summons thereof was served on him at Shirdi. On the day previous to the hearing of the case, the doctor asked permission of Sai Baba to leave Shirdi so as to be able to be present for the case. Sai Baba advised him to start the next day. Accordingly he did so and remained present in the court on the day next to the date fixed for the hearing. There he came to know that his case was not called out on the earlier day as the Magistrate was otherwise busy. On the day on which he remained present, the plaintiff and his witnesses were examined but being satisfied that there was no prima facie case against the doctor, it was dismissed.

Once, when a party in Shirdi village, hostile to Appa Kulkarni, filed a complaint of misappropriation of funds against him, the Deputy Collector called him for giving an explanation. Appa was frightened and approached Sai Baba. Sai Baba assured him and said, "The Deputy Collector is at Nevase. First go to the temple of Mohiniraj at Nevase, bow to him and then tender your explanation before the Deputy Collector." Appa did as instructed. After hearing him the Deputy Collector exonerated him of the charge and told him that he was convinced of his innocence. When Appa returned to Shirdi and praised Sai Baba, the latter said, "What did I do? The Doer and He who gets done is Narayana. He makes impossible things possible for a devotee."

It was alleged against Adam Dalal of Bandra, that in a mortgage transaction his bond in favour of mortgager was fabricated. Adam was frightened and went for Sai Baba's *darshan*. Sai Baba assured him and said, "All will be well." And so it happened. The mortgager was

committed to sessions in which Adam became a witness
for the prosecution and he was freed from anxiety.

Once, when jesting and joking took an ugly turn, Sai
Baba, by a remark of his, applied the healing touch which
ended the controversy. Two devotees were engaged in
serving Sai Baba and there was a possibility of their faces
dashing against each other. Seeing this the lady with a
sense of humour, known as Mavshibai, jestingly said to
the old male devotee, Anna Chinchanikar, "What, you
want to kiss me? Even though so old you have no sense of
shame!" Hearing this Anna Chinchanikar was visibly
agitated. But Sai Baba pacified both by his remark. He
said to Anna, "Why are you so highly excited? What is
wrong in kissing the mother?" This piece of humour
saved the situation and there was laughter in which both
the devotees joined.

On another occasion when a controversy was
erupting between a *Ramadasi* and Madhavrao
Deshpande, Sai Baba pacified the *Ramadasi* by
counselling him. A *Ramadasi* used to sit in the
sabhamandap opposite Sai Baba and do *parayana* (a full
reading of the text in a specified number of days) of
Ramayana. According to the rule laid down, he would
first recite *Vishnusahasranam* and follow it by *parayana*
of *Adhyatma Ramayana*. After many *parayanas*, while he
once engaged in a *parayana*, Sai Baba called him and
said, "There is a sharp excruciating pain in my abdomen.
Get some *senna* quickly from the bazaar." The *Ramadasi*
put a token in the *Pothi* (holy book) and went to the
bazaar to purchase *senna*. While the *Ramadasi* was away
Sai Baba got up from his seat, went to the *Pothi*, picked
up *Vishnusahasranama Pothi*, and giving it to
Madhavrao said, "Shama, I give to you this *Pothi* which
can do many things. Try reading it. Once I was in distress
and my heart was palpitating. Then by one reading of
Vishnusahasranama I got relief and repose. So daily read
slowly a line or two from it." Madhavrao replied, "I don't

want it. It is composed in Sanskrit. My speech is uncouth and I cannot even pronounce compound letters clearly." Even then Sai Baba said, "Never mind. Read it as you can and as much as you can. Take this *Pothi*." On Sai Baba's direction he accepted it. Just then the *Ramadasi* returned with the *senna*. Seeing his *Pothi* in Madhavrao's hands he was livid with anger. Forgetting the *senna* he assailed Madhavrao briskly and said, "All this is your cunning. You wanted my *Pothi*. So you used Sai Baba as a ruse to send me to the bazaar and seized possession of it. Let me see how you appropriate it." Madhavrao said to him, "Sai Baba gave me this *Pothi*. Really, I did not take it. Is your *Pothi* lined with gold? *Pothis* are so easily available in the bazaar. But Sai Baba gave this *Pothi* to me with his own hands. So I value it and propose to retain it!" However, the *Ramadasi* was not pacified and became stubborn. Then intervening, Sai Baba said to the *Ramadasi*, "Is this the fruit of your *parayana*? How is it that your mind is so unbridled and wilful? You have the *Pothi* by heart. I on my own have given it to Shama. Go to your seat and learn to think and discriminate." The *Ramadasi* was somewhat pacified. Shama was now compelled to accept the observance of the vow of *Vishnusahasranam parayana*. The *Ramadasi* accepted the promise of Shama to give in exchange *Panchar-atni Gita* and thus the controversy ended. By this one incident the weal of two devotees was served. The long-standing hostility between the two of them which erupted into the open that day changed into one of friendship thereafter.

The trouble of a person in Moglai who had fallen a victim to the strange deeds of fiends was completely cured by Sai Baba's blessings. Strange things would happen at this person's house. New clothes bought and hung on a peg would be torn or be infested with insects or weevils. The person changed his residence but even in his new house similar things would happen. Even a transfer to another town was of no avail. Finally, hearing of Sai

Baba's fame he came to Shirdi, and after taking *darshan*, recited his tale of woes before him. From that day the play of fiends ceased automatically. So the person wrote.

A candidate who has appeared for an examination knows the suspense he experiences until the declaration of results. Anant Mahadev Kulkarni along with his father came to Shirdi for Sai Baba's *darshan* in 1914 after appearing for the vernacular final examination. Having heard of Sai Baba's fame as well as kindness Anant asked Sai Baba, "Shall I pass the examination?" Sai Baba replied, "You will pass with the 114th rank." When Anant was about to leave, Sai Baba gave him *prasad* of *pedha*. When the results were declared after some days, Anant was found to have passed with 114th rank.

Knowing by inner vision that a certain action of his devotee would entail misery for him in future, Sai Baba would dissuade him from taking a false step. Purandare was employed in the railways. Once he decided to visit Shirdi with his wife and obtained Sai Baba's consent. He also got a pass from the railways for the purpose. The day before his departure Purandare got to know that the workmen were thinking of going on strike. When Purandare's superior officer also came to know of this he asked Purandare to defer his leave and assured him that he would issue a new pass in substitution. But Purandare would not change his mind and insisted on going to Shirdi. The same night Purandare saw Sai Baba with a staff in his hand in his dream. He admonished Purandare severely and said, "Don't come. What is the necessity of coming so often? I am not separate from you." So Purandare cancelled his visit to Shirdi that time. Thereby his superior officer's suspicion about him was removed. After a month when Purandare was ascending the steps of the *masjid* at Shirdi, Sai Baba said, "Hey, don't be foolish. We have to do many things. Stay where you are, take my name, etc." By these words of Sai Baba

Purandare recognised that Sai Baba had saved him from the untrue allegation which would have been otherwise attached to him that he was colluding with the strikers.

Sai Baba would assure poor devotees who would lead pure and gentle lives that God is Protector of the poor and would help them mysteriously. He had told Raghuvir Bhaskar Purandare during his first visit to Shirdi, "Build a house, I will be coming to stay there." At that time Purandare and other devotees considered this impossible. However, helping him in every way, Sai Baba made Purandare buy a plot of land and build a bungalow therein. On the day of *vastushanti* (house-warming) Purandare had a feeling that Sai Baba was accompanying him with a *jholi* (a cloth gathered up at the corners) and a staff and this impression lasted until he entered the bungalow. Purandare occupied half the bungalow and let out the other half from which he got rent which helped him meet the monthly expenses.

In 1914, Ramachandra Sitaram Dev of Andheri had an experience of how Sai Baba takes care of his devotees. At that time he stayed on his farm and there was no habitation around. Many thefts occurred then in Andheri. It was fearful and dangerous to live on an out-of-the-way farm. In such a state Dev prayed to Sai Baba. That night Sai Baba appeared in his dream and assured him that he would get ten Pathans to protect him. Next day, ten *dhobis* came to him to ask for space. Dev let out part of his land on which they had built huts for which they paid him a monthly rent. And because of their habitation there was no longer any fear of robbers.

The marriage of Kakasaheb Dikshit's son Babu was to take place. For that occasion many devotees from Harda were to go. The mother of Sadashiv Dhundiraj Nayak being seriously ill, the Nayak family even though desirous of being present, had to stay back. But Sai Baba resolved their difficulty by appearing in a dream to the Honorary Magistrate Krishnarao Narayanrao Paralkar.

Sai Baba told him, "Go and tell Sadashiv that his mother's condition won't be an impediment in his attending the marriage. After the marriage is over she will pass away on Ekadasi day." Paralkar conveyed Sai Baba's message to Sadashiv because of which the Nayak family attended the marriage without any fear or anxiety and returned to Harda thereafter. Then, as said by Sai Baba, Sadashiv Nayak's mother passed away on Ekadasi day at twelve o'clock.

As a devotee's purse fell down and was lost, Sai Baba arranged for money to be sent to him in his difficulty! Uddhaveshbua alias Shyamdas of Dahanu set off from Bombay by a steamer on a pilgrimage to Dwarka with a party of pilgrims. The tickets of all the members of the party were with Uddhaveshbua. The tickets were in two parts - one part of the steamer ticket and the other of the *machava* (a kind of boat) ticket. Separating the steamer tickets, Uddhaveshbua kept them in his purse. While standing on the deck near the railing Uddhaveshbua took out the purse which accidentally fell into the sea and the money along with the steamer tickets in the purse, vanished from sight.

Uddhaveshbua and his party had no difficulty in getting off the steamer at Dwarka as Uddhaveshbua explained the facts to the ticket collector and showed him the *machava* tickets. But the pilgrimage had just begun and Uddhaveshbua had no money left with him.

He was now worried how the pilgrimage was to be completed. His final refuge was, however, Sai Baba. Not to put out his hand for money to anyone being his rule, he immediately posted a letter to Sai Baba. Before the letter could reach Shirdi, the very night on which it was posted Sai Baba appeared in the garb of a *sadhu* at 11:30 p.m. in the dream of Gopal Giridhar and, waking him up, said, "Look, your father is stranded in Dwarka without money. Send him money." Giridhar looked around but could not see anyone. Thereafter he sat for over an hour thinking of what the dream meant, but could not come to any conclusion. Then he fell asleep. After some time the same *sadhu* appeared in Giridhar's dream again. He seemed to be very angry and directed Giridhar to remit money to his father at once. Giridhar got up a second time, woke up his wife, opened the door of his house and looked around but no one was to be seen. Then he thought that perhaps his father at Dwarka must be in need of some money. So in the morning he went to the post office and sent money to his father by a postal order. Uddhaveshbua was surprised to receive money from his son without having asked for it.

When the father met his son on return home, his son described to him how he had got intimation of his father's difficulty in a dream. When Uddhaveshbua went to Shirdi, Sai Baba remarked, "I arranged to send you money." So Uddhaveshbua realised how the powerful Sai Baba took care of his devotees and warded off their calamity.

Notes

1. *Shri Sai Leela*, June 1952, pp. 5-6.
2. Ibid., December 1951, pp. 19-21.
3. Ibid., June 1952, p. 6.
4. *Shirdi Diary of the Hon. Mr G.S. Khaparde*, Shri Sai Baba Sansthan, Bombay, entry dated 8 December 1910.

12. LOVE

The highest relationship is one of Love.
> The plain simple fare of Vidura He preferred to the delicacies of Duryodhana.
> He relished the berries tasted by Shabari and established bonds of Love,
> Out of love Hari served the King and even became a barber.

The highest relationship is one of Love.
> In Rajasooya sacrifice of Yudhisthir he cleared the leftovers,
> And out of love, forgetting His divinity drove the chariot of Arjuna.

The highest relationship is one of Love.
> The bonds of love grew in Vrindavan where he danced with Gopis,
> Surdas is not worthy of His Grace, why should he be vain?

Wealth is respected in the world, but in the *durbar* (court) of the true saint who is the Lord personified, it is loving devotion which is honoured. The notes of love from the heart of a devotee are accurately recorded in the vibrant and yet sensitive heart of the Mahatma, who is ever one with the Divine. The musical sound evoked in response is equally melodious, delicate and thrilling. In the opening *pada* (composition) there is a reference to this ancient covenant of the Lord. Many devotees of Sai

Baba have had experiences of this kind. Let us have a look at some of them.

It was the day of the Ramanavami fair in 1913-14. There was a terrific rush in Shirdi for Sai Baba's *darshan*. The Mamledar, Police Inspector and other officials were present for keeping *bundobast*. Sai Baba was seated in his usual place in the *masjid* since the morning. It was now 11 a.m. The devotees requested the police regulating the crowds to stop the queue for *darshan* for some time to enable Sai Baba to have his morning repast, but the latter said that he was not hungry. In the *sabhamandap* and further outside there was jostling in the crowd. It was summer time and everyone was perspiring. Yet there was abounding enthusiasm for *darshan* of Sai Baba in the crowds. Outside the *sabhamandap* a sixty-five year old woman was wailing all the time, "Please have pity on this poor old woman. Oh, Sai Baba, give me *darshan*." Amidst the vast crowds and the prevailing noise, who would pay attention to her?

In the meantime, Ramchandra Atmaram Tarkhad was passing that way. Hearing the old woman's cry, his attention was drawn to her. Seeing her miserable plight he was filled with compassion and catching her hand he said, "Come with me. I will arrange for you to have *darshan*." Since the police and others recognised Tarkhad, he led the old woman to Sai Baba. On seeing Sai Baba she called out to him lovingly and embraced him warmly. Tears rolled down her eyes and for some time she was choked with emotion. Placing his hand on her head, Sai Baba made minute enquiries about her household and said, "Mother, I have been waiting since long for you. What have you brought for me?" The old woman replied, "Baba, I had brought one *bhakri* (loaf of bread) and two onions with me. After I had walked and walked I got tired and sitting by a stream in the morning I ate half the *bhakri* with one onion. Now I have only the

half *bhakri* and one onion which please accept." So
saying, she untied the bundle in her sari and gave its
contents to Sai Baba - who gobbled them with relish and
said to the old woman, "Mother, your *bhakri* tasted very
sweet." Seeing this, tears stood in Tarkhad's eyes and
other devotees were overcome with emotion.

Once R.B Purandare started for Shirdi with his wife.
Giving her two *brinjals* (eggplants) Mrs R.A.Tarkhad
requested her to make a dish of *bharit* (by roasting) and a
dish of *kachrya* (by frying) out of the second, and offer
them to Sai Baba on her behalf. On reaching Shirdi,
Purandare's wife made *bharit* out of one *brinjal* and
offered it to Sai Baba. Though many other dishes had
come from others Sai Baba sampled only the *bharit* and
remarked, "This is very tasty. When we get *kachrya* we
shall have our meal." As it was not the season for growing
brinjals, in food received from others there was no dish of
brinjal. After making enquiries it came to be known that
Mrs Purandare had cut the other *brinjal* and was going
to make *kachrya* later as offering for Sai Baba. Thus Sai
Baba showed how he cares and appreciates the offering of
devotees made with a loving heart.

Sai Baba also showed recognition of Mrs Tarkhad's
love for him in December 1915. Balakram Mankar, a
devotee of Sai Baba, passed away in Shirdi. Mankar's son
called on Tarkhad before proceeding to Shirdi to perform
obsequies of his father. Mrs Tarkhad thought of sending
something with Mankar's son as an offering to Sai Baba.
Nothing else was available in the house except one *pedha*
(milk sweet). So she sent that *pedha* with Mankar's son.
On reaching Shirdi he went for Sai Baba's *darshan* but
forgot to carry Mrs Tarkhad's *pedha* with him. When Sai
Baba pointedly asked him, "Have you brought anything
with you for me?" he replied, "Nothing." To remind him
Sai Baba said again, "Is anything given for me?" He
again replied in the negative. So the third time Sai Baba
asked him directly, "Did the mother not give you

something for me before you started?" Then he was reminded of the *pedha* and begging Sai Baba's pardon, he went to his place and brought the *pedha*. That very moment Sai Baba put it into his mouth lovingly.

In 1915, when Shantaram Balwant Nachane Dahanukar was leaving for Shirdi, V.S. Samant gave him a coconut, a little packet of sugar and two annas to be offered to Sai Baba. Nachane offered the coconut of Samant to Sai Baba but forgot to give him the two annas. When Nachane asked permission of Sai Baba to leave for Bombay, the latter said, "Go from Chithali, but why have you retained two annas of this poor Brahmin (meaning himself)?" Then Nachane remembered the two annas of Samant which he immediately handed over to Sai Baba. Then again he asked leave of Sai Baba who said smilingly, "Go, now there is no objection. You must always discharge properly the responsibility you have undertaken. Or else you should not accept responsibility."

On 13 September 1918 Annasaheb Dabholkar, the author of *Shri-Sai-Sat-Charit*, had a dream. Accordingly, he sent with a devotee going to Shirdi a hundred leaves of Piper-betel, some arecanuts and eight annas. As the devotee was late by two days in starting for Shirdi, the Piper-betel leaves dried up. Nevertheless, the devotee offered them to Sai Baba telling him that they had dried up because of the delay in reaching Shirdi. When Sai Baba got up from his seat, the attendant asked him what was to be done with the dry Piper-betel leaves, as usually Sai Baba distributed all the things that were received. However, in this case he said, "Let the Piper-betel leaves remain." He would not spurn the things offered with love.

Sai Baba once appeared in the dream of the wife of a postal official posted at Burhanpur, who had never visited Shirdi before, and standing at her doorstep asked for a meal of *khichri*. The wife awoke and began looking around. She told all her family of her dream. After some time her husband was transferred to Akola. While there, the couple visited Shirdi, and served Sai Baba for fifteen days. One day after preparing the *naivedya* (consecrated food) of *khichri* she went to the *masjid*. At that time the curtain had been drawn and Sai Baba had sat down to his meal. As per rules, entry to the *masjid* at that time of the day was prohibited. Love, however, knows no fear. Pulling the curtain aside, the lady entered with the *thali* of *naivedya*. As soon as Sai Baba saw her, as if hungering for *khichri*, he said, "Bring, bring, bring the *khichri*." Then taking the *thali* from the lady's hands, he ate mouthfuls of *khichri* delightedly. Everyone sitting there was astonished that Sai Baba who normally did not partake of *naivedya* of anyone, should eat the whole of this *naivedya* and thought that there must be a reason behind it. When the husband of the lady was asked, he narrated the story of his wife's dream. All were convinced thereby that however far devotees of Sai Baba may be, he attracts them like a magnet one way or the other.

Dr. Keshav M. Gavankar has stated that in 1912 when he was seven years old, he was very sick. Medical treatment as well as *tantric* practices were of no avail. For two months he was lying semi-conscious in bed and doctors opined that without an operation he would not get well. His parents, etc., were against an operation as they believed that an operation would surely spell his end. At this time Y.J. Galwankar, son-in-law of Annasaheb Dabholkar, and author of *Shri-Sai-Sat-Charit*, had just returned from Shirdi. Galwankar was a close friend of Gavankar's uncle. He advised application of *udi* and *Sai-bhakti* as means for curing him and a vow to be made that if Gavankar got well he would go to Shirdi. He was thus cured but it took five years for the vow to be fulfilled. When Gavankar went to Shirdi and *naivedya* of *pedhas* was offered on his behalf to Sai Baba, the latter returned five *pedhas* and ate the rest. When Madhavrao Deshpande asked Sai Baba, who did not

ordinarily partake of any *naivedya*, why he did this, Sai
Baba replied that Gavankar had kept him hungry for five
years. Thus Sai Baba showed that he knew of his vow
made five years ago.[1]

Once Sai Baba appeared in the dream of Capt. Dr.
Hate of Gwalior and asked him, "What, have you
forgotten me?" Prostrating before Sai Baba, Hate went
into his garden, gathered fresh *walpapadi* (a sort of
bean), prepared a soup of *walpapadi* with undressed rice
and went to offer it to Sai Baba, when he awoke. Hate
had an intense urge to offer *naivedya* with *walpapadi* to
Sai Baba but could not make the journey to Shirdi
leaving aside his work. So he wrote to his friend in
Bombay requesting him to personally go to Shirdi and
offer *naivedya* with a cooked dish of *walpapadi* and said
that he was remitting money by money order.
Accordingly, Hate's friend went to Shirdi, made the
necessary purchases except *walpapadi* which was not
available. In the meantime a woman vendor arrived with
a basket of vegetables and Hate's friend got *walpapadi*
too. Thereafter *naivedya* was prepared as advised and
offered to Sai Baba. Without touching any other dish in
the *naivedya*, Sai Baba partook of *walpapadi*. This was
an example of how Sai Baba helps a devotee to fulfil his
good resolve.

The love-stream of Sai Baba continues to flow
uninterruptedly even after his *samadhi*. Sagun Meru
Naik had an experience of this in 1922-23. He had a
dream in which he saw that the *naivedya* of butter-sugar
which used to be offered to Sai Baba earlier at the
morning *arati* had been stopped. So he enquired of the
Sansthan and it was confirmed that the practice had
been stopped. Sagun knew that Sai Baba liked butter
very much. So at his own expense he began offering
naivedya of butter-sugar at the morning *arati*. Now, the
Sansthan offers this *naivedya* at the morning *arati* but

Sagun also continues his practice of offering this *naivedya*.[2]

When Das Ganu along with his party (which possibly included Pundalikrao) returned from Jagannath-Puri, he happened to meet Vasudevananda Saraswati (alias Tembe Maharaj). At that time Das Ganu told him that he would be going to Nanded via Shirdi. Immediately placing a coconut in the hands of Das Ganu, Vasudevananda asked him to give it to Sai Baba with his *pranams*. When Das Ganu's party reached Shirdi, Sai Baba remarked to Madhavrao Deshpande, "This Das Ganu is a big thief! He consumed the sweetmeat which my brother had sent to me!" Das Ganu did not understand the reference to the context and asked Sai Baba, "What sweetmeat?" "A thief and contumacious on top of that! Didn't you consume the coconut meant for me?" retorted Sai Baba. Immediately Das Ganu recollected that Vasudevananda had given a coconut to him and found that what Sai Baba had said was correct. Vasudevananda was a strict follower of Brahminism while Sai Baba did not care for external practices. The two appeared poles apart to the world but seeing the love and esteem in which they held each other, all understood that the saints were essentially one, and protection of the world was their mission. The other differences are outward and relative.

Pundalikrao prostrated before Sai Baba and begged his pardon, admitted his guilt, expressed regrets and offered to bring another coconut in lieu of the coconut he had used up. Then, rebuking him smilingly, Sai Baba said, "My brother, considering you trustworthy, had given you that thing. What's the result therof?" And then he told them, "You appear to hold yourself guilty because your ego considers yourself the doer. Actually I felt that you should all meet me and so I made coconut only the excuse for it. What is wrong if you consumed the coconut? You are all my children. So when you ate, you offered it to me and understand that I received it. Everything has happened according to my wish. There is no place for anxiety. Offer both merit earned and sin committed to me so that you will be liberated."[3]

Sai Baba would see, through inner vision, the *sattvic* desire of a devotee and would satisfy it. Thereby the tree of love of a devotee would get strengthened by watering it with faith. Once Hari Sitaram alias Kakasaheb Dikshit came at the beginning of Navaratra to Shirdi from Nagpur and stayed on till Dusshera. On an auspicious day like the Dusshera he had no fruit with him for the worship of Sai Baba and so he was somewhat downcast. After some time Sai Baba distributed grapes brought by a devotee. Dikshit gave some grapes from his share to Sai Baba which he ate. Thus, the feeling of deficiency in his *puja* troubling his mind vanished. In 1918 on Gurupoornima day, Sai Baba's *puja* was performed but there was the deficiency of *tambul* or *vida* (roll of Piper-betel leaf, arecanut, lime, cardamom, etc.). In the afternoon Sai Baba called Dikshit and asked him to get three or four *vidas*. When Dikshit brought them, Sai Baba put one in his mouth and himself removed the deficiency in his *puja* that morning. A third time Dikshit went to Sai Baba with the object of garlanding and giving him a *dakshina* of Rs.25. He garlanded Sai Baba but forgot to offer the *dakshina*. So Sai Baba reminded him and Dikshit gave the *dakshina* and was satisfied within.

Surveyor Govindrao Oak of Andheri and Krishnaji alias Annasaheb Agashe went to Shirdi for Sai Baba's *darshan*, and stayed there for two or three days. Before departing, both of them purchased a photograph each of Sai Baba for themselves which they kept in a bundle. On the way home Govindrao felt that it would have been better if he had purchased one more photograph for his brother. When the bundle was untied on reaching home they found three photographs instead of two! Both Govindrao and Krishnaji marvelled at Sai Baba's *leela*.

Chhotubai, wife of Rao Bahadur Moreshwar Pradhan, had time and again the experience of Sai Baba responding to her loving devotion and protecting her. Once all her children in her household got measles. The youngest of them was very weak. His condition became serious with high fever. Doctors gave up hope of his life. Chhotubai was continuously praying to Sai Baba. Sitting by her child day and night for four days she was fatigued. The condition of her child was deteriorating. After she had commenced *japa* of Sai Baba's name, within five minutes she dozed off and had a dream in which Sai Baba appeared and standing before her asked, "What are you doing? Your child is well. Why fear? Unhesitatingly give him food when he asks for it tomorrow around 6-6:30 a.m." The dream over, confused, she got up. She looked around but Sai Baba wasn't there. Her child was fast asleep and the family members sitting around him were happy as the child's fever had come down. The child had taken some milk and was sleeping peacefully. The face of the child which was earlier pale was now somewhat brighter. At the break of the dawn, the child began playing and asked for food at 6-6:30 a.m. which was given as per Sai Baba's advice in Chhotubai's dream. The child recovered fully in a few days.

Chhotubai had another experience of a similar kind. Her son was then in good health. At night all retired as usual. At 11 p.m. Sai Baba came in Chhotubai's dream and said, "Why are you sleeping? Get up, this boy will now get a fit of epilepsy." Chhotubai got up with a start and noticed that the boy had neither fever nor cough. Yet she collected all the medicines from the cupboard and arranged them on the table. As the boy would often get fits, hot water would always be kept ready. She sat up, prepared for the fit. There was, however, no sign of the impending fit. But as she had implicit faith in Sai Baba she sat near the boy and did not sleep. At 2 a.m. the boy suddenly raised his hand and lost consciousness.

Chhotubai woke up everybody. She told them that she was all ready for the contingency, thanks to Sai Baba's warning. Hearing this, all of them were amazed. The boy returned to consciousness after half an hour. Next morning, the doctor came and after four to five days he was all right. Thereafter he never had any fit of epilepsy.

Once Pradhan's elder son had typhoid. The elder sister of Chhotubai, wife of Pradhan, vowed to take the boy to Shirdi if he got well. Within fourteen days thereof the fever subsided. Four or five days thereafter the boy was permitted to sit up in bed. Against medical advice the elder sister now started for Shirdi with Chhotubai and the boy. On the journey, the boy was indisposed and Chhotubai was frightened. She feared that if anything untoward happened to her son she would become a laughing stock. Her elder sister who had vowed to make a trip to Shirdi was on tenterhooks. At Kopargaon station a man asked, "Shall I get you a tonga?" Hearing this the boy asked, "Have we reached Sai Baba's house? Now help me to sit up." When his body was touched he was found to have no fever. The boy wanted to get up but Chhotubai took him in her lap. On reaching Shirdi he was taken to the *masjid*. Sai Baba held him up in both his hands and made him stand. The boy stood up effortlessly. Chhotubai had doubts about how the boy who had been confined to bed for so many days would be able to stand. But he stood firmly and ate a banana and a mango given to him by Sai Baba. Then as if reminding Chhotubai of the thoughts that crossed her mind in the train, Sai Baba asked, "Well, will the world now laugh at you for having taken the risk of bringing him here?"

Once when Chhotubai was in Shirdi she was engaged in the worship of Sai Baba. In the middle of the worship Sai Baba said to her, "Go to your place. Your puja is there." When Chhotubai returned to her place of halt she found her child bawling. It wouldn't quieten down. When she pacified it she returned to the *masjid*. Then Sai Baba said, "Now complete the puja."

Chhotubai once saw Sai Baba in her dream. Sai Baba said to her: "Look, I have come here for your sake. Now offer *haldi-kumkum* (turmeric - a powder prepared from turmeric coloured with lemon juice, alum, etc.) at my feet." Accordingly, Chhotubai applied *haldi-kumkum*, garlanded and worshipped Sai Baba. Interpreting her dream, Nanasaheb Chandorkar told Chhotubai that she should get silver *padukas* made, go to Shirdi, get Sai Baba to touch the *padukas* with both his feet and install them in her *puja*-shrine. In a few days Chhotubai had an opportunity to go to Shirdi when she carried the silver *padukas* with her. She thought that after her daily worship of Sai Baba was completed, she would get him to touch the *padukas* with his feet. When she went to the *masjid* she noticed that even though all other *bhaktas* had worshipped Sai Baba he had put only one foot on the ground. So she was in a quandary about how she should get the *padukas* touched by both his feet. As soon as Chhotubai came to worship him, he placed his second foot also on the ground, and directing her as to which *paduka* should be placed on which foot, asked her to complete her *puja*. Chhotubai did as directed and worshipped him. When Chhotubai began to pick up the *padukas* after the *puja*, Sai Baba took them in his own hands and gave them to Chhotubai in Nanasaheb Chandorkar's presence. Then he remarked to Nanasaheb, "Nana, look, she is cutting both my feet and taking them away."

Pandurang Bendre desired that he should have Sai Baba's *padukas* for his daily *puja*. So he got silver *padukas* made and took them to Shirdi. When he approached Sai Baba, Kakasaheb Dikshit was sitting by him. Bendre handed over the *padukas* to Dikshit. When Dikshit was about to give them to Sai Baba, the latter said to him, "Give him the *padukas*." Bendre was not satisfied. In the afternoon Bendre returned with the *padukas* and gave them to Madhavrao Deshpande for being handed over to Sai Baba. Knowing the devotee's desire, Sai Baba gave the *padukas* with his own hands to Bendre. In addition, he gave him a coconut whereby the devotee was fully satisfied.

In 1913, when Atmaram Haribhau Chaubal went to Shirdi for Sai Baba's *darshan*, he carried with himself silver *padukas* which he had specially made to order. When he showed them to Sai Baba, the latter took them in his hands and remarked, "How beautiful!" Then he inserted his two great toes in the *padukas* and added, "How nice they look. Take them and keep them in your *puja*-shrine and worship them." Accordingly Chaubal would worship them. In 1930, on the 13th day of the waning moon in *Ashwin* (October-November), when Chaubal got up early in the morning and wanted to have *darshan* of the *padukas*, one of the them was missing. They were installed on a low wooden stool. The missing *paduka* was not found either under the low wooden stool or anywhere near. Notwithstanding the loss of one *paduka*, Chaubal continued with the daily *puja* of only one *paduka*. After two months he found one morning that even the second *paduka* was missing and could not be traced. Then he and his family wondered whether they had incurred the wrath of Sai Baba! With the intention of purchasing new *padukas* he went to Bombay. The day on which he went to Bombay he did not find *padukas* readily available. So he was disappointed and continued with the *puja* of the photograph of Sai Baba. The kind master must have thus tested his devotee for nine months. When he was convinced that his devoteee just could not forget the *padukas* he was filled with compassion. And one day the *padukas* were found neatly placed under the low wooden stool. This was a *leela* of Sai Baba. The whole household of Chaubal heaved a sigh of relief and was overjoyed.

Sai Baba would accept things sent to him with love and guide his devotees. The wife of Vinayak Shankar Giridhar had an experience of this kind. When Giridhar went with his friend to Shirdi she sent with him a garland of roses strung together by her. When Giridhar garlanded him, Sai Baba said, "This is a garland of love." Sai Baba would keep the garland on only for a second. He not only uttered the above words but the same night appeared in the dream of Giridhar's wife and said, "The garland which you gave me is one of love. Continue to garland me thus often."

"Even if my man is a thousand crore miles away, I will drag him here just as a young one of a sparrow is brought with a string tied to its leg." Many have experienced the truth of this saying of Sai Baba. Let us examine some such instances. Lakhmichand of Delhi was first employed at the Churchgate office of B.B. & C.I. Railway and later with Ralli Brothers. In 1910 he saw in his dream a bearded *sadhu* surrounded by his devotees. He bowed to him respectfully. Later Lakhmichand went to the house of Dattatreya Manjunath Bijur for the *kirtan* by Das Ganu. According to his usual practice, Das Ganu kept a photograph of Sai Baba before him while performing *kirtan*. As soon as Lakhmichand saw the photograph, he identified it as that of the *sadhu* whom he had seen in his dream. Unexpectedly he got all information about Sai Baba. But he was a stranger to Shirdi and did not know whom to go with, how to have *darshan,* etc.

One day at 8 p.m. Lakhmichand's friend Shankarrao came to his place and asked him, "Will you come to Shirdi? I had first intended to go to Kedgaon but I have changed my mind and wish to go to Shirdi." Lakhmichand borrowed Rs.15 from his paternal cousin and set out for Shirdi. On the way Shankarrao performed *bhajan*. They met two or three Muslims with whom Lakhmichand made enquiries about Sai Baba. Their replies satisfied him. He wanted to buy guavas at Kopargaon but forgot. After the tonga crossed the river Godavari he was reminded of it. Just then he saw an old woman with a basket on her head following the tonga. When the tonga was stopped he came to know that she had guavas. Gladly, Lakhmichand had the pick of the guavas and paid for them. Whatever remained in the basket the old woman voluntarily gave to Lakhmichand for being presented to Sai Baba on her behalf. Then they drove straight to Shirdi. Lakhmichand had *darshan* of Sai Baba, and pesented him with a garland and fruits. Sai Baba immediately said, "They perform *bhajan* on the way and ask others (about me). Why should they ask others? They should see everything with their own eyes, whether the dream is true or false. What was the mecessity of coming for *darshan* with borrowed money? Is your desire now satisfied?" When he heard his own account from Sai Baba's mouth, Lakhmichand had no doubt about Sai Baba's omniscience. During their stay in Shirdi, Lakhmichand once had pain in his waist. Sai Baba said, "It is good you are hungry. There is pain in your waist for which you require medicine. Today *sira* (sweet semolina) is being prepared. Perform the morning *arati*." Lakhmichand had the desire to eat *sira* that day. After the *arati* he had *sira* in his meal by eating which his pain in the waist stopped.

When Lakhmichand visited Shirdi a second time, a thought crossed his mind that Nanasaheb Chandorkar and Kakasaheb Dikshit were old devotees and bigwigs. If a garland were to be offered to Sai Baba through them, Sai Baba would surely accept it. So even though he was present he was about to entreat one of the two to garland Sai Baba when omniscient Sai Baba said, "Oh, are you not big? You too are big. Come and garland me and offer *naivedya*, etc."

Ramlal was an inhabitant of Bombay. Sai Baba gave him *darshan* in his dream and asked him to come to him.

Ramlal had not seen him before and so he did not know who he was. In the afternoon of the same day, while Ramlal was walking along the road, he saw a photograph resembling the person seen in his dream. He asked the shopkeeper whose picture it was and where the said person stayed. The shopkeeper gave him the information sought in answer to his questions. Later Ramlal went to Shirdi and stayed there till Sai Baba's *nirvana* in 1918.

Sai Baba helped in ingenious ways those who wished to have his *darshan*. One such instance is that of Ganesh Gopal Mahajani of Samantwadi, Thane, who was keeping indifferent health and was debilitated. His pious mother desired that her son should have *darshan* of a *Mahatma* like Sai Baba and Mahajani agreed with her. He had heard of the fame of Sai Baba. But he was employed as a clerk in Makanji Khatan Mills on a salary of Rs. 15 per month and the to and fro expense of travel to Shirdi was also about the same. The expense involved came in the way of satisfaction of his desire.

Once a water pump in Shirdi went out of order and R.A.Tarkhad, the Manager of Khatan Mills, decided to send his engineer to Shirdi on a particular day to repair the pump. Mrs Tarkhad also decided to go to Shirdi with the engineer. When Mahajani came to know about it he went to Dadar station on the said day with a garland and fruits for being sent to Sai Baba with them. R.A. Tarkhad had come to Dadar station to see his wife off. When he saw Mahajani he said to the latter, "Do you wish to go to Shirdi? A member of my family for whom the ticket was purchased is unable to go. Take this extra ticket for Shirdi." Mahajani jumped at the offer and gladly proceeded to Shirdi. He sent a message to his mother about his sudden departure with someone going to Thane, and thus had the *darshan* of Sai Baba.

Even after Sai Baba's *nirvana*, obstacles in the way of those devotees anxious to go to Shirdi, suddenly disappear. Anandrao Dolas of Kandivli had an experience of this kind on 10 March 1952. He desired to be present for the Ramnavami festival at Shirdi. So he asked his head clerk and applied one month in advance. As Anandrao's assistant fell ill his application for leave was not sanctioned. As the festival of Ramnavami drew near Anandrao prayed to Sai Baba to somehow get his leave sanctioned or else he would resign, but have his *darshan* at Shirdi at Ramnavami. Resolving thus in his mind, he went to the office the next day and asked the head clerk about his leave. By Sai Baba's grace the latter went to the higher office and got 15 days' leave sanctioned for Anandrao.

Sai Baba helped even student-devotees to fulfil their desire to go to Shirdi. Ramachandra Vithoba had an experience of this kind. He saw his friend Dattu, son of Bapusaheb Shirsathe, preparing to go to Shirdi and felt sorry he could not take the trip to Shirdi due to his financial condition. His mother was at Talegaon and there was no one around who could pay for his travel expenses. Ramachandra had come to believe in Sai Baba due to Dattu. Some time before Dattu's setting out for Shirdi, Ramachandra's mother suddenly arrived there and seeing the eagerness of her son to go to Shirdi, paid for his travel expenses. Ramachandra's faith in Sai Baba was thus strengthened.

The following incident took place after Sai Baba's *nirvana*. Bapusaheb Shirsathe, a devotee of Sai Baba, desired that his whole family should go to Shirdi for Sai Baba's *samadhi-darshan*. One of his sons who was a Government official agreed to accompany him. However, the other son who was a non-believer, flatly refused to accompany his parents. His father was pained but felt that Sai Baba would bring him round. The wife of the non-believer son was with her parents at Ahmednagar at that time. As the son was travelling to Ahmednagar he got down at the earlier station and was strolling on the platform. There he noticed his wife who had started for

Shirdi, as Bapusaheb's family was to go to Shirdi at that time. So willy-nilly he also went with her to Shirdi. Slowly he got experiences as a result of which he came to believe in Sai Baba.

The nephew of Dr. D.M.Mulky, a medical practitioner, was a patient of chronic osteomyetitis which was treated by the best surgeons of Bombay without any effect. The boy's wound in the bone was fully healed by the *udi* and loving and merciful *drishti* (glance of Sai Baba). Dr. Mulky himself earlier had twice made a vow when he was cured of two ailments, but he did not keep his word. Once, he even came as far as Manmad to fulfil his vow, but because of the tirade of a booking clerk at Manmad Railway Station against Sai Baba, he was prejudiced and proceeded to Bombay from Manmad. He now decided to spend his remaining leave in Alibag. For three consecutive nights he heard in his dream the words, "Do you still have no faith in me?" This induced him to go over to Shirdi, but he did not feel it proper to leave a case of typhoid in hand. Finally he said to himself that if the temperature of the patient came down that very day, he would start for Shirdi the next day. The patient's fever came down the same afternoon and he left for Shirdi. He stayed in Shirdi for four days. Before he made his *pranams* and went away, he learnt from Sai Baba that he would find an order on his table `transfered to Bijapur on promotion', which indeed happened. After this incident Dr. Mulky came to appreciate the greatness of Sai and the significance of his *darshan*.

The story of how Sai Baba's great devotee, Hari Sitaram alias Kakasaheb Dikshit, was inspired to go to Shirdi and how Sai Baba facilitated his visit is amusing and delightful. When Dikshit was in London, while getting into a train he tripped and impaired his foot. In 1909 he spent a few days in his bungalow at Lonavla when he chanced to meet his co-alumnus at Elphinstone College, Bombay, Nanasaheb Chandorkar, after many years. They exchanged notes about the events in their lives in the intervening years. Then Nanasaheb asked Dikshit, "Do you really desire that the limp in your foot should be completely cured? Then come for my Guru's *darshan*. He is all powerful and can cure any physical, mental or spiritual ailment and show you the true path to God." Due to Nanasaheb's loving description and *rinanubandha* (affinity by virtue of ties of former births), not caring for his physical disability, but for the sake of spiritual well-being, Dikshit expressed a strong desire to meet his (Nanasaheb's) *guru*. He obtained all information from Nanasaheb and when he visited Ahmednagar in his election campaign for his candidature for the Bombay Legislative Council, he put up with his friend Sirdar Mirikar. After his campaign work was over, he had a strong urge to go to Shirdi and discussed the matter with Mirikar. He wished to know who would take him and accompany him to Shirdi. Sirdar Mirikar and his son Balasaheb were thinking over the matter as to who should accompany Dikshit to Shirdi. But Baba had his own plans for Dikshit.

In Shirdi, Madhavrao Deshpande received a telegram from his father-in-law stating that his mother-in-law was very ill. Taking Sai Baba's permission Madhavrao left Shirdi and reached Ahmednagar at 3 p.m. As he emerged from the station he was seen by some common friends of Mirikar and Dikshit. They conveyed the news to Mirikar and Dikshit. Kakasaheb Dikshit's disquiet ceased immediately. Where could he meet a better companion than Madhavrao to take him to Sai Baba? When Madhavrao visited the abode of his father-in-law, he found his mother-in-law to be well. Sirdar Mirikar sent for Madhavrao and requested him to take Dikshit to Shirdi. It was decided there and then that Madhavrao should accompany Dikshit on the night train to Shirdi. There was a rush on the train but the guard, recognising Dikshit, arranged for both of them to travel in the first

class compartment. Then Madhavrao regaled Dikshit
with many tales and *leelas* of Sai Baba. Dikshit was
thrilled to hear them. They did not know how the time
passed.

In the morning the train reached Kopargoan where
they met Nanasaheb Chandorkar. He had also started
for Shirdi for Sai Baba's *darshan*. At this unexpected
meeting all the three were astonished. Later Dikshit met
Sai Baba who said to Dikshit, "Expecting you, I sent
Madhavrao straight to Ahmednagar." Dikshit was
overwhelmed and his hairs stood on end. This was the
first meeting of Dikshit with Sai Baba. Later he became a
staunch devotee of Sai Baba, built a *wada* in Shirdi and
had the fortune of intimate contact with Sai Baba. After
the *nirvana* of Sai Baba, he suddenly passed away while
travelling in the suburban train, singing the praises of
Sai Baba.

Joshi of Thane who could not go with his friends and
family to Shirdi vowed that unless he had *darshan* of Sai
Baba at home, he would not accept him. Caring about his
devotee, how Sai Baba gave him *darshan* at home is an
astounding experience. A Konkani gentlemen came to
Sai Baba for *darshan*. When he asked for the consent of
Sai Baba to leave, the latter said, "Will you do a thing for
me?" The gentleman readily agreed. Sai Baba then gave
him a packet of *udi*, and told him, "Go by the Mail and
whoever asks you for an inch of space to sit by you in the
train, give him the packet." The gentleman replied, "I
will certainly do as I am told. But if I don't meet any such
person on the way I will let you know by post."

The gentleman then proceeded to Kopargaon and
travelled by the Mail as told by Sai Baba. Till Kalyan
Station no one came to ask him for 'an inch of space to sit
by him.' He did not know that the Mail would halt at
Thane. So thinking that nobody was likely to ask him for
space to sit he was about to pen a postcard to Sai Baba. In
the meantime the Mail halted at Thane. The

compartment of the Konkani gentleman was crowded. As the train was about to start a man came panting into the compartment. The Konkani gentleman's child was sleeping beside him. Pointing to the inch of space near the child the man who came panting said to him, "Please give me some space to sit, I am feeling giddy." The Konkani gentleman immediately took the child in his lap, gave the man space to sit and also the packet of *udi*, telling him the whole story behind it. The man was none other than Joshi. He accepted the packet of *udi* with reverence and with the feeling that he had had *darshan* of Sai Baba without going to Shirdi.

In 1921 Raosaheb Y.J. Galwankar set out with his family on a pilgrimage of Kashi-Prayag. After visiting many a holy shrine and bathing in holy *kunds* (pools/springs) and rivers, he arrived at Prayag where he was taken to all the holy spots. At Bharadwaj Ashram he was filled with a desire to have the *darshan* of a holy person and silently prayed to Sai Baba for it. He had told his guide that besides seeing holy spots he was anxious to see holy persons. Within a few minutes after they left Bharadwaj Ashram, the guide stopped the tonga and pointing to a venerable man with a long beard falling over his breast said, "This Mahatma visits Prayag rarely, once in many years. He is widely known for his saintliness. He does not allow people to approach him and does not accept money." Seeing the venerable figure so soon after his prayer to Sai Baba, Galwankar went near him despite his guide's protest. The saint, far from being angry, welcomed him with arms raised by way of blessing and said, "Come child." Galwankar's mother, wife and other ladies in the party also approached the Mahatma, despite the guide's protest and were blessed by him. Galwankar had three annas in his pocket which he gave to the Mahatma. Much to the surprise of the guide the Mahatma received the money, looked at the coins with a pleasant countenance and accepted them.

Little did the guide know that Galwankar was a staunch devotee of Sai Baba, that Sai Baba is in touch with saints everywhere through his astral body and fulfils the good desires of his devotees.

In 1928 Justice M.B. Rege of Indore High Court went to Dakshineshwar to see places and things of interest. He got the service of a local man to act as his cicerone. The cicerone showed him the figure of Kali that Ramakrishna Paramahamsa worshipped. He looked at Kali standing outside the worship room and passed on. He was anxious to see the tiny image of Ramlal who sported as a living boy with Ramakrishna, and told his guide to show him Ramlal. The guide took him to one of the temples and showed him a huge image and said, "This is Ramlal." Rege said this could not be true. The man replied that he as the local man should know, and that Rege, as a stranger, could not be better informed. Rege fell silent.

Just at this juncture, a *pujari* of these temples came and inquired if he was from the Deccan. Rege replied that he was. Then the *pujari* said he would show him round Kali and every other image at close quarters and with full detail. Rege said he had just seen them. Then the *pujari* insisted on his visiting them again. He did not want any money from Rege. The reason for his persistent request was that he had been instructed in a dream the previous night that a devotee from the Deccan would be coming on the following day and that he was to take him to all the images and help him to worship them. Thus assured, Rege followed him. He took Rege inside the sanctum sanctorum and told Rege that he was free to touch the image and worship as he liked. Next, he said he would show Rege the figure of Ramlal. Rege told him that he had been shown a huge figure of Ramlal by his guide. The *pujari* berated the guide for deceiving Rege and then took him to the tiny image of Ramlal that Paramahamsa had played with and placed it in Rege's lap. Thus all his expectations were fulfilled beyond measure - all through the grace of Sai Baba.

Madhavrao Deshpande had an experience of the satisfaction of his *sattvic* desire. Once Sai Baba simultaneously received pressing invitations to the thread ceremony of the son of Kakasaheb Dikshit and to the marriage of the elder son of Nanasaheb Chandorkar. Instead of attending himself, Sai Baba deputed Madhavrao Deshpande to attend the thread ceremony at Nagpur and the marriage at Gwalior. As Benares is not far from there, Madhavrao thought of going on a pilgrimage to Benares and then to Gaya. When he mentioned his idea to Sai Baba, the latter said, "Yes, you go. I will speedily complete the pilgrimage of Benares and Gaya and return before you."

Madhavrao borrowed Rs.100 and started. On the road he met Appa Kote. On learning that Madhavrao was proceeding to Benares, he immediately joined him, having no money with him. To Madhavrao, Dikshit gave Rs.200, Chandorkar Rs.100, and Jathar (the father of Chandorkar's daughter-in-law) Rs.100. Thereby, Sai Baba provided for the expense of the pilgrimage of Madhavrao. Moreover, Jathar arranged for Madhavrao's accommodation at Benares and Ayodhya in the temples belonging to him.

Madhavrao spent two months and twenty-one days in these two places and after visiting Prayag proceeded to Gaya. In the train he heard that there was an outbreak of plague in Gaya. The train reached Gaya at night. Madhavrao and Appa Kote spent the night in a *dharmashala* (a building erected for the accommodation of travellers). The following morning a *panda* (Brahmin priest at the place of pilgrimage) who met them told them to hurry up as all other pilgrims had started. Madhavrao asked him guardedly whether there was an epidemic of plague in his locality. The *panda* assured them that there was no plague in his locality as they could see for themselves. So Madhavrao and Appa Kote went with the *panda*. On seeing his spacious house both of them were pleased, but the reason for their greater happiness was that in the room where they sat a photograph of Sai Baba was just opposite them. Seeing Sai Baba's photograph Madhavrao was overcome and tears began flowing from his eyes. The *panda* thought that he was crying because of their fear of plague. So he assured him again that his locality was free from plague and proceeded to tell him that if he did not trust him he could enquire with others to satisfy himself, but not cry unnecessarily. Then Madhavrao narrated to the *panda*, the account of his travel, how he had started from Shirdi, how Sai Baba had remarked that he (Sai Baba) would return before Madhavrao after completing the Benares Gaya pilgrimage, how he had realised the truth of Sai Baba's remark on seeing the photograph which caused the emotion of joy to surge in him. This explanation removed the *panda*'s misunderstanding of the situation. Then Madhavrao asked him how the photograph of Sai Baba came to be there, to which the *panda* replied, "Twelve years ago, I had a paid contingent of two to three hundred persons who attended to the pilgrims from Manmad and Puntambe. In course of time I heard of Sai Baba and went to Shirdi. I had the *darshan* of Sai Baba and while I was moving about in the village with the intention of purchasing a photograph of Sai Baba, I saw one hanging on the wall in the house of a person. With the permission of Sai Baba, the person gave it to me."

It suddenly struck Madhavrao that that person was none other than himself. But as many years had elapsed neither the *panda* nor Madhavrao could recognise each other. After the explanations, however, both were filled with joy and the *panda* also recollected that Madhavrao had been his host during his visit to Shirdi. So the *panda* felt like returning this act of kindness. He was not lacking in resources. He had elephants in his stalls. So he was very hospitable to Madhavrao and Kote. Using the palanquin for himself, he seated Madhavrao on the elephant and showed him all the places of interest. Then with pomp he led them to Vishnupad where he arranged for their *puja* and *abhishek* to the deity and *pindadan* (offering of the ball of rice) to the manes of ancestors. Considering themselves blessed and praising Sai Baba and singing of his mysterious *leelas*, Madhavrao returned to Shirdi.

The story of Shri Sai Vishwa Mandir in Tarkas Bhuvan on Relief Road in Kalupur area of Ahmedabad, is another instance of the satisfaction of the *sattvic* desire of devotees. Ramshankar Tripathi apprised his close friend, Linubhai Sayyad, of the experiences he got after returning from Shirdi. Linubhai had already visited Shirdi and had some experiences of his own. After Tripathi told Linubhai of his experiences, the faith and devotion of Linubhai was strengthened and the two of them felt that they should share their experiences with other seekers.

So in August 1948 they decided to form a Mandal. Initially, they would meet at a place and do *bhajan*. At this time they came to know of the devotion and faith of Sheth Ratilal Chimanlal Shah.[4] Linubhai got introduced to him and apprised him of their activity. Sheth Ratilal Chimanlal Shah was inspired to establish a Sai Mandir and reserved the third floor of his house for this purpose. He suggested that all the activities of the Mandal shuld be carried on from there.

From 23 December 1948, a beginning was made of the regular activity of Shri Sai Mandir in Tarkas Bhuvan. Every Thursday there would be *stavan* (songs in praise), *bhajan*, and *swadhyaya* followed by *arati*. Even now the programme is generally the same but there is a marked increase in the number of devotees. For the convenience of the devotees the hall is kept open the whole day. Besides Thursdays, Ramanavami, Guru Poornima and Vijayadashami festivals are celebrated.

As the accommodation in Tarkas Bhuvan was found insufficient, a three-storeyed building near Bala Hanuman in Khadia Shobharam Surti Pol has been purchased for housing the *mandir*. Necessary alterations will be effected in the building and an idol of Sainath will be installed according to the prescribed religious rites and the temple will be declared open soon. Then it will be kept open daily for *darshan* for the convenience of the public.[5]

Sai Baba also made a person his devotee, satisfied his *sattvic* desire and compelling the present writer to accept *guru-padukas*, showed the importance of *Guru* worship to the people. Sai Baba fully convinced Vasantrao Vishnushastri Panashikar of his omnipotence and oneness with Brahman. Initially, Panashikar was opposed to the keeping of a photograph of Sai Baba in the Vitthal *mandir* in 129 Fanas wadi, Kalabadevi, Bombay, but his opposition soon faded away due to his experience. He told all who met him that though Sai Baba was no more in flesh and blood, like the Maruti-incarnation Samarth Ramdas and the foremost saint Shri Akkalkot Swami, Sai Baba also manifests himself for the welfare of the people. He established Shri Sai Seva Sangh in Bombay and keeping a photograph of Sai Baba respectfully in Vitthal *mandir* started its *puja, bhajan, arati,* etc.

He also thought of establishing Sai Baba's *padukas* in Gujarat-Maharashtra. His economic condition was not such as to accomplish his objective. So he prayed to Sai Baba and his prayer was answered. *Padukas* were installed in his Vitthal *mandir* with the assistance of devotees. He also donated *Padukas* to Sai devotee Kulkarni of Pune. On Kulkarni's suggestion, he also thought of donating *padukas* to the present writer and pressed him to accept them. Since the writer had taken *sannyas* about that time, he expressed his inability to accept them, in fact, avoided accepting them. But determined Panashikar started *satyagraha*, went on a fast and coming to Ahmedabad informed the present writer of his having been on fast since ten days. He undertook the responsibility of meeting all expenses including travel lodging and board of himself and his companions and told the writer that unless he consented to accept the *padukas*, he would not give up his fast. Considering the determination and the fasting since ten days of Panashikar, it appeared to the present writer as if through him Sai Baba was impressing on him the importance of *guru-padukas*, even for a *sannyasin*, and urging him to accept them as a symbol of Sadguru Sai Maharaj as the eternal, pure, immovable witness of the Creative Power, and not to torment a loving devotee by disappointing him. So he consented.

Soon Panashikar returned to Bombay, and on 12 June 1954, equipped with weighty silver *padukas*, a photograph with silver ornamentation, all things required for *puja*, two chowries, flag, etc., left by Janata train for Ahmedabad with a party of fifteen or sixteen male and female devotees.

En route, at Balsar, Navasari, Surat and Baroda railway stations, the *padukas* were honoured by devotees and doing *bhajan* they reached Ahmedabad and put up at Lallubhai Dharmashala as arranged. At the Dharmashala *puja* and *arati* of the *padukas* were performed at 3 p.m. and the *padukas* were taken in procession with pomp in B.D. Raval's car to the residence of the present writer in Khajuri Pol. There *puja-archa* and *abhishek* for offering *padukas* were performed at the hands of B.C. Shukla, Secretary of Bhavnagar Sai Samaj. Rameshbhai and his wife Kamalaben sang melodious *bhajans* and in the presence of devotees, the *padukas* were offered ceremoniously to the present writer. Then Mrs Kumudben Raval welcomed the party from Bombay on behalf of the present writer and after distribution of *prasad* the party left for Bombay the same night.

Even though his men may be thousands of miles away, devotees realise that their thoughts to the minutest detail are known by Sai Baba through his inner vision. If a devotee has a desire and Sai Baba thinks it is worthy, he satisfies it. When Smt. Krishnabai Prabhakar first came for Sai Baba's *darshan,* the latter gave her a four-anna coin. Krishnabai kept it in a casket and would worship it. One day, Krishnabai purchased a coconut from a female vegetable vendor and while paying for it the four-anna coin from the puja was inadvertently given. When Krishnabai discovered her error, she was unhappy and began praying constantly to Sai Baba for getting it back. In the evening the female vegetable vendor came to her and said, "Take this four-anna coin which is from your puja. I don't want it." Krishnabai was happy beyond words and gladly gave the vendor another coin.

Sai Baba was guided solely by the interest of the devotee in deciding whether to permit a devotee to extend his stay in Shirdi, or staying for the number of days the devotee intended to stay. When Wagle, a government servant, went to Shirdi for Sai Baba's *darshan,* he felt like extending his stay, but was in two minds as the leave he had applied for was expiring. Sai Baba said to him, "Why are you afraid? Have no anxiety. There is no need to worry." On the fourth day, Sai Baba himself said to Wagle, "Now, go today." Wagle returned to Bombay and reported for duty but no one questioned him why he had been absent or overstayed his leave.

The case of Kaka Mahajani was just the opposite. He went to Shirdi with the idea of staying for a week and participating in Gokulashtami festival. On his arrival in Shirdi, Sai Baba called him immediately, "When are you going back?" Mahajani did not know what to say but replied, "Whenever you tell me to." Sai Baba said, "Start tomorrow." When Mahajani reported at his office on returning to Bombay, he learnt that the managing clerk of the firm had suddenly fallen ill and the Senior Partner had posted a letter to him in Shirdi asking him to come back immediately.

Sai Baba's love was not limited to human beings but also extended to the mute and dumb creation. A bull in Shirdi was dedicated to Lord Shiva and was allowed to roam and graze freely all over the village. It would enter the fields and garden and cause damage. Therefore the villagers contributed Rs 3 each for the expense of sending it to a *pinjrapole* at Yeola. The bull was entrusted to Bhiku Marwari along with the money and he took it away for being left at the *pinjrapole*. He returned and told the villagers that he had discharged the responsibility entrusted to him.

That night Sai Baba appeared in the dream of Bayaji Appaji Patil and said, "Why are you sleeping? I have been tied at the door of a butcher." He woke up and consulted the others. They concluded that the bull had been left with a butcher and not left at the *pinjrapole* in Yeola. So Bayaji started at once, went to Yeola and searched for the bull at the two *pinjrapoles*. It was not found there and he was informed that Bhiku Marwari had not brought it there. Then Bayaji went round and looked for it near the butcher's quarters. He saw the bull lifting its head over the wall. It was there at a butcher's place. It was to be cut up that very day by the butcher who told Bayaji that he had bought it for Rs.14 from Bhiku Marwari. Bayaji got it released after paying the butcher its price and placed it in a *pinjrapole*. Bhiku Marwari was charged, convicted and sentenced to two months' imprisonment.

Considering Shri Krishna a human being like himself and forgetting his divine nature, when Arjun would get vexed with him, Shri Krishna would pacify him. Such *leelas* would also happen in the *durbar* od Sai Baba. Once

Shankarrao Gavankar and Lala Lakhmichand of Bombay went to Shirdi, and as they were ascending the steps of the *masjid,* found Sai Baba in a temper. Notwithstanding his mood, Shankarrao went up but Sai Baba ordered him out! So, feeling hurt, he and Lakhmichand went to one side of the *masjid* and resolved not to go back unless sent for. Hardly two minutes had passed when Sai Baba sent for them and gave them *darshan* first!

The boss of Kaka Mahajani, Dharamsey Thakkar, Solicitor of Bombay, who went to Shirdi, called on Sai Baba. Sai Baba gave Thakkar grapes containing seeds to eat. He disliked grapes with seeds. But out of respect for Sai Baba he sucked the grapes and kept the seeds in his fist. Sai Baba again gave him some more grapes which he politely refused. But as Sai Baba insisted he accepted them. This time he found that all his grapes were seedless while those given to others were with seeds! Than a thought occurred to him that Sai Baba should next give grapes to Mahajani which Sai Baba did. So he was convinced that by his inner vision Sai Baba knew the thoughts of others and could satisfy them if he so desired.

A tailor of Shirdi named Martand was very sick. There was no one at home to nurse him. He suffered much but there was no help. One day he was lying near the road when Sai Baba passed that way and told him to go to Nanasaheb Dengle of Nimgaon where he would be cared for. Dengle was very considerate and said, "Consider this as your house and stay here. Yesterday night Sai Baba appeared to me in a dream and asked me to take care of you. Don't worry." Martand was touched and stayed at Dengle's for some days. With proper nursing he recouped and returned home healthy to attend to his business.

Sai Baba rarely left the limits of Shirdi. If he did go visiting it was to Nimgaon and Rahata that he would go. Khushalchand Seth of Rahata was a devotee of his. Once

Sai Baba felt like meeting Khushalchand Seth whom he had not seen for some days and said to Kakasaheb Dikshit, "Take a *tonga* to Rahata and tell Khushalchand Seth it's many days since he met me and ask him to call on me." Dikshit went by a *tonga* to Rahata and met Khushalchand Seth who had just got up from his afternoon nap. He said to Dikshit, "Just before you came he gave me *darshan* in my dream and also the message which you have brought from him. I wish very much to come to Shirdi but my son has gone out with the cart." Dikshit told him that knowing this Sai Baba had sent him with a *tonga* and requested Khushalchand to accompany him. Khushalchand Seth readily agreed, came to Shirdi and was very happy to meet Sai Baba in person.

If a devotee felt that he was not as dear to Sai Baba as another devotee who was favoured by the latter to render a particular service or given a particular thing, Sai Baba would remove his imaginary grievance by satisfying his desire. Sai Baba said that there was no differentiation in his *durbar*. R.V. Modak and Prof G.G. Narke had experience of this. Seeing Sai Baba smoke a chillum given him by Nulkar, Modak felt that he should receive a chillum of Sai Baba's at his hands so that he could keep it in his daily *puja*. Next day when Modak went to the *masjid* for *darshan*, Sai Baba asked Madhavrao to give two chillums to Modak.

Similarly once when Prof. Narke was in Shirdi, he saw the present writer being entrusted by Sai Baba with the task of collecting noon *bhiksha*. Prof. Narke felt that as he was not as advanced as the present writer he would not be entrusted by Sai Baba with that task. Imagine his surprise when next day the present writer could not go to the *masjid* and he was entrusted with the said responsibility! That made him realise that in Sai Baba's eyes all were equal.

In accordance with the saying of the Lord in the *Bhagavad Gita,* 'In any way that men love me in that same way they find my love', Sai Baba also satisfied his devotees in appropriate ways and every devotee thought that he was dearest to him. Once M.B. Rege, Judge of the Indore High Court, decided to visit Shirdi during Ramanavami in 1915 and to present Sai Baba with a costly gift. He purchased a fine lace embroidered cloth for Rs. 85, made of a type of Dacca muslin produced at Chander which could be folded into a 6"x 6"x 1" packet. He made up his mind that if Sai Baba cared for his love he should not return the same to him but should retain and wear it. Each devotee went and presented his cloth openly to Sai Baba which was placed on him and then at the end the attendants returned them to the owner thereof. When Rege bowed to Sai Baba, he shoved his tiny packet under his seat cushion (*gadi*). None noticed what was under the *gadi*. When Sai Baba got up he said, "Clear off all that lies on the gadi and dust it." When the *gadi* was removed Sai Baba saw the muslin packet and said, "What is this? Muslin!" and spread it out. Then he further said, "I am not going to return this. This is mine." He then wrapped it around his body and remarked to Rege, "Don't I look nice in this?" By this *leela* and these words of Sai Baba, Rege was immensely pleased and considered himself to be blessed.[6]

Three years earlier he had satisfied him in a similar way. In 1912 he went for Guru Poornima day to Shirdi. He saw the devotees at Manmad, each having a basket of flowers, garlands, etc. He was pained at the thought that he had forgotten to take a flower garland for his *guru*. When they reached Shirdi all garlanded Sai Baba except Rege who observed with sorrow that he had no garland to offer him. Immediately Sai Baba lifted up the bundle of garlands around his neck and said to Rege, "All these are yours." Rege was thus satisfied and convinced that Sai

Baba was ever with him and knew all his thoughts and aspirations.[7]

Even after his *nirvana*, Sai Baba continues to satisfy the desires of his loving devotees by various means. The Hon. Magistrate of Harda in Madhya Pradesh, Krishnarao Narayan Paralkar would feed a hundred Brahmins every year in remembrance of Lord Dattatreya. If for any reason he could not feed a hundred Brahmins any year, he would feed two hundred Brahmins the next year. In accordance with this practice, in 1925, he decided on a Monday to feed two hundred Brahmins on a coming Saturday. On Tuesday at 5 a.m. while he was performing *bhajan*, Paralkar heard an inner voice. 'If you feel that I should participate in the meals on Saturday, invite Kakasaheb Dikshit.' Paralkar wonderd how far it was proper to call Dikshit all the way from Bombay only for a meal. While he was thus hesitating came the clear answer at *puja* time, ' Why are you confused? Write a letter to Kakasaheb Dikshit and feed him along with the Brahmins and thus know that you have fed me.' On Wednesday Paralkar wrote a letter to Dikshit.

Saturday dawned, but there was neither a letter from Dikshit nor had he arrived. So Paralkar with tears in eyes approached Sai Baba's photograph, prayed to him and after bathing, sat down for his *sandhya* (morning prayer). Just then a telegram was received from Dikshit in which it was stated that he was arriving along with Madhavrao Deshpande. Paralkar was overjoyed. He went to the station with his friends to receive the honoured guests. At meal time the two guests sat down for meals to the joy of Paralkar and all those present.

The bonds of love thus grew in Vrindavan.

Notes

1. *Shri Sai Leela*, June 1949, p. 14.
2. *Shri Sai Leela*, December 1952, p. 52.
3. This account is based on verses 125-183 in Chapter 51 of *Sri-Sat-Sat-Charita* and pp. 122-124 of *Sant Kavi Dasganumaharaj - Vyakti ani Vangmaya* (Marathi) by A.D. Athavale.
4. The account of this unforgettable experience of the devotee has been described in the next chapter - *Sagunaroopdhari*.
5. The *mandir* was opened years ago. It is open on Thursday from 7 a.m. to 9 p.m. and on other days from 7 a.m. to noon and 5 p.m. to 8 p.m. for *darshan*.
6. *The Devotees' Experiences of Sri Sai Baba*, Part I, pp. 11-12.
7. *The Devotees' Experiences of Sri Sai Baba*, Part I, p. 9.

13. SAGUNAROOPDHARI

Arjuna, listen to my testament: the word is abroad that I the Lord assume form for the sake of My devotees for I am one with My devotees and My devotees are one with Me.

Tulsidas

For the sake of My devotees, whenever they are in trouble, out of tender love, I rush to their rescue and protect them.

Surdas

By doing *keertan* with loving devotion, the devotee experiences that the Lord manifests Himself. [80]

Narada Sutra

Brahman which is without qualities or form assumes form for the sake of devotees. The devotee loves God and because of loving devotion the Lord yields to him, i.e., the Lord serves His devotee and wherever and in whichever activity the devotee needs help, He runs to his aid. For honouring the *hundi* of Narsi Mehta, for easy delivery of Kunverbai, for performing obsequies, for avoiding excommunication of the devotee, He assumed many forms. To Eknath He came in the form of servitor Shreekhandya, became Vithu Mahar for the sake of Damaji, helped Janabai in grinding, pounding, beating into shape cowdung cakes, and washing clothes; for saving the Pandavas, lengthened the dress of Draupadi and earned the blessings of Bhishma; rescued the son of *Guru* Sandipani from the netherworld, served in the

sacrifice, removed the leftovers, drove the chariot of
Arjuna - in short did not feel ashamed or below His
dignity to do any work or assume any form. Blessed is the
devotee and blessed is the Lord. Words are inadequate to
describe the significance of the loving devotion whereby
the form of the Lord becomes manifest. The devotee and
the Lord are one. The sorrow of the devotee is the sorrow
of the Lord who is not at rest unless He assumes form and
removes it. This is the ancient truth and this is the test of
the devotee as well as the Lord. The *sanatana* Sainath
had warded off the calamities of His devotees. That the
truth of the ancient covenant of the Lord to become the
devotee of His devotees is also valid in this age was
brought home to the devotees by Sai Baba when he was
in flesh and blood and also after his *mahasamadhi*.

For the sake of Nanasaheb Chandorkar, Sai Baba
once assumed the form of a wood-gatherer, another time
that of a Mahar and a third time that of an office peon.
During the first incident Nanasaheb Chandorkar who
was in Ahmednagar district in the summer season had
started for the fair held on Harischandra mountain,
along with his office crowd. By the time he had climbed
half the distance it was noon. Nanasaheb's throat was
parched by the scorching heat of the sun and fatigue of
climbing and he was panting. His companions looked for
water near about but none was to be had. His
companions advised him to climb slowly with pauses for
rest. Nanasaheb told them that there was no strength
left in him to proceed further unless he had water to
drink and he was not in a condition to go further. He
wished that Sai Baba were there and then there would
have been no want of anything. His companions said to
him, "Nana, Sai Baba is not here, so get on steadily with
patience and grit." But Nanasaheb was adamant and
would not budge an inch.

Here in Shirdi, sitting in his usual place, Sai Baba
remarked to Madhavrao Deshpande sitting near him,

"Nana is in trouble." In the meantime Nanasaheb noticed a Bhil carrying a burden of wood and asked him where he could get water. The Bhil replied, "Just below the rock you are sitting upon is water." When the rock was lifted clear water was found beneath it. Nanasaheb had his fill and slaked his thirst and went ahead as if nothing had happened.

After some days when Nanasaheb went to Shirdi, Madhavrao asked him, "Were you in some trouble ten or fifteen days back?" When asked why he was asking this question, Madhavrao apprised Nanasaheb of the words uttered by Sai Baba. Then Nanasaheb recalled that he had been to Harischandra mountain fair where he was panting with thirst for lack of water. Then he realised that Sai Baba had assumed the form of a Bhil wood-gatherer to protect him.

The second incident took place at the time when Nanasaheb went from Shirdi to Kopargaon to have a dip in the Godavari during an eclipse. As soon as the eclipse commenced a Mahar came shouting '*De dan sute grahan*' (give in charity and the eclipse will pass off). Nanasaheb gave him four annas. At that very moment, showing a four-anna coin to a devotee sitting by him, Sai Baba said, "See, I have brought these four annas from Nana." After Nanasaheb returned to Shirdi, when asked how much he had given in charity for the eclipse, he said that he had given four annas to a Mahar. From this incident Nanasaheb and others had an idea of how Sai Baba, apparently sitting in Shirdi, travelled in space assuming different forms for the welfare of his devotees.

The third incident occurred when Nanasaheb was a Mamledar at Jamner. His daughter, Minatai, had severe labour pains as the time for delivery drew near. So the Chandorkar family prayed to Sai Baba for a smooth and safe delivery. No one in Shirdi knew anything about this except Sai Baba, who by his inner vision was aware of

everything. The passionate cry for help from a devotee
reaches the Lord without delay wherever He may be.

While all this was happening in Jamner, Ramgirbua
in Shirdi felt an intense desire to visit his place in
Khandesh. So he approached Sai Baba for permission to
go. Sai Baba would call him by the pet name Bapugir. He
said to him, "Do you wish to go? Do go but rest for a while
and then proceed. First go to Jamner. Halt at Nana's
place, meet him and then go further." To Madhavrao
Deshpande sitting near him Sai Baba said, "Copy out the
arati of Adkar for Nana." Then handing over a packet of
udi to Ramgirbua he said, "Give this packet and the text
of the *arati* to Nana." Ramgirbua said to him, "I have
only two rupees with me. How can I reach Jamner with
this amount?" Sai Baba replied. "Go with your mind at
ease. Everything will be provided." With faith in Sai
Baba's word Ramgirbua left.

In those days there was no railway connection right
up to Jamner. Alighting at Jalgaon, the journey onwards
had to be made by other transport. Ramgirbua purchased
a ticket up to Jalgaon by paying the fare of Rs. 1-14
annas. He reached Jalgaon by 2.45 a.m. He had now only
2 annas. left in his pocket. So with an anxious mind he
got out of the station, and he saw at a distance a robust
man with a beard and whiskers, dressed in breeches and
a buttoned-up tunic. He wore a turban and had boots on.
The man came near and enquired of passsengers, "Who is
Bapugir of Shirdi?" Ramgirbua advanced and said, "Why,
I am Bapugir of Shirdi. What do you want of me?" The
man replied, "Chandorkarsaheb has sent me with a
tonga. Please get into it and let us go." Ramgirbua was
relieved of his anxiety.

The tonga sped along. At the break of dawn it stopped
at Baghoor near a stream. Unyoking the horse the driver
took the horse to the water. Then he brought water for
both himself and Ramgirbua to drink, and spreading out
a repast of mangoes, *gulpapadi* (a sort of cake made with

jaggery) and *pedhas* before Ramgirbua, he said, "Let us refresh ourselves." Ramgirbua was suspicious about the driver's caste. Sensing his distrust the driver assured him thus: "I am not a Muslim. I am a Garhwali Rajput. There can be no objection to sharing food with me. Moreover, these refreshments are sent by Nanasaheb for you." Thus persuaded, the two of them had refreshments.

The driver now yoked the horse and they reached Jamner in the morning. On entering the town Nanasaheb's *kucheri* (office) was sighted. The tonga stopped for Ramgirbua to relieve himself. When he came back and looked around, the tonga, the horse and driver had all disappeared. Ramgirbua wondered what had happened. So he walked up to the *kucheri* and getting to know that Nanasaheb was at home, went to his residence and sat on the verandah. Nanasaheb called him in. Ramgirbua handed over to Nanasaheb the text of the *arati* and the packet of *udi* given by Sai Baba. At that moment Nanasaheb's daughter was in insufferable labour pains and *Navchandihavan* was being performed and *saptashati* was being recited. Nanasaheb called his wife and gave her *udi* for administered in water it to their daughter and himself started reciting the *arati* sent by Sai Baba. Just then a message came from the delivery room that as soon as the *udi*-water was given to the daughter, she safely delivered a child. Then Ramgirbua asked Nanasaheb, "Where is the driver of the tonga? I can't see him anywhere near. And where is the tonga?" Nanasaheb exclaimed, "Which tonga? How was I to know that you were coming so that I could send a tonga?" Hearing this Ramgirbua was astonished and narrated to Nanasaheb the whole account of his travel right from setting out. Nanasaheb too was agape with wonder and realised that it was all a *leela* of the master-actor Sai who had devised the whole plan for warding off the trouble of his devotee.

For the wife of Ramachandra Atmaram Tarkhad, Sai Baba assumed the forms of a hungry dog and pig. Eating the food offered by Mrs Tarkhad he expressed satisfaction and stressed the duty of a devotee to offer food to a guest, whether a human being or any creature, animal or bird, which is present. The incident occurred thus.

Once while she was in Shirdi it was meal time and food had been served in *thalis*. In the meantime, a dog came and stood there. Mrs Tarkhad served a piece of *bhakri* to the dog. Just then a hungry pig covered with mud arrived there. Mrs Tarkhad gave it a piece of *bhakri*. She did this naturally. In the afternoon at 3 p.m. when she went for Sai Baba's *darshan*, he said to her, "Mother, you fed me today and I was filled. I was hungry and you satisfied my hunger. Always act thus. I tell you, this alone will be useful to you in the end. This is the way to practise kindness. We should first give bread to the hungry before we eat. Remember this carefully." She could not follow what Sai Baba was saying. She said, "How could I have given you food here? I am myself dependent and eat whatever I get on payment of money." Sai Baba replied, "I am filled by partaking *bhakri* you served with love. When you had sat down for meal a dog suddenly came there and you fed it with *bhakri*. Then a pig covered with mud came and again you gave it *bhakri*. I am one with both of them. Inasmuch as you fed them you have fed me."

This very truth Sai Baba taught Lakshmibai Shinde, in his inimitable way. After the evening prayer, Sai Baba was once standing facing south, in the direction of the Marwadi's house and shop. Other devotees were also with him. In the meantime Lakshmibai Shinde came there and bowed at Sai Baba's feet. Sai Baba said to her, "I am hungry." Lakshmibai replied, "I will make a *bhakri* and bring it. Here I go and will be back soon." So saying she went and returned with *bhakris* and side dish (cooked

vegetable and *chatni*). She served the fare on a leaf and
placed it before Sai Baba. He picked it up and placed it
before a dog. Immediately Lakshmibai questioned him
thus: "Baba, what is this you have done? I went posthaste and making *bhakris* brought them to you which
you serve to a dog! I was under the impression you were
hungry. What kind of hunger is this? You did not even
taste a bit thereof and I fretted for nothing." Then Sai
Baba said to her, "Why grieve for nothing? Know that the
satisfaction of the hunger of a dog is feeding me. A
creature may be dumb or have speech, the hunger of both
is alike. Those who feed the hungry in fact feed me."

Sai Baba looked after not only the material well-
being of a devotee, but also his welfare. He also looked
after the spiritual welfare of animals. One morning Sai
Baba told Mrs Jog, "Mother, in the afternoon a she-
buffalo will come to your backdoor. Feed her well with
puranpolis with *ghee* applied to them." Mrs Jog faithfully
prepared *puranpolis*, offered *naivedya* to Sai Baba, and
in the afternoon noticed a she-buffalo standing at her
back door as said by Sai Baba. She was pleased and fed
the she-buffalo with *puranpoils* with *ghee* liberally
applied to them. She was at first happy that the she-
buffalo consumed *puranpolis* to her heart's content but
was upset when in a short time the buffalo sat down, was
indisposed and gave up the ghost. She examined all the
vessels used for cooking including the one in which *puran*
was cooked to see whether any foreign body or insect had
fallen into it, but found nothing of the sort. She was
fazed. For one thing, from a spiritual point of view, if the
buffalo had died because of being overfed, the sin of her
death would be on her head. On the other hand, from the
practical point of view if the owner of the buffalo came
there and got to know that she had died because of
feeding her *puranpolis*, he would hold Mrs Jog
responsible for her death. The protector of devotees is
ultimately the Lord. So she took refuge in Sai Baba and

apprising him of the facts admitted that she was disconcerted. Sai Baba assured her that there was no reason to worry. He said, "Her owner cannot harass you. Spiritually, you have committed no wrong. There was only one desire left in the buffalo, viz., to eat *puranpolis*. As soon as I saw this I satisfied her desire through you. She will be released from the *yoni* (class or nature) of buffalo and will get a good birth. There is no need for anxiety." With this explanation Mrs Jog realised that Sai Baba cared for the welfare not only of human beings but also of animals.

Sai Baba assumed the form of a black dog for Bala Shimpi as well as Mhalsapati, ate rice at their hands and cured them of chronic fever. Hansraj had asthama. In order to prevent him from eating curds Sai Baba, in the form of a cat, would lap up the curds. Therefore, Hansraj gave two blows to the cat, the marks of which Sai Baba showed on his body to the devotees. This incident has been described earlier. While Upasanibua was staying in the Khandoba temple, for accepting the *naivedya* Sai Baba assumed the form of a dog but Upasani shooed him away. Sai Baba had brought this to the notice of Upasani. Once while Upasani was cooking Sai Baba assumed the form of an old man and peeped in which was resented by Upasani. Sai Baba had indicated to Upasani that he was that old man and cautioned him not to do so again. A third time Sai Baba assumed some other human form and suggested to Upasani to drink warm water for his irregular breathing. This has also been referred to earlier.

The son of Ramachandra Atmaram Tarkhad was a sincere devotee of Sai Baba. Once his mother wished to go to Shirdi and the son wanted to accompany her. There was, however, an impediment in his way. He worshipped and offered *naivedya* to a photograph of Sai Baba regularly, so who would do the *puja* and offer *naivedya* in his absence? The father undertook the reponsibility. So the son went with his mother and the two of them stayed in Shirdi for some days. In between, on one occasion when the son and his mother went to the *masjid*, they bowed to Sai Baba and sat by him. Sai Baba said to them, "I had been to Bandra today as I do every day, but I did not get anything to eat or drink and had to return hungry. The door was closed yet I entered freely. Who was to stop me? The owner was not at home. I had to suffer pangs of hunger as I was not fed. I had to turn back in the heat of the sun." Hearing these words Tarkhad's son guessed that his father must have forgotten to offer *naivedya* to Sai Baba's photograph. So he wrote to his father at Bandra and came to know that the day on which Sai Baba had uttered the above words his father had forgotten to offer *naivedya*. By reminding the Tarkhad family thus, Sai Baba wanted to make them aware that the *naivedya* offered to him with love is accepted by him in the same spirit and hence the importance of being regular, for strengthening the bond between the devotee and his *aradhya-daivat*.

Sai Baba also assumed form not only to counsel his devotees but also to gladden their hearts or to satisfy their intense desire. In 1918 Gulveshastri went to Shirdi for Sai Baba's *darshan* with *ganga-jal* (Ganges water), and performed *abhishek* to Sai Baba with it. Then he asked leave of Sai Baba for going to Sajjangad of Samarth Ramdas Swami for Ramanavami.

Then Sai Baba said, "I am there as well as here." Gulveshastri proceeded to Sajjangad. On Ramanavami day Sai Baba gave him actual *darshan* and Gulveshastri performed *charan-seva* for a while. Thus satisfying him Sai Baba vanished.

Similarly when Damodar Ghanashyam Babre alias Anna Chinchnikar had come and stayed in Shirdi, his wife was alone at Chinchni. There was an outbreak of plague at Chinchni in the meanwhile and the servants of Chinchnikar had left. Mrs Chinchnikar was frightened.

Sai Baba gave her *darshan* ten to twelve times to assure and cheer her up.

When the wife of Vinayak Shankar Giridhar of Malad was down with pneumonia, Sai Baba appeared to her in the form of Lord Dattatreya and protected her.

Once, when R.B. Purandare's wife was unwell, Sai Baba gave her actual *darshan*, applied *udi* on her forehead and saved her. On the day of *vastushanti* (housewarming) when Purandare set out with Sai Baba's photograph, he had the exhilarating feeling of Sai Baba accompanying him with his *jholi* and *sataka* (baton), which lasted until he reached his house and put down Sai Baba's photograph. When Purandare's mother and wife felt an intense desire to go to Pandharpur for the *darshan* of Vitthal-Rakhmai, Sai Baba gave them *darshan* of Vitthal-Rakhmai in Shirdi itself.

The mother of Shankarrao, a friend of Shantaram Balwant Nachane, was a devotee of Vitthal of Pandharpur. She went to Shirdi but was disappointed as she could not go to Pandharpur. The *udi* given to her in Shirdi turned into *abir* (fragrant powder composed of sandalwood, zedoary, cyperus, rotundus, etc.) and she felt that her pilgrimage to Shirdi was the pilgrimage to Pandharpur.

Police Sub-Inspector Somnath Shankar Deshpande, son of Nanasaheb Nimonkar, once stayed in Shirdi in the absence of his father for the service of Sai Baba. Madhavrao Deshpande was sitting on a step of the *masjid* and Sai Baba was seated in his usual seat. Suddenly Sai Baba appeared to Somnath in the form of Maruti. There was the Maruti body. Only he did not see if Maruti had a tail. Seeing that form Somnath told Madhavrao at once to take Maruti's *darshan*.

To Adam Dalili of Bandra, Sai Baba once came as a Brahmin and begged for something, and a second time as a Marwadi who said he was hungry. The first time Adam gave him two annas and the second time he gave him four annas and sent him to a Marwadi hotel for his food. Later, when Adam went to Shirdi, Sai Baba dropped significant hints showing that he had visited Adam in those forms, and speaking about his second visit said, "When I went to this man he sent me to the Marwadi hotel to eat."

When Govind Keshav Rege was suffering from some acute ailment and lost all hope, Sai Baba appeared to him in the form of a *sannyasi* and assured him that he would get well from the third day, and it happened as Sai Baba had said. Many devotees have experiences of Sai Baba having assumed *sagunaroop* in their domestic difficulties, mental problems, spiritual conundrums and having helped them and removed their difficulties. Some of these experiences have been narrated earlier. But there are many experiences which flabbergast us. Let us note them here.

A devotee, Haribhau Keshav Karnik of Dahanu, alighted at Dhond while travelling from Shirdi to Pandharpur. He learnt there that the Passenger train ticket would have to be changed to a Mail ticket by paying the difference. There was very little time and he felt like evacuating his bowels. He was in a quandary as to whom he should entrust his baggage with while answering the call of nature and while getting his ticket changed. Suddenly, Sai Baba appeared to him in the form of *hamal* (porter), showed him the lavatory and looked after his baggage. By the time Karnik returned, it was time for the Mail to arrive. So the *hamal* said to Karnik, "Get into the train while I get your ticket." So saying he went to the second platform, exchanged the old ticket for the new and as the train started, gave Karnik his ticket and disappeared without asking for his porterage.

Shrikrishna Purushottam Patil of Andheri had gone to Akkalkot via Shirdi. On his return trip he decided to break the journey at Poona as he was short of money. He was to borrow some money from his friend in Poona and then proceed to Bombay. For the sake of this devotee, Sai Baba assumed the form of a Brahmin and appearing in Patil's compartment started a conversation with him. In the course of their talk, when the Brahmin came to know the reason of Patil's breaking the journey at Poona, he said, "There is an epidemic of plague in Poona. I will buy a ticket for you up to Bombay. After reaching Bombay send the cost of the ticket by money order." So saying he got off at Poona and got a ticket up to Bombay for him. Then he said that he would be back after having tea but never returned. He was not seen again by Patil. Thus protecting Patil from the incidence of plague in Poona, Sai Baba had purchased a ticket up to Bombay for Patil!

When Govind Raghunath alias Annasaheb Dabholkar first went to Shirdi, he got into the local train at Bandra Station thinking that the Manmad Mail stopped at Dadar. To give him correct information Sai Baba asssumed the form of a *Yavana* and got into his compartment as the train started. Seeing his luggage the *Yavana* asked Dabholkar whither he was bound. When Dabholkar told him that he intended to catch the Manmad Mail at Dadar, the *Yavana* informed him that the Manmad Mail did not halt at Dadar and that he should therefore proceed to Boribunder. So Dabholkar went to Boribunder where he found Hari Sitaram Dikshit waiting for him. On hearing Dabholkar's account Dikshit immediately appreciated Sai Baba's concern for Dabholkar even at his first visit to Shirdi.

The whole family of Harda's Honorary Magistrate, Krishnarao Narayan alias Chhotubhaiyya Paralkar, including his wife, sons, daughters-in-law, etc., started on a Sunday, Mahashivaratri Day, at 3 p.m. for the *darshan* of Siddhanath of Nemavar. As some fault developed in the wheel of the cart, they arrived late in the evening on the bank of the Narmada when it was dark. They had to cross over to the other bank of the river. The

cartman accompanying Paralkar tried to persuade the
boatman to ferry them across and promised him double
the money. But, being dark, fearing that ferrying them
across in violation of the law would expose him to
punishment, the boatman declined. All were
disappointed and Chhotubhaiyya's wife exclaimed,
"Baba, thy will be done" and asked the cartman to take
them to a temple for the night's halt. Just then a *fakir*
arrived there with his small white mare. He said to the
boatman, "I have come here after wandering the whole
day, ferry me across." The boatman also said "No" to the
fakir. Then the *fakir* approached Paralkar's cartman and
the following dialogue ensued between the two of them:

Fakir: Do you also want to cross over to the other
side?

Cartman: Yes.

Fakir: You should not have come so late.

Cartman: There was a fault in the wheel because of
which we were delayed.

Fakir: In whose territory are we?

Cartman: Where we are standing is British Indian
territory and on the yonder bank is Holkar's
territory.

Fakir: Does not matter. I will go to the station and get
a permit and the boatman will then willy-nilly
have to take us.

So saying the *fakir* went a dozen paces and vanished.
The boatman who had so far been refusing to ferry the
Paralkars across, now himself came and said, "Come, I
will ferry you across," and began picking up their
baggage. Because of her earlier experience
Chhotubhaiyya's wife said, "What will be your charge?
Let us fix it now." The boatman replied, "Madam, you
may pay me whatever you like. If you don't wish to pay,
don't, but now please get into the boat." The sudden
change in the conduct of the boatman, the Paralkars
attributed to the *fakir's* influence and they were

convinced that Sai Baba had assumed the form of the
fakir to remove the impediment in their way.

Sai Baba had assumed the form of a *gosain* for
Uddhavesh alias Saisuta Shyamdas. The facts are as
follows. After the pilgrimage of Dwarka, Narayan Lake,
Sudamapuri, Porbandar, Junagadh and Somnath,
Uddhavesh proceeded to Girnar. On a Thursday morning
he started climbing Girnar. He had covered some
distance when due to heat and thirst he fainted and fell
down. Fortunately for him he did not fall on the right side
or else it would have proved a fatal leap into the valley
below. An old woman and an assistant were
accompanying Uddhavesh. The assistant wished to rush
to the Ambaji Kund below to get some water for his
master when a *gosain* arrived there with a *lota* full of
water, and calling the old woman said, "Granny give him
this water to drink. What will he do without it?" The old
woman and the assistant had a passing doubt about the
gosain's caste when he said, "Give this water to him
without any reservation," and sprinkled some water on
Uddhavesh's face and stood near his head.

The sun was overhead and it was hot and no water
was easily available. So the old woman made Uddhavesh
drink the water. Then he regained consciousness and saw
the *gosain* standing by him. "Son, drink the whole of this
water. I am now busy and will see you on my way back,"
he said to Uddhavesh and went away. After about 45
minutes Uddhavesh felt refreshed. Slowly climbing the
steps, he had *darshan* of Lord Dattatreya's *padukas*, and
descending to the place where he had fainted, waited for
over an hour for the *gosain* to return. But he was never
seen again. Later when Uddhavesh went to Shirdi, to
remind him of the incident Sai Baba remarked, "Oh, I
have seen him often, also given him water to drink!"
From this remark Uddhavesh realised that the *gosain*
was none other than Sai Baba who had saved his life.

Sai Baba would assume that form which would be conducive to the spiritual progress of the devotees and gladden their hearts. Rao Bahadur Moreshwar Pradhan, after having stayed in Shirdi for many days, decided to prepare special *naivedya* and to invite devotees for the *naivedya* meal. Sai Baba consented and asking Pradhan to invite Babu, nephew of Dada Kelkar, said, "I will also come. Prepare *naivedya*." Next day, food was cooked for the *naivedya* meal. Babu was invited and all was set. *Thalis* were arranged, Sai Baba's being first, next being Babu's and then those of the other devotees. As the devotees were about to commence the meal, a crow came, picked up a *puranpoli* from Sai Baba's *thali* and flew away. Then Pradhan who was aware of Sai Baba's omniscience as well as other devotees knew that Sai Baba had kept his word by coming in the form of a crow.

God is ever ready to repay the debt to His devotees. There is no rule as to the manner in which He will repay it. The Almighty prefers the manner in which the work of a devotee will succeed or his calamity will be warded off. In March 1952 the trouble which Dr. Dhirajlal Shah of Baroda was facing was warded off by giving medical suggestions. Dr. Bansilal, thirty-five-year-old son of Dhirubhai, was suffering from pneumonia. There was no want of doctors, *vaids* and surgeons. Medical treatment and nursing were being well attended to. Thereby the pneumonia subsided but the fever continued regularly for two months. Best allopathic and ayurvedic treatment failed to make any difference to the fever.

Then it so happened that while Dr. Dhirajlal sat down for his prayer he saw a mass of pus in his son's body. Since his mind was under stress due to his son's condition, he dismissed the thing as a figment of his imagination and paid no attention. Moreover, such a thing was against medical opinion. The doctors were unanimous in their opinion that there was no pus in the body. But how would Sai Baba remain quiet? He brought the suspended mass of pus to the notice of Dr. Dhirajlal a second and then a third time. So Dr. Dhirajlal got an expert surgeon to carry out minute examination of Bansilal, and a four-ounce mass of pus was found in a suspected place. Then an operation was performed and after two pounds of pus were removed, Dr. Bansilal recovered rapidly.

Govind Raghunath alias Annasaheb Dabholkar, author of *Shri Sai-Sat-Charita* in verse form, had a dream on the day of *poornima* in *Falgun* (March) 1917. In the dream Sai Baba appeared in the garb of a *sannyasi*, and after saying, "I will be coming for lunch today," he vanished. Being the day of *Holi* festival Dabholkar had invited a few relations and friends for meals. Pursuant to the dream, Dabholkar also felt that Sai Baba would come as a guest in some form and partake of the meals. So he informed his wife of his dream and asked her to cook for one more guest.

At noon, *Holi puja* was performed according to the rites. Relatives and friends began arriving. *Rangoli* was drawn in front of the house, low stools were arranged for guests to sit and *thalis* were placed before them. In the centre of the main row, *rangoli* decoration was drawn round the bigger low stool and a *thali* placed before it. Food was served in all *thalis* and Dabholkar was waiting at the door for the guest of his dream to arrive. When told that the food had been served in all *thalis*, bolting the front door he came and was about to sit down for meals when there was a knock at the door and a voice was heard enquiring, "Is Raosaheb in?" Dabholkar went posthaste and saw two persons standing at the door: one was Ali Mohammed and another was Ismu Mujavar, Shagird of Saint Maulana. Seeing that Dabholkar had got up from his meals, they begged his pardon and, taking out a packet and removing its outer wrapping of newspaper, revealed an image of Sai Baba. "It is our earnest request to you to agree to keeping this." On seeing Sai Baba's image, the hair on Dabholkar's body stood on end and he was overcome with emotion. Bowing with love to the image, Dabholkar asked, "Where did you get this image?" Ali Mohammed said, "We purchased it in a shop." Then Dabholkar asked, "How were you inspired to bring the image to my place at this time? Tell me." Ali Mohammed replied, "It is a long story. As your family members are waiting for you to join them at meal I will narrate it to you at some other convenient time."

As the image arrived on the *Holi* festival day as indicated by Sai Baba, rites of installation of the image and its worship were gone through and thereafter all had their meals. From that time, every year on the *Holi* festival day this image is worshipped similarly every year.

Nine years after this incident, Dabholkar happened to meet Ali Mohammed, whom he questioned about the story of this image. Ali Mohammed said that he had purchased that image with love in the bazaar and had hung it along with photographs of other saints in his house. Then he fell ill and his house was under the care of his brother-in-law. The Murshid of his brother-in-law was Abdul Rahman who was against any images. So removing all pictures of saints in the house of Ali Mohammad he had them immersed in the sea at Chimbai near Bandra.

After getting well, when Ali Mohammed returned to his Bandra residence he did not hope to see any picture of holy persons, but to his utter surprise on the wall opposite the front door, he saw the image of Sai Baba on the wall as before. He wondered how this picture had escaped his brother-in-law's attention. So removing it from the wall he hid it in a cupboard lest it should meet the same fate as the other pictures at the hands of his brother-in-law. However, thinking that it was not convenient to keep it at his residence he had wanted to find for it a suitable household. So he and Ismu Mujavar had met in confidence and decided to present it to Dabholkar. So they had gone that day and at that hour to the latter's place. Inscrutable was the *leela* of Sai Baba that he had appeared to Dabholkar in his dream and informed him that he would come to his house for lunch in any form. Thus Ali Mahommed also got confirmation that his decision to present the image to Dabholkar was correct.

Sai Baba gave Appa Kulkarni an experience of how holy persons strive day and night for their devotees. In 1917, when the First World War was going on, government officials had to tour for recruitment of soldiers. At that time Kulkarni was transferred to Thane for this work. Balasaheb Bhate, a former Mamledar who had retired prematurely from service and settled down in Shirdi, had given a photograph of Sai Baba to Kulkarni which he worshipped daily. While he was posted at Thane, he had an intense desire to go to Shirdi for Sai Baba's *darshan*. But it was not possible for him to get leave. By inner vision Sai Baba became aware of his longing.

Now Kulkarni went on duty to Bhiwandi with the idea of camping there for eight days. Two days after he went, a strange thing happened at his residence in Thane. A *fakir* resembling the picture of Sai Baba came and stood at their door. So the inmates of the house asked him if he was Sai Baba. The *fakir* replied, "I am not Sai Baba. I am a servant of Sai Baba. On his order I have come to enquire about the well-being of the family." Then the *fakir* asked for *dakshina*. Kulkarni's wife respectfully offered him a rupee which he accepted. Giving her a packet of Sai Baba's *udi*, he said, "Keep this with the picture of Sai Baba. May God bless you. Sai Baba will be waiting for me." So saying he left.

On the same day Kulkarni had planned at Bhiwandi to go to the interior but he had to cancel his programme as his horse was unwell, and he returned to Thane in the afternoon. When he came to know that a *fakir* resembling Sai Baba had visited his house earlier in the day, he was upset that he had missed his *darshan*, and that only a rupee had been given him as *dakshina*. With a heavy heart he went out in search of the *fakir*. He searched in the *masjids* and *takias* (Muslim travellers resthouses) of the town but to no avail. Disappointed he returned home and had his meals.

Later he went out for a walk with his friend. After going some distance he saw a man approaching him rapidly and stopped. From his appearance he seemed to be the same *fakir* who had visited his home earlier in the day. As soon as the thought occurred to Kulkarni that the *fakir* resembled Sai Baba, the *fakir* extended his hand on which he placed a rupee. The *fakir* asked for more. Kulkarni had in all three rupees and his friend three, all of which he gave to the *fakir*. When the *fakir* asked for still more, Kulkarni said he would give him more if he accompanied them home. The *fakir* agreed and Kulkarni returned home with him and the friend. On returning home he gave him three more rupees yet the *fakir* was not satisfied. Then Kulkarni said, "I have a ten-rupee note but no change." Then the fakir asked for the ten-rupee note and as soon as he received it he returned nine rupees to Kulkarni and went away. Kulkarni had resolved in his mind to give *dakshina* of ten rupees. Thus, Kulkarni was pleased that to fulfil his resolve and to remove his anguish after being deprived of *darshan*, Sai Baba had appeared to him in this particular form.

For his devotee Balkrishna Vishwanath Dev, Mamledar of Dahanu, Sai Baba assumed the form of the trinity. A day for the concluding ceremony for the various religious observances of Dev's mother had been fixed up for which Dev proposed inviting a hundred to two hundred Brahmins. Dev also sent a respectful invitation to Sai Baba by writing to Bapusaheb Jog. Sai Baba said to Jog, "I always remember him who thinks of me

constantly. I do not require a coach, train or aeroplane to
travel. The moment a devotee calls out to me lovingly I
respond to him instantly. Write to him that I, you and a
third person[1] will go. The recipient will be happy." Jog
replied to Dev accordingly who was delighted.

Then it so happened that a month before the day fixed
by Dev for the concluding ceremony, a Bengali *goshala -
activist sannyasi* — visited Dahanu and the
stationmaster suggested to him to meet Mamledar Dev
for funds for his *goshala*. As luck would have it, Dev came
to Dahanu Station at that moment and on the Bengali
sannyasi being introduced to him Dev told him that he
would help him if he returned after three to four months.

The day of the concluding ceremony dawned. At 10
a.m. that day the aforesaid *sannyasi* got down from a
tonga opposite Dev's house. A little vexed, Dev remarked
to his son, "Do you notice that *sannyasi*? Instead of four
months he has come so soon after his last meeting for
funds for his *goshala*." Sending off the tonga the *sannyasi*
came in and reading the expression of restless
preoccupation on Dev's face said, "I haven't come for
money. Today I wish to have a meal." The following
dialogue then ensued between them.

> *Dev*: Regard this as your own house.
> *Sannyasi*: But I have two boys with me.
> *Dev*: No problem. It's good. There is yet time for the
>   meals. Tell me where you are putting up so that I
>   can send for you.
> *Sannyasi*: What is the necessity for sending for me?
>   What time shall I come?
> *Dev*: At noon come with the boys.

Accordingly at noon the Brahmins sat down for the
meals. The *sannyasi* also came with the two boys and the
three of them ate heartily. After the conclusion of the
meals, the guests were honoured with *pan, attar*
(perfume) and *gulabpani* and the gathering of Brahmins
dispersed. The *sannyasi* and his two companions also

departed. After all invitees had left, Dev wondered why Sai Baba who was to come with Jog and another had not turned up. With a sad heart Dev wrote to Jog at Shirdi why he was deceived by Sai Baba and why he had not kept his word.

Jog approached Sai Baba with Dev's letter. Before Jog could read the letter, Sai Baba exclaimed, "Ask him why he had invited me if he could not recognise me? Look, for the sake of my promise I will give up my life but my word will never go in vain. Does he remember that when I went unexpectedly in the garb of a *sannyasi*, he was afaid I would ask for funds? I removed his suspicion and told him that I would be coming only for meals with two others. Accordingly I joined in the meals with two others." Jog wrote a detailed letter to Dev on reading which, tears of joy flowed freely from his eye and he wondered silently at Sai Baba's mysterious *leela*.

That Sai Baba takes as much care of the son of a devotee after the devotee's death is seen from an experience of Shripad Balkrishna alias Baburao Dev published in *Shri Sai Leela* of September 1952 on pp. 35-39. On December 31, 1951, Dev fainted, fell down, sustained an injury and was hospitalised for many days. While a patient in the hospital he remarked to a friend named Shantaram who called on him—how could he expect to be as fortunate as the daughter of Nanasaheb Chandorkar for whom Sai Baba had sent *udi* at Jamner in 1905? Shantaram said, "Your father was a staunch devotee of Sai Baba and you are a dutiful son of your father. Why won't Sai Baba send *udi* for you from Shirdi?" Next day Shankarrao Lathore, a friend of Dev who visited him at the hospital said to him, "I returned from Shirdi only yesterday. While I was there I told Vitthalrao of the injury sustained by you in an accident and he has sent specially for you *udi* and *prasad* which I have brought with me." Dev was reminded of his conversation with his friend Shantaram a day earlier and he realised that though thirty-three years had elapsed since his *samadhi*, Sai Baba was as active and concerned about his devotees as he was when he was in flesh and blood.

Sai Baba always remarked, "Though the Spirit may depart from my earthly tabernacle, know this for certain that my bones will assure you from the *samadhi*, and not only I, but my *samadhi* will speak to you. It will communicate with whosoever takes refuge in it."[2] Devotees of Sai Baba experience the truth of this promise even today.

Sai Baba told Jog twenty-four hours before his *samadhi*, "I haven't shown you anything. Out of my three and a half *kalas*, I have'nt shown you even one-fourth thereof. However, people will have experience thereof hereafter." Jog interpreted this remark to mean that Sai Baba intended to give experience of his vast and mighty powers to devotees after his *samadhi*. Later, he came to know that by these words that Sai Baba was suggesting that he would become one with Om.

Seth Ratilal Chimanlal, inhabitant of Ahmedabad, residing at Tarkas Bhuwan, Relief Road, Shahpur, had an amazing experience of Sai Baba's powers. The incident took place on May 22, 1945. Seth Ratilal boarded the Madras Mail going to Ahmedabad at Adoni at 10 a.m. He was travelling by a second class[3] compartment in which his co-passengers were Jagadish Munshi, solicitor son of K.M. Munshi, his wife, Naidu, an agent of the Central Bank, and Gopalrao, a well-known cotton merchant and Chairman of the Cotton Marketing Committee. Nothing of note happened until 4 p.m. and all the above gentlemen passed time in playing cards, joking and chatting.

The Mail was now passing through the Nizam's territory and reached Gulbarga. Suddenly, without any overt cause Ratilal became uneasy in his mind. The country was then passing through the trauma of partition and Ratilal was aware that the Nizam's dominion had become a hotbed and centre of intrigue and militant activity. Whatever the reason, Ratilal was seized with anxiety. He tried to make his companions aware of his apprehensions but they laughed them off as being a figment of his imagination. Since Seth Ratilal had full faith in his inner prompting, he stopped participating in all light-hearted activity and started remembering and repeating the name of Sai Baba.

Half an hour must have thus passed and the train neared Gangapur station. Just then an armed gang raided the train and started looting and indulging in violence. Seeing this Ratilal's companions were no doubt frightened, but coming to their senses they joined Seth Ratilal in *namasmarana* of Sai Baba as the only way of salvation open to them at that time. Sai Baba immediately came to their rescue in a mysterious manner. He was seen to have assumed the form of a burly Pathan[4] and guarded Ratilal's compartment and created an optical illusion whereby the armed gang spread out to other compartments and directed their attention to passengers therein without causing any harm to Seth Ratilal and his co-passengers in the compartment! The train thus limped its way to Sholapur where statements of all the passengers were recorded by men from the Collector's office who had come to survey the damage caused by the Razakars' party. Then it came to light that only Ratilal's compartment had been spared by the armed raiders! How come? was the query on the tip of everyone's tongue. "All this is the grace of Sai Baba," said Seth Ratilal and his companions with one voice.

Balakram Mankar was employed as the head of a department in Makanji Khatau Cotton Textile Mills and was earning a good salary. After his wife expired he retired from worldly interests and settled down in Shirdi. After some time Sai Baba instructed him to stay by himself in Machhindergad for doing *tapas*, and gave him 10-12 rupees. Mankar was reluctant to leave Shirdi as he thought that he would be deprived of the *darshan* and the company of Sai Baba, but the latter told him that he would benefit by his spiritual discipline in Machhindergad. So Mankar proceeded there.

In Machhindergad Sai Baba once gave him actual *darshan* when Mankar was wide awake. Mankar asked Sai Baba, "Why did you send me so far away?" Sai Baba replied, "Your mind was restless while you were in Shirdi. So to steady your mind I directed you to go there. Earlier you thought that my existence was confined to the three and a half cubits length of this body in Shirdi. Look carefully now for yourself whether I am not there as well as in Shirdi. My object was to make you aware of this."

After the prescribed period of stay, Mankar left Machhindergad to go via Poona to his residence at Bandra, a suburb of Bombay. He proposed to travel to Dadar from Poona by train and stood in the queue before one of the windows at Poona Railway Station to purchase a ticket. An unbelievable thing happened there. An utter stranger, a barefooted Kunbi peasant with a piece of cloth worn around his loins, a *kambal* thrown across his shoulders and a rag tied round his head, who was far ahead of Mankar in the queue, purchased a ticket up to Dadar. Seeing Mankar, he approached him and enquired where he was going. As soon as Mankar said "Dadar", the Kunbi handed over a ticket up to Dadar to Mankar and told him that he suddenly remembered some urgent work in Poona due to which he had revised his plan at the last moment. Mankar gratefully accepted the ticket and put his hand in his pocket to take out the money with which to pay the Kunbi. In the meanwhile the latter disappeared in the crowd around and was lost from view. Mankar tried to search for him in vain. The train had pulled up on the platform. Mankar waited at the entrance of his compartment until the train steamed out of the platform. Who could have been the generous and desireless peasant who obliged him? He could only guess. Who else could it have been except the compassionate Master Sai Baba?

It is said of Narsi Mehta, the famous saint of Junagad, that when he had been to the bazaar to purchase *ghee* for *shraddha*, on being invited to a *bhajan*, he forgot all about *shraddha* at his home and the Lord had to assume the form of Narsi Mehta and attend the *shraddha* ceremony at his residence. This story shows that it is the covenant of the compassionate Lord that if you are in distress for His sake, He is ever anxious about you.

As per this dictum, for a teacher-devotee of his, Dattatreya P. Kandalgaokar, a resident of Dadar, Sai Baba had assumed the devotee's form! This devotee had started a *parayanan saptaha* (reading performed in seven days) of the *Pothi, Shri Sai-Sat-Charit*, and during this *saptaha* he would not go out of his house. So his daughter, staying at Bandra, would visit him every evening, taking along his night meal and would immediately go back. The *parayana* over, Kandalgaokar went out on the evening of the seventh day for making purchases for the concluding ceremony on the eighth day. His daughter came as usual and waiting for a long time left without meeting her father. It was dark by the time she reached Bandra station and the road to her residence was desolate and hence fearsome. Sai Baba was naturally concerned about the safety of his devotee's daughter and knew that she would be apprehensive. So he assumed the form of her father and joining her at Bandra reached her home. She pressed him to come in but he excused himself on the plea that he had to make a lot of preparations for the next day, and left.

Next day when the daughter visited her father she rebuked him for not coming in, in spite of her pressing invitation, and the devotee came to know that Sai Baba had assumed his form to ward off the fear of his daughter and see her home safely. Thus the devotee had an experience of the kindness, compassion and love of Sai Baba for his family and a recognition of having received the *saptaha* of *Shri Sai-Sat-Charit*.

For the concluding ceremony of a vow of Mrs Chandrabai R. Borkar, Sai Baba had given her *darshan* in the form of a *fakir* and begged for alms. When Chandrabai was at Pandharpur, she decided to observe *kokila-vrata* during the month of *Shravan* (July-August), and went to Kopargaon for the purpose. Every morning and evening she would do circumambulation of Dattaghat, when she had the feeling of having *darshan* of Sai Baba. Then on Thursday, a young fakir arrived at the Dattaghat and asked her for alms of *jaggery-bhakri* and garlic *chutney*. Chandrabai told him, "In the month of *Shravana* (July-August) we abjure garlic and onion from our diet. I have come here to hear the notes of a koel. How shall I serve you sweet *bhakri* and onion?" Even though she excused herself thus she was not sure whether she had done the right thing. So next day she proceeded to Shirdi and taking Mrs Jog with her went for Sai Baba's *darshan*. Immediately Sai Baba remarked, "She did not give me *jaggery-bhakri* and garlic *chutney* and has now come here." Chandrabai was now convinced that by giving her *darshan* and asking for alms, Sai Baba wanted to perform the concluding ceremony of her vow and muttered to herself, "I have come here to offer you alms." Jog's wife, without hearing her, said to Sai Baba, "She has come for your *darshan*." Sai Baba replied, "She is the sister of my seven births. Wherever I go she comes in search of me." It was as if he was suggesting that the store of the meritorious deeds of a *bhakta* compels him to perform the concluding ceremony of his vow by assuming a form.

For the sake of his devotee, Rao Bahadur S.B. Dhumal, after his *mahasamadhi*, by his invisible powers, Sai Baba had affixed overnight thousands of signatures of Dhumal on papers of the Nasik Local Board of which the latter was the President. One evening, the peon of the Local Board brought the papers for Dhumal's signature as usual. In the meantime, a visitor for whom Dhumal had much regard, came in and stayed talking with him till midnight. So the signing of papers had to be postponed till the next night. As Dhumal was going out of town for the day, he sent back the papers of the previous day without signing. When he returned that night, he found only that day's papers brought for his signature. When he called for the previous day's papers he found that they bore his signature. The peon had been sent away the previous evening and his presence was required during the signing as each signature had to be blotted by the peon. Yet thousands of signatures of Dhumal were found affixed to the papers. He had no other explanaton for it except the superhuman powers of the compassionate Sai Baba.

Shantaram Balwant Nachane had twice experienced that even after his *mahasamadhi* Sai Baba assumes a form. In 1926, his son Harihar alias Sainath, who was eight or nine months old, was playing with other children in the house. The older children were bursting crackers. A match lighted by one of the children which was thrown away fell on Harihar's clothes and his clothes caught fire. No one noticed what was happening to Harihar. His mother was engaged in some domestic chore. Suddenly a *fakir* appeared before her and pointing to the place where the children were playing said, "See what is going on there." She at once went there and noticed what had happened. With great presence of mind and resourcefulness she put out the fire. Though the front half of the frock was burnt, Harihar came off entirely unscathed without sustaining any burns. This was evidently due to the same cause as the sudden appearance of the *fakir*. The *fakir* disappeared as suddenly as he had appeared. The family of Nachane realised that the person who had appeared in the nick of time to caution Harihar's mother, was none other than Sai Baba.

The second wife of Nachane passed away in 1929. For immersion of her ashes and other obsequies Nachane wished to go to Nasik. Knowing that his devotee was in a confused state of mind due to grief at the loss of his wife, Sai Baba assumed the form of a peon and travelling with Nachane up to Nasik, right up to the twelfth day he remained with him, extended him sympathy and took enormous trouble for him. At Victoria Terminus Nachane found a fellow-passenger in a peon. Even before the train started the fellow passenger befriended him. The following conversation ensued between them:

Peon: Where are you going?

Nachane: Nasik

Peon: Why don't you carry any bedding? The nights are chilly.

Nachane: I find it unnecessary. I am in no mood to mind these things. It is eight days since my wife died leaving a three-year-old son to be taken care of by me.

The peon then called a friend and got a blanket and a bedsheet for Nachane.

Nachane: How can you get these things so quickly?

Peon: Our quarters are very near. It is the J.J. School of Arts. Have this bedding please.

Nachane: (Accepting the bedding) What is your name? May I know who you are?

Peon: I am a peon at that school. My name is Ganapati Shankar. You may go to sleep now. Have no anxiety. I am also going to Nasik. I shall wake you up when we reach Nasik

Nachane: What takes you to Nasik?

Peon: Simply to see Nasik. My Sahib is gone to Simla and I get this chance of travelling to Nasik.

Then Nachane lay down.

Peon: Do take good care of your money or if you like, I will keep it for you in this steel trunk of mine, if you give it to me.

Nachane handed over Rs.80 to him and went to sleep. At Ghoti Station the peon woke him up and both had tea together. The peon paid for both. They got off at Nasik Road Station and got into a bus. Then the peon told Nachane that he should not go to a *panda* (priest) as he would fleece him. He would settle everything for Nachane. Nachane agreed, accompanied the peon and did everything according to the latter's instructions. Then he attended on Nachane as a peon would till the twelfth day ceremony. The *panda* was not well informed, so the peon instructed him about the fine points of the ceremony. He also showed Nachane where to immerse the ashes. Accordingly, Nachane stood at that particular hollow and held the ashes in position by pressure of the hand so that they were dissolved as though they were sugar candy.

On the twelfth day the peon received a wire requiring his resumption of duty in Bombay. He accounted to Nachane for every pie given him and agreeing to call on Nachane at Andheri, parted.

After his return to Bombay, Nachane, seeing that his beneficent friend did not turn up, went to J.J. School of Arts to make enquiries with the Principal and the peons there, but he was told that there was no such person by that name known to them. Who was this person who had taken such enormous pains and rendered such splendid assistance to Nachane? Who else could it be but Sai Baba?

In 1942, when the Quit India Movement was going on, a Sai-devotee, in order not to get entangled in any

undesirable activity, decided to leave Bombay and went
to get a railway ticket. In such a situation Sai Baba
assumed the form of a Pathan, purchased a ticket for him
and arranged for his accommodation in a compartment.
On his reaching Surat, Sai Baba appeared to him in the
form of a Victoria-driver and said to him, "Come, I know
your place. I will take you home. Pay me whatever you
like." The driver then seated him in his Victoria and
drove him home. On reaching his place the devotee asked
the driver, "What shall I pay you?" "Give me the eight
annas in your pocket," was the reply. The fare in those
days was actually Rs. 1.50 to Rs. 2. Gladly accepting
what was given the driver disappeared and was never
seen again.

Notes

1. The third individual was none other than the present writer -
    Swami Sai Sharan Anand, formerly known as Vaman
    Prangovind Patel. The translator came to know this fact on
    enquiry.
2. *Shri Sat-Sat-Charit*, chap. XXV, verses 105-106.
3. In those days there were four classes of railway travel,
    namely, first class, second class, intermediate class and third
    class.
4. Seth Ratilal saw a Pathan outside his compartment - *Shri
    Saileelakhyana* (Gujarati) by Swami Sai Sharan Anand, Chp.
    23, verses 79-83.

14. UDI

'Mirthful sportive Ram has come, has come with sackfuls of *udi*'. This refrain only, he (Sai Baba) would sing at his own sweet will, full of joy.

Shri Sai-Sat-Charita, XXXIII, 29

The holy meritorious, off-white ash produced by the perpetually burning *dhuni* in the *masjid*, which Sai Baba would apply on the forehead of his devotees when they approached him for taking leave to depart, he would call *udi*. 'U' (as in full) means up and 'i' (as in pin) means to go. Learned men interpret 'i' also to mean go up, ascending on high, soaring into the heavens. So that which causes the dawn of good fortune in this and the other world for devotees of Sai Baba is called *udi*. She is the mother of Sai devotees, the divine Kamadhenu (legendary cow mentioned in the *Mahabharata*). She removes sufferings, destroys fear and calamity, gets rid of pain or sorrow, does not burn and ever gives happiness. It is not pungent, bitter, sour or saltish to the taste but sweet and pleasing. It has divine medicinal or healing virtues, and it destroys laziness, dullness of understanding, disease, sin, etc. Sai Baba has created it out of great compassion for the welfare of his devotees. If it is always taken with singular devotion and loving heart, there is no doubt that it leads to salvation.

It has been stated earlier that initially Sai Baba would dispense medicines to patients, but later he commenced administering to all *udi* from the perpetually burning sacred fire. The refrain quoted at the beginning of this chapter is the line which was mouthed by Sai Baba.

Many devotees have experiences of patients having been completely cured of mental disorders, intoxicating influences of spirits or drugs, lunacy, nightmare, hemiplegia, labour pains, cholera, plague, tuberculosis, paralysis, rheumatism in the joints, dropsy, diabetes, typhoid, pneumonia, scabies, lice in the hair, chest boil or tumour, intestinal disorders, chronic osteomyelitis, appendicitis, insomnia, snakebite, scorpion bite, etc. - in fact, from the most simple to the most complicated diseases. It is not possible to give a complete list of patients and their diseases for lack of space. But devotees continue to get experiences even after the *nirvana* of Sai Baba by partaking of *udi*. Taking refuge in Sai Baba and partaking of *udi* with loving devotion, certainly proves beneficial. It will, however, be apposite to give a few experiences here.

Vasudeo, the son of Shantaram Balwant Nachne, ate some Pharaoh's serpents thinking them to be peppermints. As a result Vasudeo experienced a stinging sensation and his tongue was protruding. He was taken to a doctor who administered an emetic which did not act. Then Nachne gave Sai Baba's *udi* and *tirtha* which acted at once and he vomited all the poisonous stuff which he had swallowed.

By partaking of *udi*, childless women are known to have got children, and lactating women having no milk in their breasts, having milk.

A lady in the household of Hasmukhlal Wadilal, Banker of Lakha Patel Pol, Sankdi Sheri, Ahmedabad, a M.B.B.S. lady doctor and a female teacher from Baroda, by partaking of *udi* and remembering Sai Baba, delivered safely within fifteen minutes.

Udi is also useful in the delivery of female cattle. One such instance is narrated by Rajaballi Mohammad of Turner Road, Bandra, in his statement dated September

27, 1936[1] thus: "Five years back, my she-buffalo was in great travail, in trying to calve. Pained at her suffering, I sent for the veterinary surgeon. He tried his best, especially as I was the Chairman of the Sanitary Committee of the Municipality, he would be glad to help me in such a difficulty. But he could do nothing. Then I remembered Baba's *udi*. I placed some *udi* on the head of the buffalo and hoped that Baba would kindly come to its aid. In about ten minutes, she safely calved; there was no more trouble. There are numerous cases in which I have used Baba's *udi*, with signal success. I take it myself in this way. I apply a bit of it over my chest, eyes, forehead and think of Baba. Then all my difficulties are overcome."

That Annapoorna Devi (a name of Parvati or Bhawani - akin to Anna Perenna of the Romans, hence applied to a female cook under whose management the daily provision seems blessed and increased) could be invoked through Sai Baba's *udi* was experienced by the wife of the devotee Bala Nevaskar for whose death anniversary guests were invited for meals. On that occasion three times the number of guests expected arrived. So, on the instruction of Bala's mother, his wife put a fistful of *udi* in all the vessels of cooked food which were covered, and the covers were partially lifted only for serving. Thus, not only all the guests were fed but the quantities cooked still remained in the vessels.

The most remarkable experience of *udi* was that of Pradhan in 1932. A resident of Sandhurst Road, Bombay, he was employed as a clerk in the Revenue Department. His youngest son had high fever for four days. Then his pulse became slow and irregular and suddenly stopped. An M.B.B.S. doctor who examined him pronounced him dead. Pradhan was frightened but could not believe that his son was dead. He still had hope. So, he applied Sai Baba's *udi* to the forehead of his son, and, holding Sai Baba's photograph before his son, prayed fervently. The doctor remarked that all this was useless as his son's life had already departed. Pradhan replied, "Sai Baba is God. He will save my son." Thus forty-five minutes passed. Then the boy suddenly revived, sat up and began playing as if nothing had happened.

Notes

1.   *Devotees' Experiences of Sri Sai Baba*, Part II, pp. 91-92.

15. DAKSHINA

Works of sacrifice, gift and self-harmony should not be abandoned, but should indeed be performed; for these are works of purification.

Bhagavad Gita, XVIII, 5
(translation by Juan Mascaro)

Acts of sacrifice, almsgiving and austerity should not be given up: their performance is necessary, for sacrifice, almsgiving and austerity are a means for purification to those who rightly understand them.

Bhagavad Gita, XVIII, 5
(translation by Swami Prabhavananda
& Christopher Isherwood)

For pleased with thy sacrifice, the gods will grant to thee the joy of all thy desires. Only a thief would enjoy their gifts and not offer them in sacrifice.
Holy men who take as food the remains of sacrifice become free from all their sins; but the unholy who have feasts for themselves eat food that is in truth sin.

Bhagavad Gita, III, 12-13
(translation by Juan Mascaro)

Please the devas:
Your prayer will be granted.
But he who enjoys the devas' bounty
Showing no thanks,
He thieves from the devas.
Pious men eat

What the gods leave over
After the offering:
Thus they are sinless.
But those ungodly
Cooking good food
For the greed of their stomachs
Sin as they eat it.

Bhagavad Gita, III, 12-13
(translation by Swami Prabhavananda
& Christopher Isherwood)

'In this southern direction which is your deity?'
'Yama'. 'In what is Yama based?' 'In sacrifice'. 'In
what is sacrifice based?' 'In faith. It is as a result of
faith that the host gives *dakshina*. In faith is
dakshina based.' 'In what is faith based?' 'In the
heart. Because through his heart does a man
understand. Faith is based in the heart.'

Brihadaranyaka Upanisad, 3.9.21

The basic principles we can deduce from the quotations
are:
1. Works or acts of sacrifice, *dan* (gift/almsgiving/
   liberality to the poor/offerings presented) and *tapas*
   (austerity) are not to be abandoned but practised.
   These purify a learned/wise man.
2. Gods gratiated by acts or works of sacrifice will
   grant your desires/prayers. So know him to be a
   thief who enjoys their gifts without offering thanks
   to them.
3. Sacrifice is based on *dakshina* (offerings
   presented). It is satisfied through *dakshina*.
   Dakshina is based in faith, which means belief in
   God with a desire to offer with devotion.
4. A devotee should not go to God or *Guru* empty-
   handed.

There is no religion or sect in this world which does
not praise selfless *dan*. In Hinduism, the *shrutis*, the

smritis and the *Puranas* are one on this point. The difference of opinion can arise only about the place of *dan* and the worthiness of the recipient. The commonly accepted principle is that according to one's capacity, *dan* should be made at the appropriate time and place to a worthy person or cause. It may at once be stated here that a man of tranquil wisdom or who has overcome the three *gunas* (forces), or is firmly established and absorbed in Brahman is undoubtedly worthy of *dan*. Such *dan* is conducive to the welfare of the donor. The way of a devotee is different. He to whom everything is God personified or a manifestation of God, no blame attaches if he accepts *dan*. It is hardly necessary to state that he is beyond the commonly accepted principle of place, time and worthiness.

Those who have attained the perfect stage are without any desire. They rarely ask for or accept *dakshina*. Initially Sai Baba also did not accept *dakshina* from anyone. In spite of refusal, if anyone left *dakshina*, just as *dakshina* in a temple in an uninhabited forest is taken away by anyone, so also, the *dakshina* left before Sai Baba would be taken away by anyone. Even when he started accepting *dakshina*, he would not accept more than two pice. But in the last ten years of his life there was a sudden spurt in the number of persons visiting him. Then he would accept anything from one pice to Rs. 500-1000 at one time. He would rarely accept a currency note, and, if he did, would immediately convert it into coins. He would accept *dakshina* only by day. After evening he did not accept *dakshina* and whatever was the collection of the day would be disbursed by nightfall. At night nothing would remain. He would distribute about Rs. 75-100 every day as under: Bade Baba or Fakir Baba Rs. 30 to 55, Tatya Patil Rs. 15-25, Little Amani Rs. 2, Jamala Rs. 6, Dada Kelkar Rs 5, Bhagi Rs. 2, Sundari Rs. 2, Bayaji Patil Rs 4, Lakshmibai Rs. 4, and the *fakirs* and poor people at least Rs. 8. He would purchase baskets of fruits when available and distribute them. Chakra Narayan, Christian Fouzdar of Kopargaon in 1918 observes in his statement, "He was clearly and unmistakeably unattached... Whatever he got, he scattered with a liberal hand. When he died, we took possession of his cash; that was only Rs 16. Yet daily he was paying or giving away hundreds of rupees. Often we noticed that his receipts were smaller than his disbursements. Wherefrom came the excess for him to disburse or pay? We could not make out. This made me conclude that he had divine powers."[1]

Sai Baba did not ask everyone for *dakshina*. Nor did he accept *dakshina* from all. If anyone went for his *darshan* with a resolution to give a particular amount Sai Baba would remind him if he gave less to fulfil his resolve. If any devotee sent *dakshina* through some other devotee and if the other devotee forgot to hand it over to Sai Baba, the latter would remind him and recover that amount. From anyone who would go merely with the object of testing him and not giving him *dakshina*, Sai Baba would not ask for *dakshina*. The wife of one such person who returned home without having given any *dakshina* to Sai Baba, saw in a dream, her husband's wallet fall in the lavatory receptacle. She narrated the dream to her husband who, being filled with penitence, sent that money to Sai Baba by money order. Sai Baba also did not accept *dakshina* from such person who had become *sattvic* and purified by giving *dan* generously, and who had not much to benefit by such *dan* to him. If any person who had vowed to pay a certain amount to a deity was remiss in carrying out his obligation, Sai Baba would ask him for that exact amount and save him from the sin of plighted word. The experience of the visitor from Goa narrated earlier bears this out. Even towards a person who would not give *dakshina* when asked, Sai Baba's behaviour would be as kindly as before and it would not undergo any change. Sai Baba who would look

after the material well-being of a devotee visiting Shirdi,
would, in order to reduce the latter's greed and purify
him would also say, "I don't accept anything gratis from
anybody. For one I return tenfold and raise him on the
path of knowledge, etc."

Sometimes Sai Baba indicated by asking for *dakshina*
the raise due to a devotee in the pipeline. Rao Bahadur
Sathe who got an increase of Rs. 50, Daji Hari Lele who
too got an increase of Rs. 50 and Somnath Deshpande
who received an increase of Rs. 10 had an experience of
this when they went for Sai Baba's *darshan*.

In 1917 Gajanan Narvekar was getting high fever.
He sent his son to Shirdi with a *dakshina* of Rs. 500. As
soon as this *dakshina* was paid to Sai Baba, immediately
Sai Baba started shivering and got fever. A devotee who
was sitting by Sai Baba said to him, "How is it that you
have got fever?" Sai Baba said, "I have to carry the
burden of him whose *dakshina* I accept." Once when Rao
Bahadur Moreshwar Pradhan was in Shirdi, he gave a
dakshina of Rs. 500 to Sai Baba. How Sai Baba
undertook the responsibility of taking care of his whole
family has been described before.

It is not as if by asking for *dakshina* Sai Baba merely
removed the worldly sorrows of devotees or looked after
the material well-being of devotees. Many devotees have
experienced many a time that Sai Baba asked for
dakshina to stress some moral principle or to suggest the
usefulness of some spiritual practice. We have already
referred to the experiences of Mule Shastri and
Annasaheb Dabholkar. Now we will examine the
experiences of some other devotees visiting Shirdi.

When Raghuvir Bhaskar Purandare of Perry Road,
Bandra, visited Shirdi, he was fond of worshipping and
praying to Lord Vishnu. Sai Baba encouraged him to
continue this *upasana*. Whenever he went to Shirdi, Sai
Baba would ask him for *dakshina* of only two rupees.
Once Purandare asked him why he always asked for Rs 2

only. Sai Baba then said, "It is not these rupees I want. I want *nishta* (concentrated faith) and *saburi* (patience combined with courage)." Purandare replied, "I have already given these." Sai Baba told him, "Keep up *nishta* and be strict and anxious to fulfil all promises. You should always have truth with you. Then I will always be with you, wherever you are and at all times."

In 1914 when Prof. G.G. Narke had stayed in Shirdi for 13 months, Sai Baba asked him several times for *dakshina* of Rs 15. Narke had no money at that time as he was without employment and Sai Baba knew that fully well. So when he was with Sai Baba alone, Narke said to him, "You know I have no money and why do you ask me for Rs 15 dakshina?" Sai Baba answered that he knew Narke's impecunious condition well enough. "But," he added, "you are reading *Yoga Vashista* now. The part you are reading is specially important. Get me Rs 15 *dakshina* from that." Getting money out of reading *Yoga Vashista* and deriving valuable lessons therefrom and giving the money to Sai Baba meant of course lodging the lessons in his heart, where Sai Baba stayed as his *Antaryami* (inner Controller).

In 1915, a vaccinator, Tryambak Govind Samant, a devotee of Ganesh, went to Shirdi for Sai Baba's *darshan*. He had only five rupees with him. He gave one rupee by way of *dakshina* to Sai Baba. Sai Baba asked him for one more rupee but Samant was reluctant to give that. Sai Baba was, however, determined to get that one rupee out of him. So a verbal tug of war between the two went on for some time and ultimately Samant parted with one more rupee. Then turning the two rupees upside down Sai Baba had a good look at them and placing his hand on Samant's head said, "You have given these two rupees to the one-lettered (God). Now you may go. Ganu Mahar will bless you." But Samant did not understand then the meaning of these words of Sai Baba.

Samant had performed one crore *japa* of the mono-syllabled *mantra* of Shri Ganesh. By his blessing Sai Baba had reminded Samant that he had appeared to him when the latter was twenty-one years old in the form of Ganu Mahar and initiated him into this mono-syllabled *mantra*. But Samant was upset at having had to part with one rupee more to Sai Baba and in the rush of going to Bombay, could not make head or tail of Sai Baba's blessing.

As Samant came to the main road after leaving Shirdi, he learnt that all the tongas going to Kopargaon had left. And, as he had no faith then in Sai Baba, he was more agitated as a result of this. Just then a tonga came from Rahata. A Gujarati gentleman was seated in it. He stopped the tonga and asked Samant to get into it. Samant forgot that he did not have sufficient money on his person. Then the following conversation ensued between them.

Gujarati: Well, have you been to Sai Baba?

Samant: Yes.

Gujarati: What a *fakir!* You give him one and he asks you for more!

Hearing this Samant was astonished. It was as if the gentleman was echoing the thoughts in his own mind. He wondered how he could know them.

On reaching Kopargaon, the Gujarati gentleman paid the tonga fare and also purchased a ticket up to Dadar for Samant. Then spreading out a towel on the platform, both of them sat down to a good repast and travelled together up to Dadar. Before alighting at Dadar Station Samant asked the gentleman for his name and address. The gentleman replied, "My name is Ganu Marwadi. I stay on the upper storey of the *chawl* behind the *Masjid* station." Samant noted the address and returned to Bassein at 9 p.m. Next day, he went to the address given by Ganu Marwadi for returning his money. There the

whole population was Muslim and, of course, Ganu
Marwadi could not be traced.

Samant now began to think seriously over the
matter. He recollected that when he was twenty-one
years old he was going from Triambakeshwar to some
other place and he had to pass through a forest. Some
robbers had then caught him, taken him to a cave and
threatened to kill him. At that time he had prayed
fervently to Shri Gajanan and he heard a voice calling
out 'Jai Malhari', and he had been freed from the hands of
the robbers. A second time when he missed his way in the
forest he had prayed to Shri Ganesh and a man afflicted
by black leprosy stood before him and said, "My name is
Ganu Mahar. You have missed your way. I will show you
the way but you must not turn back and see." On
agreeing to this Samant ahead with Ganu Mahar behind
went on conversing all the time. When they reached the
correct way Ganu Mahar suddenly ceased speaking. So
Samant turned and looked back but there was no one.
This experience also came back to his mind when he
thought of the past coolly. Now with the latest experience
of Ganu Marwadi he was convinced that he who had
freed him from the clutches of the robbers, Ganu Mahar
who met him in the forest and Ganu Marwadi who paid
for him to reach home without spending any money, were
three forms assumed by none other than Sai Baba.
Thereafter, Samant began worshipping Sai Baba in the
form of Ganapati.

On reading the description of *samsar* (worldly life) in
the books on Vedanta philosophy, Hari Sitaram alias
Kakasaheb Dikshit, thought that the illustrations such
as rope-serpent, gold and ornaments, earth and earthen
vessels, are not of one kind. Even though rope-serpent
means a rope, it appears to us as a serpent; similarly
even though Brahman, the world does not appear to us as
such. In the mirage the vapour floating over sands
appears at a distance like water. Gold, when beaten into

shape by a goldsmith, is turned into golden ornaments. Earth, when shaped by a potter, becomes an earthen vessel. Out of the four illustrations, in the first two, the thing which is in a particular position does not appear as it is but as something different; but in the last two illustrations gold and earth out of which the things referred are made, are clearly seen. Dikshit was perplexed as to which of these illustrations are applicable to the worldly life. Even after thinking he could not come to a satisfactory conclusion. He desired intensely to know the truth.

In the meantime a man came from Sai Baba with a message that he wanted a hundred rupees from Dikshit. Dikshit had only one rupee with him at that time. So explaining the position to the messenger, Dikshit sent his prostrations to Sai Baba. After the messenger lℯft, it occurred to Dikshit that Sai Baba clearly knew through his inner vision who had how much money. Here there was no one having a hundred rupees with him. So the doubts which had arisen in his mind on reading the books on Vedanta must have had something to do with the figure of one hundred. With this thought uppermost in his mind, Dikshit prayed before Sai Baba's photograph for guidance.

Within five minutes of his prayer the meaning became clear to him and his doubt was resolved. It occurred to him that there is no inconsistency between the two sets of illustrations and both of them are applicable to the *samsar*, and they indicate different aspects. *Samsar* is like one hundred. Hundred means one with two zeroes. Similarly *samsar* is existence. Or Brahman and the illusory world of name and form are superimposed on it. The illustrations of gold and ornaments, earth and vessels, indicate that the basic substance is the ground. Just as there is gold in the ornaments thereof, and earth in the vessel made from it, similarly the ground is the Spirit and it is indestructible

and not illusory. Even if these zeroes disappear there is
no danger or harm caused to the One. Name and form are
illusory, and as they only appear, they are zeroes. Rope-
serpent and mirage are the illustrations indicating this.
Like name and form, the rope and water are illusory and
only appear, i.e., they are also zeroes. Thus Dikshit was
convinced of the appropriateness of these two types of
illustrations.[2]

Another time Dikshit was sitting by Balasaheb Bhate
and reading the second chapter of *Eknathi Bhagwat*.
During this reading Gopalrao alias Bapusaheb Buti
brought a message for Dikshit that Sai Baba had called
him for a *dakshina* of sixteen and a half rupees. This
time, too, Dikshit had no money with him except a rupee
given to him by Sai Baba on Guru Poornima day. Buti
had been directed by Sai Baba to sit by Dikshit and listen
to the reading from *Eknathi Bhagwat*. From all this
Dikshit guessed that the answer to the sixteen and a half
rupees puzzle must be in the reading of that day's part of
the *Eknathi Bhagwat*. Buti sat there as directed.

When the remaining part of *Eknathi Bhagwat* was
being read, the stanza '*kayena vacha,* etc.', also came. In
this part King Janaka has asked what is *Bhagwat
Dharma* and out of Brahman-knowing nine sons of
Rishabh, the eldest son gave an exposition of the
Dharma. The essence of this exposition is found in the
stanza '*kayena vacha,* etc.' which means 'Whatever I do
through my body, speech, mind, organs, intellect, ego as
well as nature (*prarabdha-karma* at birth), I offer to
Narayan who is beyond everything, after pronouncing
His Name.'

As soon as the reading of the extensive and
instructive commentary of Eknath was completed, a
messenger from Sai Baba came to call Buti. So Dikshit
was further strengthened in his belief that there must be
a connection between this stanza and sixteen and a half
rupees. So he began mentally adding up the things

mentioned in the stanza which totalled 15 1/2: body 1, speech 1, mind (*manas*) 1, organs 10, intellect (*buddhi*) 1, ego 1, nature 1/2. But Sai Baba had asked for 16 1/2 rupees. So on scrutinising the commentary of Eknath, he understood that though there is mention of *chitta* (discursive faculty including memory) in the original stanza, in Eknath's commentary on this stanza there is exposition also on *chitta*. If added to the above sum the total works out to 16 1/2. From this Dikshit understood that Sai Baba's object in asking for Rs. 16 1/2 *dakshina* was that all these 16 1/2 things must be offered to the Lord.

It also occurred to Dikshit that Sai Baba had asked him to get not 16 but 16 1/2. So what was the reason for his putting emphasis on this 1/2 rupee, i.e., nature? On deep thinking it appeared to him that even in this Sai Baba's purpose was to centre his attention on one special principle. It is possible to offer whatever actions other organs perform consciously. But Eknath has shown the way to offer the actions which happen automatically according to one's own nature and in which there is no purpose and hence are difficult to offer to God. It is worth remembering. Instead of thinking that I offer to God this action which I have performed, it is best to regard that God is the doer of this action and I am only the instrument. Just as a *munim* engages in trading worth crores of rupees not of his own but on behalf of his master, similarly all these actions which happen through me are God's. If this feeling is cultivated desirelessness and selflessnes will also develop. And when this takes place, the action being His whether it is conscious or natural, the resolution to offer everything to God will not be necessary. Thus Dikshit understood in entirety Sai Baba's purpose in asking for *dakshina* for Rs. 16 1/2.

Uddhaveshbua alias Shyamdas of Dahanu, also had an experience of being instructed by Sai Baba through the latter's demand for *dakshina*. We have seen in

Chapter XI that when Uddhaveshbua started on a
pilgrimage to Dwaraka, while taking out his wallet from
his pocket, it fell into the sea and he was naturally upset.
Yet he attempted to read *Jnaneshvari* as per his usual
practice but could not concentrate in the given
circumstances. So he resolved that, unless Sai Baba told
him, he would not read any *Pothi-Purana*. It was easy for
Uddhaveshbua to carry out this negative resolve.

After returning from the pilgrimage to Dwaraka,
Uddhaveshbua went to Shirdi but Sai Baba did not give
him any instructions. Then he returned home and
continued with his negative resolve. Two to three years
passed thus during which there was no occasion for
Uddhaveshbua to visit Shirdi. Still he would through his
letters manage to get Sai Baba's blessings and *udi* from
Shirdi.

Once he wrote to Chidambar Keshav Gadgil,
Mamledar who was then at Shirdi with the object of
getting Sai Baba's blessings and *udi*. Gadgil read out
that letter to Sai Baba and asked what reply he should
send. Sai Baba said, "Call him here soon." Gadgil wrote
accordingly to Uddhaveshbua who presented himself
before Sai Baba within seven to eight days.

The next day after his arrival Uddhaveshbua went to
worship Sai Baba who asked for a *dakshina* of eleven
rupees and Uddhavesh paid it. Every day continuously
for ten days Sai Baba went on asking him for eleven
rupees and Udhaveshbua went on paying. On the
eleventh day when Sai Baba asked for eleven rupees,
Uddhavesh said, "My ten organs and mind, I offer to
you." Sai Baba replied, "They are mine anyway. Who are
you to offer? I have already taken them." Then seeing
Uddhaveshbua's firm faith, Sai Baba said to him, "Go to
Bapusaheb Jog in the afternoon, ask him for eleven
rupees and bring him here."

At 3.30 p.m. Uddhaveshbua went to Jog, conveyed to
him Sai Baba's message and after listening to the

reading of *Eknathi Bhagwat* went in the evening to Sai Baba with Jog. But Sai Baba did not talk either with Uddhaveshbua or Jog. This happened continuously for three days.

On the fourth day when Uddhaveshbua went with Jog to Sai Baba, after listening to the reading of *Eknathi Bhagwat*, Balasaheb Bhate was sitting there. Sai Baba asked Jog, "Well, Bapusaheb, how much did you spend today?" Jog said, "Sixty-one rupees." "How?" asked Sai Baba. Jog replied, "I gave fifty rupees to Buti and eleven to Uddhaveshbua." Then turning to Uddhaveshbua, Sai Baba asked, "Have you got your eleven?" Uddhaveshbua replied in the affirmative but interrupting him Sai Baba said, "No, no, you haven't got them. Let us see tomorrow. Read the *Pothi* too." When all the three of them returned to the *wada*, Bhate asked Uddhaveshbua what the whole matter about eleven rupees was. Uddhaveshbua told him that though he had said 'Yes' to Sai Baba he had not understood the deeper meaning of Sai Baba's statement, but he was trying to find out. After some thinking Uddhaveshbua felt that Sai Baba's reference to eleven rupees must be concerned with his decision not to read any *Pothi-Purana* unless Sai Baba directed him to do so.

Next day at 3.30 p.m. while Uddhaveshbua was engaged in *charan-seva* of Sai Baba, the latter asked him, "Have you got your eleven rupees?" Uddhaveshbua said, "If you are speaking with reference to the reading of *Pothi*, I have understood. But which *Pothi* should I read?" Sai Baba replied. "Read that *Pothi* in which there is a dialogue between you and me." Uddhaveshbua did not understand and asked, "Shall I read the *Bhagavad Gita*?" Again Sai Baba said, "Read only that in which you and I talk to each other." Uddhaveshbua thought that Sai Baba was asking him to read not Gita but *Jnaneshvari* as before. As soon as this thought arose in his mind Sai Baba said, "Go to Bapusaheb and get the *Pothi*." From that it became clear to him that Sai Baba was asking him to read *Eknathi Bhagwat*.

When Uddhaveshbua went to Jog as directed, Jog was getting ready to read the *Pothi*. Uddhaveshbua took the *Pothi* from Jog and went to Sai Baba. Sai Baba took the *Pothi* in his hands and opened it at the eleventh chapter. Pointing to it, Sai Baba said, "Take, read this. Read as it is and think of the meaning when alone. Listeners do not require the meaning. For them you should read as it is. Now go. Keep taking my name daily." The joy that Uddhaveshbua experienced was indescribable. At that time some devotees who were present there were discussing whether the *guru* ever tells to read or recite a particular *Pothi*. They were also satisfied by Sai Baba's reply as it conveyed to them the message that as the faith of the devotee, likewise is the experience that the *guru* gives to him. The *guru* stimulates the faith of the devotee and never misses the chance to suggest a way conducive to the devotee's welfare. There are no fixed rules in this matter. Beyond all rules is the rule of singular devotion and it is by singular devotion that the *guru* is won over.

Once Ramachandra Atmaram Tarkhad went with his family to Shirdi and gave as *dakshina* the sum he had taken for the purpose. But even thereafter Sai Baba entreated his wife to give him *dakshina* of six rupees. As she had no money of her own, when she returned to the place of her halt she started crying. When Tarkhad asked her why she was crying, she narrated her predicament. Tarkhad explained to her that Sai Baba did not want silver rupees but six enemies (vices)[3] of man to be offered to him so that she may become pure and desireless. He also told her, "If you want to test the truth of what I have said, sit here and say to Sai Baba - I offer to you from the bottom of my heart the six enemies (vices) - and when we later go to him let us see what he has to say." Mrs Tarkhad did as told.

In the afternoon when the two of them went to Sai Baba he asked her, "Mother, have you brought my rupees?" Mrs Tarkhad replied, "I have already given them to you." Sai Baba queried, "Have you really given?" She said, "Yes, I have really given." Sai Baba asked, "You won't turn back?" From this Mrs Tarkhad was convinced that the demand for six rupees was for the offering of six enemies (vices) to Sai Baba.

Notes

1. *Devotees' Experiences of Sri Sai Baba,* Part I, p. 125.
2. All substances have three aspects, name, form and essence which are known only after transcending name and form.
3. *Kama* = Passion; 2. *Krodha* = Anger; 3. *Lobha* = Greed; *Mada* = Pride; 5. *Moha* = Delusion; 6. *Matsar* = Envy.

16. BODHAPADDHATI WAY, MODE & MANNER OF INSTRUCTION

To know the Eternal, let a man devoted to spiritual life humbly approach a *Guru* devoted to Brahman and well-versed in the scriptures.

To a disciple who approaches reverently, who is tranquil amd self-controlled, the wise teacher gives that knowledge, faithfully and without stint, by which is known the truly existing, the changeless Self.

Mundaka Upanishad
(translated by Swami Prabhavananda)

Those who themselves have seen the Truth can be thy teachers of wisdom. Ask from them, bow unto them, be thou unto them a servant.

Bhagavad Gita, IV, 34
(translation by Juan Mascaro)

or

Those illumined souls who have realised the Truth will instruct you in knowledge of Brahman, if you will prostrate yourself before them, question and serve them as disciple.

Bhagavad Gita, IV, 34
(translation by Swami Prabhavananda & Christopher Isherwood)

Let a man devoted to spiritual life wishing to know the Eternal, surrender to a *Guru* who is well-versed in the scriptures and devoted to and established in Brahman.

Srimad Bhagavatam XI, 3:21

Just as a thing around one's neck is not seen through delusion/confusion of mind, so also the Atman is not known unless the ignorance is removed by the instruction of a *Guru*.

Shri Yogavasista

He who is well versed in the scriptures, ever established in the bliss of the Brahman and a teacher of wisdom is My very embodiment.

Eknathi Bhagwat XI:28

He is the real Sadhu, who can reveal the form of the
    Formless to the vision of these eyes:
Who teaches the simple way of attaining Him, that is
    other than rites or ceremonies:
Who does not make you close the doors and hold the
    breath, and renounce the world:
Who makes you perceive the Supreme Spirit
    wherever the mind attaches itself:
Who teaches you to be still in the midst of all your
    activities.
Ever immersed in bliss, having no fear in his mind, he
    keeps the spirit of union in the midst of all
    enjoyments.
The infinite dwelling of the Infinite Being is
    everywhere: in earth, water, sky and air:
Firm as the thunderbolt, the seat of the seeker is
    established above the void.
He who is within is without: I see Him and none else.

Kabir
(from *One Hundred Poems of Kabir*, LVI translated by
Rabindranath Tagore)

'My *leela* is inscrutable' would say Sai Baba. This is literally true. In all our educational institutions, instruction is imparted in the waking state. Sai Baba's way and mode was to impart instruction in the three states of waking, dream and *samadhi*. Moreover, the ordinary experience is that instruction can be had only from a teacher with form but even after his *samadhi* and dissolution of the body, Sai Baba continues to impart instruction as before. Towards his devotees Sai Baba had imperishable and infinite love and his mode of instruction was stimulated by compassion. He was neither mercenary nor greedy. As he was ever established in *sahaj samadhi* and the highest bliss, some persons would form the impression that he was asleep. That it was only an appearance and not the reality was the experience of the devotees. After his *samadhi*, some persons feel that he is no more but actually he is ever awake and active as before.

While the emphasis in educational institutions is on knowledge of things unseen (*parokshajnan*), in the case of Sai Baba, it was on the knowledge of the Self or the Spirit based on experience (*aparokshajnan*). Because of his omniscience and omnipresence as a result of his unity with Brahman, without being told he would know the sorrows, sufferings, calamities and also impediments in the spiritual path of the devotees, and could ward off the sorrows and calamities and suggest an instantaneously useful remedy. He does not make the mistake of giving a beginner the higher lesson, unless he is well grounded in the lesson in hand. Briefly speaking, he has the knack of imparting knowledge according to the capacity of the recipient.

Sai Baba would understand the difficulties of the devotees without being told and he guided them, removed their doubts, answered their queries, by merely watching over them like the tortoise (not by whispering a *mantra* into the ear), sustained and protected them, persuaded them by loving talk, and sometimes turned them away by feigning anger. These were some of the features of his way and mode of teaching. He taught his devotees to practise self-restraint, to live in the world with detachment, to believe in God and love Him, to love the parents, *guru*, holy persons, the poor and the downtrodden and even the dumb creation, to engage in activities selflessly considering yourself only as an instrument, to read sacred texts, to purify the heart and reflect therein.

He never discoursed to groups or gatherings. He had different ways of dealing with different individuals. If he desired to convey a moral lesson to a group he would do so through a tale or a parable.

Hindus, Muslims, Parsis, Christians, men of diverse religions, sects and views would come for Sai Baba's *darshan*. He would look with an equal eye on them all and confirm them in their spiritual practice. If anyone did not have any particular spiritual discipline, Sai Baba would guide him according to his capacity, inclination and aptitude. He was not a partisan of any religion or sect and did not wish to found and add one more sect to the already innumerable sects existing in our country. He did not wish to found a seat, *gaddi, ashram* or *peetham* and so did not have to trouble himself about appointing a successor. His selflessness and great renunciation would leave an indelible impression on his devotees who therefore believed that his advice would be in their interest and for their welfare.

He allowed those whose end was near or whose worldly responsibilities had been discharged to remain with him or encouraged them to retire from a life of worldly activity. When others sought his permission to retire from worldly life, he declined to give his consent and stopped them. He was against young people who were capable of earning their livelihood retiring from worldly life out of idleness. He also did not favour throwing one's burden on society by begging for alms. We will now examine some cases of his devotees to whom he gave appropriate directions according to their circumstances and potential.

1. Sakharam Hari alias Bapusaheb Jog along with his wife came for Sai Baba's *darshan* one Ramanavami day. Seeing that the couple had no progeny and they were in the evening of their life, as well as seeing Jog's potentiality, Sai Baba allowed them to stay in Shirdi. Sai Baba gave him *darshan* in the form of Akkalkot Swami as desired by Jog and after Megha's death entrusted the duty of worship - *arati* (the ceremony of waving a platter containing a burning flame) to him. Jog discharged this responsibility diligently and with devotion until Sai Baba's *samadhi*.

Jog's life in Shirdi was one of austerity. The couple would get up at 3 a.m. every day throughout the year and bathe with cold water at the well behind the Dikshitwada. Then Jog would attend to his *sandhya puja archa* and every alternate day, when Sai Baba rested for the night in the *chavadi*, he would attend to the morning *arati* of Sai Baba. After finishing his remaining regular discipline he would go to the *masjid* at the time of morning repast of Sai Baba. Then he would either accompany Sai Baba to *lendi* or recite the *Bhagavad Gita* at home until Sai Baba returned from *lendi*. He would help in the preparation of *naivedya* (an offering of a platter containing the whole meal or an eatable to an idol or holy person) of Sai Baba and after noon *arati* go home along with a guest sent by Sai Baba for lunch. In the afternoon at about 3.30 p.m. he would again call at the *masjid,* come back and read *Eknathi Bhagwat* until it was time for the evening round of Sai Baba.

Many a time Sai Baba would send devotees to Jog when he read *Jnaneshvari* in the morning or *Eknathi Bhagwat* in the afternoon under the guise of asking for *dakshina* (money given to Brahmins, holy persons or gods), and would direct them to listen to the *parayana* (the perusal or reading through of a holy text especially a *purana*).

On the day when Sai Baba would spend the night in *chavadi*, Jog would attend to the night *arati* at 9.30 p.m. at the *chavadi* (the village hall). Jog discharged these duties uninterruptedly for years until the day of Sai Baba's *nirvana*.

2. After the wife of Balakram Mankar passed away, Sai Baba directed him to stay in Shirdi, and lead a life of the Spirit. He got Mankar to do *tapas* in Shirdi as well as Matsyendragad and blessed him by giving him *darshan* in Matsyendragad in the waking state. On the direction of Sai Baba he would read *Panchadasi*. He died in Shirdi before Sai Baba's *nirvana*.

3. Upasani had come to Sai Baba for *darshan*. Seeing his preparation, Sai Baba advised him much against Upasani's wish, to stay in Shirdi for four years doing *tapas* but he fled away after three years much to his detriment.

4. Govind Raghunath alias Annasaheb Dabholkar retired from government service in 1916 on reaching the age of superannuation. A friend of Dabholkar who was also a devotee of Sai Baba requested Sai Baba to give Dabholkar another paid employment to assist him in meeting his family expenses. Then Sai Baba said, "He will certainly get some service but let him serve me now. He will have a happy life. To the end of his days, he will have abundantly and will not want for anything. If he devotes himself to me with faith, all his tribulations will end."[1]

5. Sagun Meru Naik came from Hyderabad in the company of a *sowcar* of that State, who was a devotee of Sai Baba. After five months'stay in Shirdi, when he asked Sai Baba for leave to depart, Sai Baba told him clearly that he had not brought him from a long distance for nothing. He asked Sagun to stay in Shirdi engaging himself in some activity and said that he would prosper.

From that time Sagun made his home in Shirdi. Even now he carries to the *Samadhi Mandir* in the morning a dish of butter mixed with sugar candy and does not have his lunch without offering consecrated rice with *ghee* (clarified butter) in the *dhuni* (sacred fire). Sai Baba arranged for his stay in Shirdi and helped him to set up a teastall as well as a shop for sale of Sai Baba's pictures, *arati* books, articles like agarbatti, camphor, etc., required for *puja*. Sagun began taking interest in gardening and tending cows and was associated with the Sansthan in rendering services to Sai Baba.

6. If there is anyone who was compelled to give up his post in the Police Department and made to tread on the spiritual path, it is Ganpat Dattatreya Sahasrabuddhe alias Das Ganu. Sai Baba did this looking to his intelligence, capacity to compose on the spot, and, of course, his potential. When Das Ganu paid his first visit in the company of Nanasaheb Chandorkar for Sai Baba's *darshan*, with his inner vision, Sai Baba said, "Tell him (Das Ganu) that composing *lavanis*, participating in *tamashas* (farcical plays) and service in the Police Department are to be given up." He gave up the first two things but dilly-dallied about resigning from his post in the Police Department. In 1898-99, Kanhya Bhil, a dacoit came to know that his movements were under surveillance by Das Ganu. So Das Ganu's life was under a threat. By surrendering to Shriram, Sai Baba's grace and because of Das Ganu's defence by the Patil who sheltered Kanhya Bhil, Das Ganu escaped with the skin of his teeth. At that time he was only a *havaldar*.

Once Das Ganu went to a place of pilgrimage on unauthorised leave and standing in the waters of Godavari with his face in the direction of Shirdi, affirmed that if he escaped punishment for the offence of absenting without prior permission, he would tender his resignation. Fortunately for him a gang of robbers was rounded up at that very place and feigning that he had been to that place in search of the robbers he avoided punishment. He was aspiring for promotion as *Fauzdar* and in the process forgot his pledge. Now he passed in the Departmental examination for the *Fauzdar's* post and was transferred. The road to the place of his new posting passed through Shirdi. He wanted to avoid Sai Baba as he would hold him to his pledge.

As fate would have it, while he was passing through Shirdi, Sai Baba accosted him. Dismounting from his horse Das Ganu prostrated before Sai Baba who took him to the *masjid* and said, "Ganu, who had affirmed with water of Godavari in the hollow of his palms that he would resign?" Das Ganu still disregarded him. So Sai Baba added, "How will you avoid me? Better resign from your post or you will have cause to repent."

A few days after this Das Ganu was involved in another scrape. An amount of Rs. 32 by way of fine was realised from a convict in Das Ganu's station for being paid into the treasury. In Das Ganu's absence his assistant pocketed the amount. As the convict was not released, he filed a complaint and an enquiry was ordered. Das Ganu was suspended and there was a possibility of his being punished. This time he again resolved that if he was exonerated of the charge he would leave his employment. He was acquitted and as per his resolve, he finally resigned from the Police Department.

After he quit the Police Department in 1912, as per Sai Baba's direction he made his abode in Nanded in Nizam's Dominions and supported himself by performing *kirtans* (celebrating the praises of God with music and singing). Then by Sai Baba's grace he got some land at little cost. He was able to live well on the income from the farm. He did his bit in spreading Sai Baba's fame in Bombay. His tasteful *kirtans*, full of devotion, became so popular in Bombay that wherever he performed there would be a crowd. Keeping a photograph of Sai Baba before himself, bare-bodied except for a *dhoti* around his loins, he would perform *kirtans*. He did not follow the usual practice of circulating the *arati-patra* among those present at the end of the *kirtan* to collect money. He performed only for the sake of spreading the *bhakti* movement. As a result of these *kirtans* in Bombay, a large number of people were attracted to Sai Baba and were blessed with his *darshan*.

Das Ganu was a prolific composer and became known as a *santkavi* (composer of *padas, kavyas, stotras, akhyanas* on saints) of Marathi language. In his *Arvachin Bhaktaleelamrit*, chapters 31, 32 and 33, and *Shrisantakathamrit*, chapter 57 are compositions devoted to Sai Baba. Sai Baba sometimes asked his devotees to read these regularly on Thursdays. For his own reading the present writer translated them in poetical form into Gujarati. Coming to know that Sai Baba in his lifetime had given permission to the present writer to publish the Gujarati translation, Das Ganu pressed this writer to publish it which he did in 1934 under the title *Bhavasudha*.

7. Abdul of Nanded was destined to serve Sai Baba. Sai Baba appeared in the dream of his *Murshid Fakir* Amiruddin in 1889 and asked him to send Abdul to Shirdi. Abdul came to Sai Baba and served him until his *mahasamadhi*. Sai Baba took care of him as a father does of his son, and made him study the *Quran*.

8. Balasaheb Bhate was at college a free thinker, an inveterate smoker and a veritable *charvaka* (a thinker who was an atheist and believed that death is the only emancipation), and whose creed may be thus summed up, 'eat, drink and be merry for tomorrow we die'. He became a *Mamledar* and was an efficient officer much liked by his boss the Collector, who was an Englishman. He was *Mamledar* at Kopargaon for about five years between 1904 and 1909. Bhate would scoff at his educated friends who met him on their way to Shirdi, and would describe Sai Baba as a madman. His friends asked

him to see Sai Baba just once and then form his judgement. In 1909 Bhate camped at Shirdi and met Sai Baba day after day. On the fifth day Sai Baba covered him with a *gerua* garment. From that day Bhate was a changed man. He did not care for earnings or work. From that day up to his death, he only wished to be at Shirdi to serve Sai Baba, to live and die in his presence. Sai Baba bade his friend Kakasaheb Dikshit draw up an application for leave for one year and with Sai Baba's help Bhate's signature was got on it. The Collector gave him one year's time to see if he would return to his old self. However, at the end of the year, he still continued to be mad after his *guru* and was granted compassionate pension of about thirty rupees as one afflicted with 'religious melancholia'. Asked for the reason for his change, Bhate had said that the putting of the *gerua* garment on him by Sai Baba marked the crisis. His original frame of mind had been removed and in its place quite a new frame of mind was put in. After that, attending to worldly duties—especially official duties—had become unthinkable. He then lived at Shirdi, attending to his *Nitya Karma*, *Upanishad*-reading, etc., before Sai Baba who would occasionally offer comments on that reading.

9. Kakasaheb Dikshit once asked Sai Baba in 1912, "Shall I retire from the Solicitor's profession and spend my life here in Shirdi?" Sai Baba asked him why it was necessary for him to leave the legal profession. Dikshit replied that he could not carry on his practice truthfully. Then Sai Baba said to him, "Let others do what they like. In your profession you should engage yourself in work you can do truthfully. It is not necessary for you to give it up." Therefore, Dikshit did not give up legal practice but spent as much time as he could in Shirdi serving Sai Baba devotedly with faith. On Sai Baba's direction Dikshit had made it a rule to read *Eknathi Bhagwat* in

the morning and *Bhavartha Ramayan* at night, and he stuck to it until the end of his life.

10. Prof G.G. Narke who returned from England in 1912 as a qualified Geologist and Mining Engineer, had no permanent employment for some years, but secured temporary prospecting jobs. His mother was, therefore, anxious about his future. At Sai Baba's instance, Narke went to Shirdi and stayed there without employment for thirteen months, but did not care. Sometimes he had stray fancies that a *fakir's* life was good for him. In 1914 on a certain day, Sai Baba had got ready a number of *kafnis* (cloaks worn by mendicants, covering the whole person except the head and forearms) which he presented to some people. Narke, who was watching the distribution of *kafnis* from a distance, hoped that one might be conferred on him so that he could wear it on special occasions like *bhajans* in honour of Sai Baba. Sai Baba stopped distribution even when many *kafnis* remained with him. Then he called Narke and placing his hand on his head stroked it and said, "Do not blame me for not giving you a *kafni*. That *Fakir* (evidently God) has not permitted me to give you one." Later, Sai Baba ensured that Narke was settled in Poona as a Professor in the Engineering College.

11. The financial condition of Janardan Moreshwar Phanse of Dahanu was not so good. He had to face many a calamity and wearied, he started for Rameshwar resolving not to come back to the worldly life. On the way he broke the journey to go to Shirdi and at the first sight of Sai Baba felt that he was a respected well-wisher of his of long standing, which feeling grew as he stayed on in Shirdi. On the eighth day he asked leave of Sai Baba who said, "Go home instead of to Rameshwar or you may be overtaken by ill-stars." So Phanse returned home and found that from the day he left home his mother had fasted and said to herself that if Sai Baba were a true saint he would change the mind of her son and send him

home. After seven days' fasting she had vowed to subsist on a diet of only milk. We have already seen how Sai Baba changed the mind of Phanse, prevented him from retiring from the world and made him start a business. If Phanse had abandoned his household it would not have been *sattvic* renunciation but demoniacal renunciation as described in chapter eighteen of the *Bhagavad Gita*, and he would not have benefited spiritually. So we conclude that only if one's renunciation was *sattvic*, only then would Baba help or else he would withhold his support.

The practical application of the moral lesson to Phanse was demonstrated in the case of R.A. Tarkhad when he visited Shirdi on December 6, 1910. He went to Shirdi to get away from the rough and tumble of his daily grind and to have peace of mind. However, his first encounter was very unpleasant. As soon as he stepped in Sathewada, a gentleman, plied him with questions: "Why have you come to Shirdi? What do you get here?" and so on. Another man came and queried: "Who is a *Sthitaprajna* (man of serene wisdom)? Will you kindly clarify at length?" Tarkhad was agitated, he lost his poise and felt that he had made a mistake in leaving Bombay and coming all the way to Shirdi. However, concealing his discomfiture, he went for Sai Baba's *darshan*.

As soon as Tarkhad bowed at his feet, Sai Baba placed his palm on Tarkhad's head and said to Madhavrao Deshpande, "Why does he do like this? Tell him something." When Madhavrao and Tarkhad emerged from the *masjid* onto the road, Madhavrao asked Tarkhad what the matter was. Tarkhad narrated to him what had happened since he had set his foot in Shirdi. Madhavrao said, "This is a *leela* and teaching of Sai Baba - living in the midst of turmoil in worldly life, to keep the mind steadfast in devotion to God. Even in the midst of trouble and anxiety of family life and employment you should direct your mind constantly toward God. Let us now go to Sai Baba and listen to what he says." As they turned back and ascended the steps of the *masjid*, Sai Baba said to Tarkhad, "Brother, keep in mind what Shama (Madhavrao Deshpande) told you." Later with these as his watchwords, without losing his balance and with full faith in Sai Baba, he could face resolutely and with detachment calamities and difficulties and hard situations. The moral to be drawn from this case is, curbing his ego, a person should conduct himself with detachment and watch events unfolding themselves instead of rejecting this and accepting that and the other thing.

Ambdekar, a devotee who was disgusted with life, went to Shirdi determined to commit suicide. He had been out of employment for seven years and had not found other suitable means of earning his livelihood. So he decided to commit suicide by jumping in the well and was sitting opposite Dikshitwada on a cart. Seeing that no one was around he was going to the well when Sagun Meru Naik came to the threshold of his house and asked Ambdekar whether he had read the *Pothi* of Akkalkot Maharaj. "Let me see the *Pothi*," replied Ambdekar and taking it in his hands turned its pages. Fortuitously his attention was drawn to the incident in which Akkalkot Maharaj had saved the disease-afflicted man attempting to commit suicide and spoken to him of the futility of suicide which only leads to rebirth for working out the remaining *karma* of the previous birth. Reading this tale, Ambdekar felt that Sai Baba had used it as an instrument to dissuade him from committing suicide. Moreover, his father had been a devotee of Akkalkot Maharaj. All this resulted in his abandoning the thought of suicide. By Sai Baba's blessing he acquired proficiency in astrology and made a lot of money. The lesson that he learnt was that running away from life and committing suicide is not the solution to one's problems. One has to face the problems and go through life to end one's *karma*.

Instead of running away from life one should work out one's *karma* virtuously and use life as a means for realising oneself. This ideal if kept constantly before one's eye can be realised through spiritual discipline. One form of spiritual discipline is to stick to the worship of family or the chosen deity which has been hallowed by tradition. Where such tradition had been interrupted Sai Baba would remind and apprise a devotee of it. In this way Sai Baba had got Mrs R.A.Tarkhad to restart the worship of Ganapati with a broken arm, Bhagavantrao Kshirsagar the worship of Vitthal, Shantaram Balwant Nachane the worship of the deity at Devpur, and Harischandra Pitale the worship of Akkalkot Swami.

The practice of repeating and meditating upon a *mantram* is a worthy form of *upasana*. "Of sacrifices (acts of worship), I am the sacrifice of silent repetitions", i.e., *japa yajna* is the best among sacrifice, says the Lord in the *Bhagavad Gita* 10:25. Sai Baba would commend a *mantra* which was suited to the mental condition of a devotee or which was being repeated by him. At the first meeting of Rao Bahadur M.V. Pradhan by pronouncing the *mantra* 'Shri Ram Jai Ram Jai Jai Ram', Sai Baba conveyed his recognition of the *mantra* given by the *guru* of the Pradhan family and encouraged him to continue the practice. He gave the *mantra* 'Raja Ram' to Mrs G.S.Khaparde and another form of Rama *mantra* to Ganesan Maharaj.

In 1910 when R.A.Tarkhad met Sai Baba for the first time he was thinking whether he should continue the practice of repetition of the *mantra* 'Shri Ram Jai Ram Jai Jai Ram'. Immediately with folded hands Sai Baba welcomed him lovingly and said, "Come Ramachandra Maharaj," suggesting thereby that the said practice would be conducive to his welfare.

To Govind Raghunath alias Annasaheb Dabholkar and Radhabai Deshmukh who believed in the devotion to *Sadguru*, he commended meditating on and the *bhajan* of

Sadguru and the twin lessons of *shraddha* (faith) and
saburi (patience combined with courage). To M.B.Rege,
Sai Baba said, "Do not read books but keep me in your
heart. If you harmonise head and heart, that is enough."
As a means of crossing the ocean of the present state of
existence (*bhavasagar*) he also commended to many
devotees regular reading of sacred texts or *Pothis* of
saints: to Nanasaheb Nimonkar *Srimad Bhagwat*
(Sanskrit) with commentary, *Bhagavad Gita* and
Jnaneshvari; to Bapusaheb Jog *Jnaneshvari* and
Eknathi Bhagwat and *Geeta Rahasya* (by Lokamanya
Tilak); to Uddhaveshbua, Kaka Mahajani and Vaman
Narvekar *Eknathi Bhagwat*; to Dr. D.M.Mulky
Jnaneshvari; to Balakram Mankar *Panchadasi*
(Sanskrit) by Vidyaranya Swami, and to Madhavrao
Deshpande *Vishnusahasranama*. To Megha and Bala
Shimpi he gave each a *Shivalinga* and to Madhavrao
Deshpande a *Shaligram* (a black stone found in River
Gandaki and worshipped as Vishnu) and asked them to
worship according to rites. Damodar Rasane brought his
son Dattatreya, after tonsuring his head, to Sai Baba for
giving him the first lesson in identification of alphabets.
Holding the hand of Dattatreya, with the aid of a pencil,
Sai Baba wrote the sacred word 'Hari' on the slate.

From the above narration, if anyone gathers the
impression that by mere worship or reading of sacred
texts the end can be achieved, he is mistaken. For the
fulfilment of all means, the grace of a Brahman-knowing
guru is always necessary. The way to earn the *guru*'s
grace was pointed out by Sai Baba to Anandrao Patankar
who came to Shirdi on hearing the fame of Sai Baba.
Patankar said to him, "I have read many books, studied
the *Vedas* and the *Upanishads* but my mind is as restless
as before. I feel that my reading and study are all wasted.
As long as the mind is not steady how can I realise the
Brahman? Hearing of your fame I have come here in the
hope that by your sacred *darshan* and blessings I will get

peace of mind." Sai Baba said to him, "Listen, a merchant had come here. There was a horse before him. He ejected nine nodules of dung. The merchant was intent and circumspect about his work. Thinking that the nodules may fall anywhere he collected them in his upper garment. Thereby his mind was concentrated and his work fructified." Patankar could not understand the riddle posed by Sai Baba and asked Dada Kelkar who clarified as under: "The merchant is the seeker, the horse is God's Grace and nine nodules of dung means the ninefold path of devotion, viz., *shravan* (hearing the attributes, excellencies or wondrous achievements of God as read or recited), *keertan* (reading or reciting), *smaran* (calling to mind and meditating upon the names and perfections of God), *padasevan* (washing, kneading and shampooing the feet of the Lord), *archana* (outward worship or religious service consisting of washing, anointing and presenting *naivedya*), *vandan* (adoration or performing *namaskar,* etc.), *dasya* (service in general in or around the temple), *sakhya* (cultivating fellowship or familiar intercourse with God), *atmanivedan* (consecration of one's self unto God). Inasmuch as you have come as a merchant here you should follow that ninefold path of devotion so that you will obtain peace of mind." Patankar felt that this clarification was apt.

Next day, when Patankar went for Sai Baba's *darshan*, in order to impress upon Patankar's mind that he meant exactly what Kelkar had explained to him, Sai Baba asked, "Well, have you collected the nine nodules of dung?" Patankar replied humbly, "They will be easily collected with your blessings." Then Sai Baba blessed him. Patankar had intellectual knowledge so that when he trod on the path of devotion he experienced peace of mind. Often Sai Baba would explain the same principle in allegorical language - "*Seetaphal* (custard apple) is better than *Ramphal* (bullock's heart fruit) for the former is easy to digest while the latter is hard to digest." He

would therefore commend the principle of *Yade Haq*
(servant of God) rather than *Anal Haq* (I am God); *Tuhi,
Tuhi* (Thou art everything, i.e., Thy will be done) rather
than *Aham Brahmasmi* (I am the Brahman).

It is easier for a man who leads the life of a recluse
than for a man in society to walk on the path of
knowledge or devotion. It is wrong for a *guru* to imagine
that his duty ends with the whispering of a *mantra* into
his disciple's ear. So Sai Baba would often say, "I am not
an ear-whispering *guru*." He had the covert aim of
standing behind the devotee and watching over his
progress, of seeing whether his devotee acted on the
lesson or not and if he was deviating, to correct him and
lead him on the straight path. Thus, wherever the
devotee might be, when he came to Shirdi, Sai Baba
would draw his attention to his mistake, and get him to
correct it. We have seen this in the cases of Nanasaheb
Chandorkar, Hansraj and others. There is one one
common principle underlying his advice, namely,
universal love which Sai Baba would do his best to
inculcate. Now we will see what other virtues he taught
his devotees to cultivate.

The fabric of life is woven with the woof of knowledge
(*jnana*) and the weft of devotion (*bhakti*). Unless
knowledge and devotion are harmonised, study, *japa* and
other spiritual practices are all incomplete.

Every minute of our life we are inching towards
death. Who does not know this truth? But a man like G.S.
alias Dadasaheb Khaparde wasted the morning and
afternoon of two days, 15 January 1912 and 19 January
1912 in idle talk. So Sai Baba asked him what he was
doing at those times. Realising the trend of the question
Khaparde became aware of his mistake. He writes in his
Shirdi Diary that when he went with Lokamanya Tilak
for Sai Baba's *darshan*, looking at Lokamanya Sai Baba
said, "People are bad, keep yourself to yourself."
Bapusaheb Jog who was then present had said that Sai

Baba had also said to Lokamanya, "You have done much for the people but now you should also take care of your soul." Within three and a quarter years thereof Lokamanya died. It is to be noted that Sai Baba had not failed to caution even a great patriot like him of the necessity to strive for salvation in this very life.

A yogi came to Shirdi and went for Sai Baba's *darshan* when the latter was eating *bhakri* with onion. A doubt immediately seized the yogi how a man who eats onion could be called a holy person. Immediately with his inner vision Sai Baba said, "He who can digest onion alone should eat it. It should not be eaten without such capacity." The yogi realised that God is omnipotent and omnipresent and in raising a doubt about the conduct of a holy person like Sai Baba, he was utterly mistaken. Moreover, in his waking state the whole world must appear to him to be pervaded by God and from this point of view too, he had committed an error. So he surrendered to Sai Baba who guided him properly and removed doubts assailing him.

A *yogi, jnani* or *bhakta* treading on the spiritual path does not waste his precious time indulging in malicious gossip. But we see in practice even men of understanding violating this principle. Sai Baba would always say, "When you speak ill of others, taunt others, I suffer." If a devotee on coming to Shirdi violated this principle Sai Baba would immediately correct him.

Mathuradas of Anjanwel sitting at Sagun Meru Naik's place was indulging in malicious gossip. Sai Baba had cautioned him then. Similarly, a devotee sitting in Dikshitwada was also guilty of a similar lapse. As the devotee went out for easing himself Sai Baba was returning from *lendi*. The devotee bowed respectfully to Sai Baba. Pointing toward a pig feasting on faeces, Sai Baba said to him, "See with what great relish the pig is feeding on the faeces. It nauseates us. Should then a human being waste his life in malicious gossip and reduce himself to the level of a pig?"

Sai Baba who taught the lesson of universal love to all said, "Nobody comes to us without *rinanubandha* (ties of indebtedness or desert in some preceding birth). So never shoo away anybody. A creature driven away thus never sets its foot on your threshold." We have seen how Sai Baba identified himself with the dog and the pig whom Mrs Tarkhad fed and how he assumed the form of a cat and bore the blows of Hansraj, an asthma patient, whom he was attempting to restrain from eating curds. Sai Baba always said:

Though I am here and you are beyond the seven seas,
Whatever you do there, I come to know at once.
Wherever you go, I am within you.
I dwell in your heart, I am always with you.
Bow always to me who am in your heart.
Know that I also dwell within the hearts of all
    creatures
Whether at your home, doorstep or on the way.
Whether it is an insect, an ant, an aquatic or aerial
    creature or an animal—a dog or a pig.
In all these I abide for ever and I pervade everything.
Do not regard yourself as separate from me, we are
    one;
Blessed is he who realises this truth.[2]

Devotees of Sai Baba had his assurance of their security. We saw in chapter nine how Sai Baba had saved Mirikar and Buti from danger to their lives by serpent bite. But people are afraid of even a trifling creature like a house lizard, who it is believed vomits poison if it falls in food or drink.

Once Sai Baba was seated in his usual place in the *masjid* and a devotee was sitting beside him. Hearing a lizard chirping on the wall behind Sai Baba, the devotee asked him, "Why is the lizard chirping? Does it portend any inauspicious event?" Sai Baba replied, "What

inauspicious event! She is very happy because her sister
from Aurangabad is coming to see her." The devotee felt
that Sai Baba was joking and evading the answer to his
question. But in a short time thereafter, a visitor arrived
on horseback from Aurangabad for Sai Baba's *darshan*.
Sai Baba was bathing at that time. The horse of the
visitor was tired and it was time for his daily feed. So
before going to the market to buy Bengal gram for his
horse he took the horse's mouth-bag, turned it upside
down and shook it. As he did this a lizard emerged from it
and ran across the floor. "Now watch the lizard," said Sai
Baba to the devotee. She went straight in the direction of
the lizard on the wall. To express their joy they embraced
and kissed each other and made circular, horizontal,
perpendicular and diagonal movements. The devotee
thus realised that even in his humour Sai Baba spoke the
truth. Sai Baba wanted to remove the fear of lizard from
the devotee's mind and to show him that all life is one.

How could one who advocated love and mercy tolerate
injustice? Once a girl sat in the *masjid* in a place opposite
Sai Baba where Hardwarbua would usually sit. When
the Bua came, the girl did not get up. As if he had
proprietary right over the seat, the Bua made the girl get
up and then he sat in her place. Nothing escaped Sai
Baba's notice. He quietly asked Hardwarbua to go to the
sabhamandap and sit there. When Hardwarbua tried
after some time to enter the *masjid* Sai Baba asked him
again to sit down in the *sabhamandap*. The Bua then
realised that as he had done injustice to the girl Sai Baba
had taken the aforesaid action to bring the injustice to
his notice.

Sai Baba did not countenance the false belief that
worldly life and spiritual life are separate and unless one
is neglected no progress can be made in the other. We will
now see some experiences in this connection. As pursuit
of spiritual life on borrowed money is against common
sense, Sai Baba had cautioned Lala Lakhmichand who

had taken a loan for his Shirdi visit about it. Thereafter Lakhmichand did not go to Shirdi by borrowing money. To one who placed a ladder for Sai Baba to get on to the roof of a house, Sai Baba gave Rs. 2. When asked why he had paid so much for such a trivial service Sai Baba said, "Give always to one from whom you get some work done, his proper hire. Do not take free service." Sai Baba also gave two lessons to Rao Bahadur Sathe, viz., not to exclude a near relation in any social function at home and not to interfere or mediate in others' affairs. The need for these lessons arose in the following circumstances. Rao Bahadur Sathe planned to hold a function in *dhanurmas* (period during which the sun is in Sagittarius), for which he invited all except his father-in-law, and went personally to invite Sai Baba. Reprimanding him, Sai Baba said, "Fetch me the *danda* ((staff)." Sathe stood quietly and realising his error begged to be forgiven. So Sai Baba was pacified and agreed to be present. Without realising that unsolicited mediation in others' affairs does not succeed, Sathe interfered in a dispute of a Marwari but Sai Baba did not like this and was cross with Sathe.

Alcoholism is detrimental both to worldly life as well as spiritual life. D.V. Sambhare alias Kolambo was addicted to drinking. Sai Baba appeared in his dream on Febrary 1, 1917 and sitting on his chest asked him, "Oh boy, what are you doing?" Only after Sambhare promised to abstain from drink did Sai Baba get off his chest. From the very next day he stopped drinking.

On February 15, 1917 came the test. The manager of the office where Sambhare was working gave a party by way of send-off for his children and Sambhare was one of those invited. Sambhare attended the party where the manager insisted on his having a peg of whisky. Sambhare pleaded that his doctor had cautioned him against drinking. In spite of it, the manager insisted. Then came miraculous help. The electric lights went out and the manager went to find out what had happened. Just then Mistry who was sitting nearby drank off Sambhare's glass believing it to be his own and the manager who soon returned thought that Sambhare had complied with his request. Thus in his inscrutable way Sai Baba helped Sambhare to keep his good resolve.

Sai Baba also watched over his devotees' conscience and morals to save them from a moral fall. Once Sathe was proposing to visit for the first time the residence of a female devotee of Sai Baba in Shirdi out of curiosity. Just before the visit Sai Baba asked him if he had gone to such and such a place. Sathe did not understand the names of places and missed the point of his question. Sai Baba then dropped the subject. Sathe then went to her lodgings and was engaged in some conversation. Very soon evil thoughts began to invade his mind. Suddenly Sai Baba appeared in front of that house and pushed open the door which had been closed but not bolted. He made some ironical signs to Sathe to convey the idea, 'What an excellent thing you are now launching into!' and disappeared. His timely intervention before any evil could take shape in action, saved the situation. Conscience asserted itself, tendencies to evil were definitely checked and Sathe retreated from the place at once and never visited it again.

Keeping one's child crying and neglecting one's own duty for the sake of attending on God or holy person does not make for spiritual progress, was the lesson impressed on Mrs Chhotubai Pradhan by Sai Baba who sent her away in the midst of *puja* to her place of halt for looking after her child.

Cupidity and evasion of obligation and boastfulness and pride also come in the way of spiritual progress and Sai Baba who knew the inner mind of his devotees watched over their habits and would draw their attention to their deficiencies to enable them to overcome them. The proprietor of a press in Bombay had gone to Shirdi and had over Rs. 18 with him, which he handed over to Sambhare in secret so that he might be able to tell Sai Baba that he had no money if the latter should ask him for *dakshina*. When the proprietor was in the *masjid* alone with Sambhare, Sai Baba asked the proprietor for Rs. 2 *dakshina*, and in order to prevent his evasive excuses added, "Take it from this man" (pointing to Sambhare). The man's ruse had been found out. He paid Rs. 2 to Sai Baba from the Rs. 18 given by him earlier.

Some months after Sambhare had given up drinking, Sai Baba did not ask him for any *dakshina* at all. Sambhare imagined that his having given up the vice, his great merit was recognised by Sai Baba by rewarding him with immunity from paying *dakshina*. Sambhare was at the *wada* boasting of this immunity in the presence of friends when at once came the call from Sai Baba. When he went to the *masjid* Sai Baba asked him for two rupees *dakshina* and Sambhare paid it.

Similarly, Bayaji Kote Patil used to boast and feel proud of great physical strength. He would do *charan-seva* of Sai Baba and then lift him and put him before the *dhuni*. Many a day he had done so. On that particular day, a *Dwadashi* day, when Bayaji tried to lift Sai Baba, he could not do so. Sai Baba laughed at him and put down his pride, and taught him not to be so proud.

Radhakrishnabai, whom H.S. alias Kakasaheb Dikshit described as the *acharya* of loving devotion, lived in Shirdi for many years and served Sai Baba faithfully. Once she happened to insult a person who had come for Sai Baba's *darshan*. Sai Baba reproached her in the presence of all saying, "Are you aware of the worth of one who ascends the steps of the *masjid*? Insulting him amounts to insulting me!"

Among persons coming for Sai Baba's *darshan* there were many who had been devotees since a long time, some who had been devotees for a few years and some very new. But Sai Baba did not discriminate between them and expressed his disapproval if anybody tried to do so.

Sai Baba restrained his devotees from actions which would feed their egotism which is an obstacle on the spiritual path. Destruction of egotism is a difficult but an inevitable discipline for a seeker. Let us see some examples of this principle. By Sai Baba's grace Nanasaheb Nimonkar who had no knowledge of Sanskrit at all began to understand *Srimad Bhagwat* and its commentary (in Sanskrit), and he advanced so far as to proceed with the *Bhagavad Gita* and then *Jnaneshvari.* All these he understood and devotees who were scholars of Sanskrit had their doubts cleared by him. Later Sai Baba stopped Nimonkar from explaining things to others so that his self-conceit may not grow. Balakram Mankar would understand the purport of *Panchadasi* but did not have complete knowledge thereof. So he approached Sai Baba who told him, "You do not have to discourse on it. Why is it then necessary to have complete knowledge? If you know enough for your purpose that is sufficient." Uddhaveshbua was also directed to read *Eknathi Bhagwat* for self-study but he was specifically warned that he should not expound, for it may feed and strengthen his ego.

Educated persons with their notions of hygiene and sanitation are apt to lose sight of humanity. Instead of trying to understand the nature of dreaded diseases and serving patients suffering from them, they create artificial barriers because of their prejudices. Sai Baba infused faith in his devotees by his bold defiance of hygiene and sanitary precautions.

When Mrs Tarabai, wife of Sadashiv A. Tarkhad, was on one occasion sitting in the *masjid,* there came a leper to the *masjid.* His disease was far advanced. He was stinking and he had little strength left in him. With much difficulty and very slowly, he clambered up the three steps of the *masjid,* moved on to the *dhuni* and then to

Sai Baba and placed his head on Sai Baba's feet. It took
so much time for him to take *darshan* that Mrs Tarkhad
who was getting the stench from him intensely hoped he
would clear off. At last when he got down slowly, carrying
a small parcel wrapped up in a dirty cloth, she felt
relieved, and said within herself, 'Thank God he is off.'
Sai Baba at once darted a piercing glance at her and she
knew that Sai Baba had read her mind.

Before the leper had gone far, Sai Baba called out and
sent someone to fetch him back. The man came. It was
again the slow process of clambering up and emitting a
foul stench all the time. And as the man bowed to Sai
Baba, the latter picked up the parcel saying, "What is
this?" and opened it. It contained some *pedha* (sweets
made of milk). Sai Baba took a piece and gave it to Mrs
Tarkhad - to her alone of all those present - and asked her
to eat it. What horror! To eat a thing brought by a
stinking leper! But it was Sai Baba's order and there was
no option but to obey. So she ate it up. Sai Baba took
another piece, swallowed it himself and then sent the
man away with the remainder. Thus, Sai Baba taught
the lesson in humility, fraternity, sympathy, endurance
and trust in the Supreme wisdom rather than in our own
notions of hygiene and sanitation for saving us from
disease.

A similar lesson he gave to Prof. G.G. Narke. In 1916,
plague was raging in Shirdi. Sai Baba used to get
sweetmeat from a *halwai* (seller of sweetmeats) in Shirdi
and sent Narke to purchase some. On arriving at the
shop, Narke found the plague-stricken corpse of the
halwai lying in his shop. He went and told his wife (who
was weeping) of Sai Baba's order. She pointed to the
corpse and said that Narke might take the sweetmeat
from the *almairah*. Narke took it trembling with fear
that by this he and others might catch the infection as
the sweetmeat would be given as *naivedya*. Sai Baba told
Narke, "You think you will live if you are away from

Shirdi, and that you would die if you stay at Shirdi. That is not so. Whosoever is destined to be struck will be struck; whosoever is to die will die; whosoever is to be caressed will be caressed."

One should not despise but treat even a poor, shabby person with consideration, was the lesson taught by Sai Baba to Hari Bapurao Shirsathe. A poor devotee of Sai Baba named Mhalsa had made her abode in Shirdi. When Shirsathe visited Shirdi, Mhalsabai blessed him and asked for money. Shirsathe gave her some and told her that he would give her more while going. When Shirsathe started from Shirdi on his return journey, he forgot his promise to Mhalsa but she had not. Instead of giving her anything Shirsathe said to her in anger, "Go get away. Does anyone give money thrice?" On his return journey Shirsathe was put to much inconvenience and trouble. In Kopargaon town he did not get a tonga to go to the station and thus missed his train and had to stay overnight there. Hence he began to think: 'Everytime I leave with Sai Baba's permission my travel is smooth. How is it that this time I am put to such trouble?'

From Manmad station another Sai Baba devotee Biharlal Vyas was a co-passenger in his compartment. They fell to talking to each other and Vyas related his experience to Shirsathe: "Today, as I started from Shirdi, the mad woman Mhalsabai came and asked me for money. Her clothes emitted such foul stench that I was nauseated. But as soon as I gave her some money, she turned back and there was a fragrance of *mogra* and other scented flowers with the breeze. I was astonished." Hearing these words Shirsathe realised that the inconvenience experienced by him on the way home was due to his ill-treatment of Mhalsa. Tears came to his eyes and he was grateful that Sai Baba had given the answer to his question through Vyas.

A similar lesson was given to Damodar Savlaram Rasane by Sai Baba. Once Rasane invited Sai Baba for a meal, but knowing that Sai Baba would not be present personally requested that he might send Bala Nevaskar Patil on his behalf. Sai Baba agreed but told Rasane that he should not humiliate Bala in any way considering him as of low caste. Rasane agreed. He prepared a sumptuous menu and spread one plate for Sai Baba just opposite his photograph, filled it with various items of food and called out 'Bala come!' A black dog came in and ate from the plate. Rasane waited reverently till it finished its meal and then other guests including Bala were served and fed. Bala was seated very near Rasane. This incident brings out clearly the fact that Sai Baba treated low creatures and men of low social status as his equals.

If this lesson was unpalatable to some, Baba had his ingenious ways of imparting it. In May 1915 Shantaram Balwant Nachane went to Shirdi accompanied by his mother-in-law and others. They put up at Sathewada. Dada Kelkar, father-in-law of Rao Bahadur Sathe, was in occupation of a part of the premises. When Nachane's mother-in-law was cutting onions for their meals, Dada Kelkar, an orthodox Brahmin, who abhorred the use of onions, got irritated and fell foul of her. She took his abuse to heart. A few hours later Kelkar's granddaughter was crying on account of severe pain in her eyes and he went to Sai Baba for a remedy. Sai Baba told him to foment the eyes with onions. Kelkar asked him from whence he was to get onions. Sai Baba always kept some onions with him and Kelkar hoped to get some from him. But the just, all-knowing arbiter Sai Baba told him, "Get them from this mother," pointing to Nachane's mother-in-law. She told Sai Baba of the morning incident and said that she would not care to give Kelkar anything, but if he ordered her she would. Sai Baba ordered the gift and Kelkar's granddaughter got relief. Thus, Kelkar realised his mistake and learnt that it was not proper to despise and ill-treat others while observing one's own traditional ways.

Another instance of an ingenious method adopted by
Sai Baba for imparting a moral lesson was in the case of
Govind Raghunath alias Annasaheb Dabholkar, author
of *Shri Sai-Sat-Charit*. Every Sunday a weekly bazaar
would be held in Shirdi. One Sunday afternoon,
Dabholkar was sitting on the right side of Baba and
doing *charan-seva*. Suddenly, Madhavrao Deshpande
spotting some groundnuts in the folds of the sleeve of
Dabholkar's coat, laughed, and as he touched the elbow
of Dabholkar, many nuts rolled down his sleeve. How
they came to be positioned there became a topic of fun
and speculation. Sai Baba said jokingly, "He is in the bad
habit of eating alone (without sharing with others). This
is the proof, if required, of his having visited the bazaar
alone and of having eaten alone. This habit is not good."
As Dabholkar had not been to the bazaar or eaten
groundnuts, he replied, "This appears to be one of your
leelas. I neither went to the market nor ate any
groundnuts. Moreover, I never eat anything without
sharing with others who are with me." Then becoming a
little solemn, Sai Baba said, "You, of course, give to one
who is with you but how will you give to those who are
not there? Do you remember me? Am I not with you?"
Then Dabholkar realised that eating food is also a
sacrificial act, and nothing should be eaten without first
offering it to or remembering God or *guru*. Another
interpretation also would be that nothing we do even in
secrecy is hidden from God or *guru* and we should
therefore be careful and circumspect in our thought and
deeds.

Once Nanasaheb Chandorkar was confused. While he
was sitting near Sai Baba two Muslim women in *purdah*
came for Sai Baba's *darshan*. Being in *purdah* they stood
for some time in the *sabhamandap*. Chandorkar,
therefore, got up and wanted to leave but Sai Baba bade
him sit down. Just then the two women came up the
steps of the *masjid* and removing thier veil took *darshan*

of Sai Baba. One of the two women was old and the other was young and very pretty. Seeing the latter, Nanasaheb was agitated and wanted to gaze at her but out of deference to Sai Baba could not raise his head. Sensing the agitation of Nanasaheb, Sai Baba patted him on the back. After the veiled women had left Sai Baba asked Nanasaheb, "Do you know why I patted you?" Nanasaheb replied, "What is unknown to you? But I wonder how in your company such tendency should raise its head!" Then Sai Baba said, "Nana, why are you agitated? When any faculty is performing its natural function, there should be no interference for it is harmful. Brahma has created this universe and if we don't admire and appreciate it, we would be lacking in aesthetics. Our instincts can be tamed gradually. If our heart is pure, what is there to fear?"

> The mind is naturally fickle but do not permit it to be impetuous
> Even if the senses are agitated, the body should be restrained;
> The senses are untrustworthy, so do not hanker after desires,
> By constant practice (and dispassion) ficklemindedness will disappear.[3]

After the intellectual understanding of the Brahman through logical reasoning, the plenary experience will follow sooner or later in the case of a seeker according to his capacity and effort. The plenary experience together with the grace of the *Guru* will lead to plenary bliss. Uddhaveshbua of Dahanu came to Shirdi in 1904 and asked Sai Baba, "When will I get a *guru* to lead me to liberation?" Sai Baba told him that he would understand after five years as it was not possible to swallow a whole *bhakri* in one gulp. After five years Uddhaveshbua had an idea of Sai Baba's powers and realised that Sai Baba could lead him on the path of liberation. Sai Baba then directed him to read *Eknathi Bhagwat* regularly. A rich but avaricious man came to Sai Baba and said, "Please show me the Brahman." Sai Baba seated him by his side and said to him, "Many people come running to me for worldly pleasures but it is rare to see one like you who seeks Brahman! I will show you not only Brahman but the whole bundle of Brahman!" So saying Sai Baba called a boy and said to him, "Go to Nandu grocer and fetch five rupees. Say Baba needs the money urgently."

The boy returned from Nandu's place and said that his house was locked. Then Sai Baba sent him to Bala grocer, but he too was not at home. Thereafter Sai Baba sent him to one or two more places but none of them was at home at that time. Would Sai Baba have not known this with his inner vision? But this was actually a test of the visitor. He who sought Brahman had a bundle of notes worth Rs.250 but he was filled with doubt and hesitation and could not bring himself to offer a paltry sum of five rupees as loan and that too for a short while! Seeing all this brisk activity he thought that Sai Baba must have forgotten all about his demand. So to remind him the visitor said, "Baba, please show me the Brahman." Turning to him Sai Baba said, "Did you not see that all this I have been doing is for this very purpose?" Sai Baba meant to convey that surrendering of five *pranas* (vital airs), five organs, ego, mind and intellect was a condition precedent to the knowledge of Brahman. But how was the avaricious man to know this? So Sai Baba told him that he had Rs.250 in his pocket and until he overcame his avariciousness and surrendered his all, Brahman was a far cry. He added, "My coffers are full. Anyone can have his pick but I have to give according to the capacity of the taker. If you keep this in mind, it will conduce to your well-being. Sitting in this holy *masjid* I never speak an untruth." The visitor thanked Sai Baba and left.

Everyone should follow the path of *dharma* prescribed for him by his *guru*. So when Swami

Vijayanand, a *sannyasin,* came to Shirdi for Sai Baba's *darshan* and after some days asked for leave to go and see his mother who was reported to be serious as per the telegram received by him, Sai Baba said, "If you were so attached to your mother, why did you take *sannyasa* at all?" He declined to give him permission and said, "We will see after a few days." He could see with his inner eye that the Swami's end was near. So he directed the Swami to go to the *lendi* and do *parayana* of *Ram-Vijaya.* Thus, the Swami passed fourteen days and completed two *parayanas.*

As he was about to commence the third *parayana*, he was seized with dangerous sickness and experienced weakness. From the *lendi* he came to the *wada* but in a short while gave up the ghost. Thus, Sai Baba steadied him on the path of *dharma* and in order to give a better start to the Swami in his next birth, Sai Baba made him study holy books prior to his end.

The devotee and the Lord, the disciple and the *guru* are one. God or *guru* bears the blows which fall on the devotee or the disciple. Passing only such burden as the disciple can bear, they make the remaining sorrow bearable by devising an effective means therefor. When Dikshit's younger daughter passed away in Shirdi in 1911, he was stricken with grief. Knowing earlier that Dikshit would have to bear the grief of his daughter's loss, Sai Baba got him to order a copy of *Bhavartha Ramayan.* By the time the daughter passed away the *Pothi* arrived and when Dikshit went with it to Sai Baba, turning the pages Sai Baba opened the *Pothi* at *Kishkindhakand.* Therein is a description of the lament of Tara after the killing of Vali and the instruction imparted to her by Rama, and Sai Baba asked Dikshit to read it. By reading this portion of the *Pothi,* Dikshit's peace of mind was restored.

If a devotee faces a problem, knowing it through his inner vision, Sai Baba does not fail to resolve the difficulty. Some years after Nanasaheb Chandorkar had accepted Sai Baba as his *sadguru*, he was transferred to Pandharpur whereby he was placed in a dilemma. Residing in Pandharpur, how could he forego *darshan* of Lord Vitthal? But would the gain be at the cost of his devotion to Sai Baba? Was there a conflict between the devotion to two of them — was the question before him. On his way to Pandharpur, Nanasaheb got off at Kopargaon and was on his way to Shirdi, when Sai Baba said to devotees sitting with him, "The portals of Pandharpur are opened for us. Let us sing His praises with delight." Saying so, he started with others singing the *bhajan*:

I have to go, to go to Pandharpur and stay there.
I have to stay, to stay there, for it is the house of my
    Lord.

Just then Nanasaheb arrived in Shirdi with his family. He prostrated before Sai Baba and requested him to come and stay in Pandharpur. Nanasaheb had not written about his visit to Shirdi to anyone nor had he sent a message. So at his sudden arrival everybody was surprised but more than anyone, Nanasaheb himself was surprised when he heard the *bhajan* for through the words thereof his dilemma had been satisfactorily resolved.

The experience of Hari Sitaram alias Kakasaheb Dikshit is also interesting. Once while going by tonga from Kopargaon to Shirdi, he passed a woman with a basket of guavas. So he stopped the tonga and bought guavas for Sai Baba. The fragrance of the guavas was so tempting that a desire arose in Dikshit to eat a guava. He mentally prayed to Sai Baba to ask why this was happening. Immediately the fragrance ceased and the desire of Dikshit died down.

While writing a commentary in verse form in Marathi on *Ishopanishad*, Das Ganu had a telling experience. In the course of writing a doubt cropped up for the

clarification of which Das Ganu approached Sai Baba.
Sai Baba said, "What is there? Go to Kaka Dikshit at Vile
Parle. His maidservant will resolve your doubt." Many of
those present thought that Sai Baba was joking, but Das
Ganu had great faith in Sai Baba's word. So he proceeded
to Vile Parle and stayed with Dikshit.

Early next morning, while Das Ganu was in bed, he
heard a girl singing in a sweet voice. Das Ganu
immediately woke up and heard her song intently. The
thought of the commentary on *Ishopanisad* came to his
mind and the riddle was solved. As he came out he saw a
Kunbi girl washing utensils. She was a relation of
Dikshit's servant. As Sai Baba's words came true Das
Ganu was very happy. Actually there was not much to
the song. It was a song which described the beauty of an
orange sari. Das Ganu was filled with compassion and
got Rao Bahadur Moreshwar Pradhan to purchase a
beautiful sari for the girl. The girl was overjoyed and
wearing the new sari played and frolicked for a day and
then tucked it away.

Next day, draped in her usual faded sari, she was
back at work but not a whit less happy. She did not
appear to feel the lack of the new sari nor was she
miserable. Wearing a faded sari by choice, her poverty
was brightened by happiness and contentment.
Happiness and sorrow are states of mind. The happiness
is in the mind and not in the sari. God permeates the
whole universe - in the poverty of the girl is His essence,
as also in the old faded sari. The giver, what is proposed
to be given and the gift are also filled with His essence.

Thus, Sai Baba taught philosophy, devotion, spiritual
discipline, morality, conduct in daily life, fellow-feeling
and divine love to all those who came to him. As
Tukaram, the famous saint of Maharashtra has said, the
ordinary talk of a holy person is instruction. This was
also true in the case of Sai Baba. Even though Sai Baba is
no more in the body, he continues to instruct and guide

his devotees and seekers, as before but only the methods adopted are naturally different. There are no set rules for their operation and their boundaries cannot be demarcated. Sai Baba makes the rules and their regulation depends on the intensity of the love of devotees for him.

We have seen earlier that Sai Baba had convincingly shown T.G. Samant that his chosen deity, Ganapati was he (Sai Baba) himself. Similarly, thirty-one years after his *samadhi*, Sai Baba showed Gangadhar Laxman Jakhadi of Dadar, Bombay, that he (Sai Baba) was even in the form of Datta.

In 1949 Jakhadi was a telegraph-master on Kalyan Railway Station. At noon as he was going to the canteen for his lunch, he saw a *sannyasin* sitting on a bench. The *sannyasin* called him, and said, "Take leave for today." The stationmaster who ordinarily used to be reluctant to grant such leave, readily granted leave to Jakhadi on that day. The *sannyasin* then narrated the account of Jakhadi's father and told him that his father had been in the service of Gopalrao Buti of Nagpur, a devotee of Sai Baba until the *samadhi* of Sai Baba in 1918. In the course of conversation, the *sannyasin* said that he himself was a devotee of Dattatreya and had come to Bombay after a pilgrimage to Mahur, and was on his way to Badrinarayan. Then the *sannyasin* asked Jakhadi to buy a ticket for him up to Hardwar. When Jakhadi asked for money the *sannyasin* told him, "Put your hand in my *jholi* (the four-mouthed bag of a mendicant *sadhu*) and take the money." When Jakhadi put his hand in the *jholi* he found it full of rupees. The *sannyasin* said, "Take all this money," but Jakhadi was not avaricious. He merely took Rs. 36 for the fare, purchased a ticket for Rs.35-12 annas and wanted to return 4 annas to the *sannyasin*. When the *sannyasin* asked Jakhadi to put back 4 annas in the *jholi*, Jakhadi found it empty. The *sannyasin*, when asked how this had happened said, "My bank is at

Mahur, Gangapur, Shirdi and such places. Whenever necessary the money comes and the need over, the money goes back. Sai Baba is an incarnation of Datta. Visit Shirdi from time to time and you will not want for anything." From that time Jakhadi began worshipping Sai Baba in the form of Dattatreya.[4]

Another Dattatreya and Sai Baba devotee, Subbarao of Guti, heard in his sleep in the first week of February, 1944, a distinct voice telling him to perform constant *japa* of Datta. Thinking that as he was in trouble Sai Baba was suggesting a remedy to relieve him from it, he decided in his sleep itself to perform *japa*. Next day in the rush of work he forgot to perform the *japa*.

The following day Sai Baba gave him *darshan* in an angry mood in his dream, and on waking up in the morning he received a telegram informing him that his son was in the hospital with acute asthma. Thereafter he would sit near Sai Baba's photograph and perform *japa*. After three days he received a letter informing him that his son's condition was improving and soon he was brought home. With *japa* and partaking of *udi* his son's condition rapidly returned to normal. In the first week he performed *Datta-japa* five thousand times and the decision to prosecute him for having a revolver was cancelled.[5]

Dahyabhai Damodardas Mehta, a hardware merchant of Bombay residing in a chawl near Madhavbag, started worshipping Sai Baba in 1945. In 1946-47 he was laid down with typhoid. There was a rumour circulating then that the spirit of a carpenter was harassing many people living in the chawl where Mehta was residing. Mehta was frightened and in order to avoid any harm coming to him he was persuaded by others to wear an amulet around his neck. However, instead of doing him any good he developed high fever. He was being treated by a doctor.

In the meantime once at midnight Mehta felt the spirit of the carpenter sitting on his chest. When he shouted, "Sai Baba, Sai Baba," he felt that Sai Baba was saying from his photograph, "Why are you afraid? I am standing here since morning with a stick for your protection, but you must tear the amulet from your neck and throw it away." Therefore, Mehta tore the amulet from his neck and threw it away. He was dissuaded against doing so but before the extraordinary strength infused in him by Sai Baba, the spirit could not prevail.

When Mehta woke up, he discovered the broken amulet lying in a corner. Then his health started improving, but due to indiscretion in his diet his condition regressed and in spite of medical treatment there was no improvement. So he vowed that he would go for Sai Baba's *darshan* and offer a *dakshina* of Rs. 101 if he were to recover. From next day his recovery began and he was restored to normalcy in a month. His illness taught Mehta two things: (1) No Sai devotee should fear any incantation or spell, black magic, sorcery or witchcraft; and (2) The might of Sai Baba is superior to any remedies devised by modern medicine.[6]

Do not show disrespect to a saint, was a lesson taught by Sai Baba to a Muslim in Ahmedabad. Ramanlal Mali, a devotee of Sai Baba, owned a shop at Bhadra in Ahmedabad. He would burn incense before Sai Baba's picture. A Muslim who would pass the shop on his way to his place of work would make fun of Ramanlal.

Once when the Muslim was returning from his work as usual, he saw an *Aulia* making a clack, clack noise with a hoe approaching from the opposite direction. Standing before Ramanlal's shop, as if to blame or censure the Muslim for his conduct, the *Aulia* said, "What, you make fun of burning incense before my picture?" and disappeared. The Muslim was wonderstruck and in a repentant mood apologised to Ramanlal. He not only came to have faith in Sai Baba as a true *Aulia,* but keeping Sai Baba's photograph started serving it.

Mrs Surjabai Kasliwal of Khamgaon in Berar had a dream in which she heard Sai Baba instructing her to do *japa* of 'Sai Baba, Sai Nath'. So, giving up the daily worship of all other gods, she started repeating the *japa* as instructed. On the fourth day, in a dream, Sai Baba showed her a *durbar* in which on four equal seats, Sai Baba himself, Shri Shantinath, Shri Padmaprabhu, and Bhagwan Mahavir were seated. When she asked Sai Baba a question, he said, "Look, here are your Shantinath, Padmaprabhu, Mahavirprabhu, ask them." On waking up Surjabai pondered on the meaning of the dream and came to the conclusion that Sai Baba wanted her to continue her daily *puja* of her gods while doing his *bhakti.*

It is difficult to say that a particular experience is only for a particular thing. Sai Baba's *leela* is sometimes suggestive of more than one thing. Ratilal Chimanlal Seth of Tarkas Bhavan, Ahmedabad, had an experience of this kind after he had offered on a Thursday 1.25 lakh *bel* leaves to Sai Baba in the form of Shiva. Next day, when Ratilal opened the door of the *puja* room, a cobra was sitting with raised hood in front of the *bel* leaves. The cobra first circumambulated the heap of *bel* leaves and then sat with its hood raised over the photograph of Radha-Krishna. Seeing this Ratilal was frightened and, closing the door of the *puja* room, postponed the programme of the immersion of *bel* leaves in the river. Three hours thereafter, devotees from out-stations came for the *darshan* of Sai Baba in the form of Shiva. When Ratilal went with them to the *puja* room, the cobra had disappeared. So he concluded that: (1) Sai Baba had given him *darshan* in the form of *Sheshashayee Bhagwan*; (2) Lord Vishnu being pleased with Ratilal's devotion to Lord Shiva, had shown his unity with Lord Shiva; and (3) By preventing him from immersion of *bel* leaves in the morning, the incident had enabled a number of out-station devotees to have *darshan*. So Ratilal was highly pleased with the outcome of his *puja* and silently thanked Sai Baba for everything.

Notes

1. *Shri Sai-Sat-Charit*, Chap. III, pp. 76-77.
2. Ibid., XV, pp. 68-73.
3. Ibid., XLIX, pp. 170-71.
4. *Shri Sai Leela*, September 1952, pp. 15-16.
5. Ibid., March 1944, p. 45.
6. Ibid., September 1952, pp. 18-19.

EPILOGUE

We had a fleeting glimpse of the glory of an individual who is a *Jeevanmukta* (eternally free), one with the perfect state of Brahman - fleeting glimpse because no proper idea of his mission can be formed from all that is written and published about him. The account that is given in the present work about his mission is only a small part of what is published about him in books and magazines. The glory of the perfect state of Brahman which has been sung by sages, saints, holy persons and devotees is but incomplete. Speech is unable to describe it fully. So sages have said:

Know him to be of childish understanding who says that the innumerable attributes of the Infinite can be counted. Perhaps it may be possible to count the particles of the earth but to sing of the qualities of the omnipotent Lord is impossible.

Srimad Bhagwat, Section 11, Chapter IV, Stanza 2

The knower of the Brahman himself becomes Brahman. This is not only an aphorism but visible truth which can be experienced. Sai Baba is a living testimony of this truth. Brahman manifests in the form of (absolute) existence, (infinite) consciousness and (eternal) bliss. It pervades everything from the atom to the universe. It is the source of creative intelligence, and so is omniscient, omnipotent. Being bliss, it destroys sorrow and poverty.

Interpreting the Vedic aphorism, 'Brahman alone is real, everything else is an illusion' to mean 'I am Brahman', do not become a literal dry *Vedantin* (follower

of the philosophy of *Upanishads*) without grounding in
the basics of devotion but obtain peace that passeth
understanding by treading on the ninefold path of
devotion. Even in the *Bhagavad Gita*, the emphasis is on
the path of devotion. This is also clear from the marks of
a dear devotee, of a man of knowledge (serene wisdom),
and of one who is beyond the three strands, qualities or
forces. Moreover, in Stanza 55 of Chapter XI of the
Bhagavad Gita, translated by J. Mascaro it is said:

He who works for me, who loves me, whose End
Supreme I am, free from all things and with love for
all creation, he in truth comes unto me.

or as translated by Swami Prabhavananda &
Christopher Isherwood:

Whoever works for me alone, makes me his only goal
and is devoted to me, free from attachment and
without hatred toward any creature - that man, O
Prince, shall enter into me.

From this it is clear that the service of personal God is
ordained. So without entertaining any narrow, sectarian
or propagandist conception of personal God, accept a
saint or *mahatma* who is one with the perfect state of
Brahman as your *sadguru* and surrendering to him,
serve him in all ways, question him and battle with the
six inimical tendencies of a human being under his
guidance with faith and patience. Thus becoming a true
Partha of Yogeshwar Krishna, triumph on the battlefield
of *samsar*. The universe is destructible and illusory, but
by devotion to *sadguru*, regarding him as the
embodiment of God, dwelling ever in God, realise
salvation for yourself and for the whole world.

We have seen that Sai Baba gives such experiences to
his devotee whereby he is convinced that whether he is
near or far, Sai Baba knows everything about his gross or
subtle existence. He is the *sutradhar* (holder and
manager of the strings) of all his tendencies. In times of
trouble or calamity, in response to sincere prayer, he

rushes to the rescue of his devotee and removes his sorrows and difficulties. Through the fear of censure of Sai Baba, a devotee remains alert or circumspect if he entertains a wicked thought in any place about anything or behaves unjustly. A devotee receives this warning or censure in a form or voice which he can recognise. Thus a devotee is circumspect not only in his worldly dealings but his treatment of the lower creation is also one of love.

"He who ascends the steps of this *masjid* is my equal. If anyone hurts him, I am hurt. If you misbehave with anyone I am pained." With such words Sai Baba has exhorted his devotees to look equally upon all. In his sight, the devotee who offers five thousand rupees a day or a poor devotee who cannot offer even a pie are both equal. He protects all with the same love as a tortoise has for her young one. The fee for such protection is one-pointed devotion and singular surrender. With him there is place for all - the man of sorrows, the seeker of knowledge, he who seeks personal ends and the man of vision.

The men of vision too, would come to Shirdi. Some of them were of the class of *acharyas*, saints and *mahatmas*. They were the very soul of Sai Baba. Since no one has mentioned anything about them, the silence on the part of the present writer is but natural and proper. However, this does not mean that those who entered as infants in the school of wisdom of Sainath remained infants permanently. Whether the entrance be at the stage of infancy or adolescence, experience for yourself the influence as well as the strength of the spiritual path. Turn to this path of welfare and abandon desires. Sainath proclaims that treading on the ninefold path of devotion you will realise yourself. There are many impediments and obstacles on the way. So take *guru* as your guide and progress under his guidance with faith and patience. And forever bliss will be yours. Be resolute.

You cannot attain realisation unless you are strong. This is the message of Sai Baba.

With love for the whole creation in his heart Sai Baba served the universe and inculcated this lesson to all. Bearing the blow of the devotee Hansraj, aimed at the cat eating his curds, Sai Baba showed his oneness with the creation. He would avert the impending calamity of the village or of his devotees. If necessary, he would take the *karmic* suffering upon himself and lighten the suffering of his devotees and the village. We saw many instances of this particularly when there was an outbreak of the epidemic of cholera or plague in Shirdi. His love did not make any distinction of caste or creed, family or *gotra*, etc. He disfavoured strongly and emphatically contempt towards the so-called lower castes. Whether the devotee was a Hindu, Muslim, Parsi, Christian, Brahmin or Shudra, Sai Baba looked upon all with an equal eye and tried to lighten the burden of all alike. Service of the creation was his creed and he sacrificed his life for this cause. He would say, "Brother, there is a thin veil like the abdominal membrane between me and God. The veil will be removed after death and then there is only God." This all powerful Sainath lies in the *Samadhi Mandir* in the universal shrine for serving his devotees.

Whatever offerings were made to him by his devotees, he would not use them himself. Fruits, *prasad*, *naivedya*, he would distribute to the poor and *sevekaris* and would only partake of the *bhiksha* he collected himself. He had no use for garments and ornaments. He wore a *kafni* of *maderpat* (thick coarse cotton cloth) and tied a piece of similar cloth around his head. Devotees had presented him with a silver throne, silver utensils, a horse, palanquin, chariot and all other regal paraphernalia. But expressing disapproval of all these presents he never made any use of them. He never sat either on the throne or the palanquin, chariot or the horse. This way he was inculcating the lesson that service must always be selfless without acceptance of anything in return.

Forgetting differences of caste, creed, sect and religion, Hindus, Muslims, Parsis and Christians participate in the festivals and worship even today as before. On the occasion of Ramanavami festival, Muslims participate in the ceremony of flag-hoisting, and Hindus participate in the *sandal* procession as Sai Baba is the focal point of both Hindus and Muslims alike who venerate him. There is equal freedom for people of all castes and religions for *darshan*, and worship in the *masjid* as well as the *Samadhi Mandir*. So, in the *Samadhi Mandir* persons of diverse religions come and obtain his blessings. He exhorted all to observe their respective personal religion conscientiously, and did not found a new religion or sect. His *Samadhi Mandir* is a shrine of universal religion. The writer prays to all to benefit from this shrine of universal religion for their own salvation.

Appendix

THE WORDS OF SAI BABA

His Advice in Brief

God is and there is nothing higher than Him. He is Perfect, Infinite and Eternal. He is Omnipotent, Omnipresent and Omniscient. He is the Creator, Sustainer and Destroyer. Surrender voluntarily and totally to His Will. Not a blade of grass moves without His Will. Trust in Him and do the right. Let the inner light (enlightened conscience) guide all your actions. Perform your duty conscientiously and with detachment regarding yourself not as the doer but only as an instrument in His hands. Surrender the fruit of action to Him so that action will not harm or bind you. Let your love and compassion flow to all creatures of God. Do not engage in controversy. Words (of others) cannot harm you. Bear with others patiently. Accept your lot cheerfully without comparing yourself with others. Do not speak ill of others. Do not give tit for tat for each is answerable for his own actions. Do not remain idle but engage yourself in some useful activity. Read the sacred texts. Be moderate in your food and recreation.

Sayings

Know that God is.
Do not believe that God is not.
God is Omnipresent.
God's Name is Eternal.

This (universe) is all a *leela* of God.

God is the Lord and the Master. There is no other Truth. His ways are unique, inscrutable and mysterious.

There is no one higher than God. How He will protect and sustain is known only to Him.

All that (i.e., other gods) is Allah.

He is the Protector of the poor.

We are all creatures of God, Allah.

He is very compassionate. We falter in our faith in Him and lack sufficient patience.

Herculean effort is necessary for the attainment of God. It is most difficult and yet He is a compassionate God. Who says He is out of reach? He is there in the tabernacle of our heart, nearer to us than the fingernail to the finger. Without unflinching faith and patience of Job, you will not see Him. One who has both these will undoubtedly find Him.

It needs insight to recognise God.

He is in the tabernacle of your heart but you must be able to recognise him.

His will be done. He will show the way and all your heart's desires will be fulfilled.

Be content with your lot.

Light dispels darkness.

Do good and God will bless you. Do evil and you will displease Him. I am everywhere and in all places and the whole world is with me.

I move everywhere and anywhere. God is everywhere.

I pervade the universe. I am both the visible and the invisible. I am unborn, eternal and everlasting. Do good and offer it to God and He will bless you. God protects the righteous. Those who sow nettles expect me to give them corn. How can I do so?

I am God's slave.

Even the learned are confused. Then what of us? Listen and be silent. One who has received His Grace is